The Immortal Marilyn

The Depiction of an Icon

John De Vito
Frank Tropea

THE SCARECROW PRESS, INC.
Lanham, Maryland • Toronto • Plymouth, UK
2007

SCARECROW PRESS, INC.

Published in the United States of America
by Scarecrow Press, Inc.
A wholly owned subsidary of
The Rowman & Littlefield Publishing Group, Inc.
4501 Forbes Boulevard, Suite 200, Lanham, Maryland 20706
www.scarecrowpress.com

Estover Road
Plymouth PL6 7PY
United Kingdom

British Library Cataloguing in Publication Information Available

Library of Congress Cataloging-in-Publication Data

De Vito, John, 1953-
    The immortal Marilyn : the depiction of an icon / John De Vito, Frank Tropea.
        p. cm.
    Includes bibliographical references and index.
    ISBN-13: 978-0-8108-5866-4 (pbk. : alk. paper)
    ISBN-10: 0-8108-5866-5 (pbk. : alk. paper)
    1. Monroe, Marilyn, 1926–1962—Criticism and interpretation. I. Tropea, Frank,
1949– . II. Title.
PN2287.M69D45 2007
791.4302'8092—dc22   2006019080

(∞)^{TM} The paper used in this publication meets the minimum requirements of
American National Standard for Information Sciences—Permanence of Paper
for Printed Library Materials, ANSI/NISO Z39.48-1992.
Manufactured in the United States of America.

For our grandmothers: Frances Cicione, Constance "Tillie" De Vito, Lutgarda "Luckie" Pesce, and Celia Tropea. Four great ladies who came from the old world to the new in search of a dream, much as Marilyn Monroe lived her life.

Contents

Acknowledgments   vii

Introduction   ix

1   Marilyn Monroe as a Character   1

2   Marilyn Monroe as Roman à Clef   83

3   Marilyn Monroe as a (Documentary) Subject   113

4   Marilyn Monroe as a Referent   139

Appendix A: Marilyn Monroe Iconography   161

Appendix B: Marilyn Monroe Filmography   189

Bibliography   199

Title Index   201

About the Authors   205

Acknowledgments

We are profoundly grateful to so many people who have been extremely helpful to us in the acquiring of all the difficult-to-find materials needed to write this book. We offer our sincerest thanks to each and every one of them: Lyn Ackerley, Elisa Birdseye, Robert Brustein, Paul Cesario, Megan Fleming, Donald Freed, Ernie Garcia of the Marilyn Monroe International Fan Club, Ken Gloss and the staff of the Brattle Street Book Store, Sue Glover, Norman Mailer, Jesse Martin, David J. Mauriello, Brian McCaffrey and the staff of Peter L. Stern and Company Book Store, Dale Notinelli of the Legend Club for Marilyn Monroe, Al Rossi, Paul Saltzman of Sunrise Films, Greg Schreiner of Marilyn Remembered, Jim Tommaney of Edge Theatre, and Butch Tuohey.

We would also like to thank the following people, who offered us their enthusiastic support: Janet Buda, Moonyean Carlton, Paula Hayes, Jimmy James, Naia Kelly, May Lo, Karen MacDonald, Andre Poulin, Betsy Sherman, and Mary DiZazzo Trumbull. It is very doubtful that this book could have ever been completed without the awesome research collections of both the Boston Public Library and the New York Public Library; the invaluable assistance of Photofest of New York in selecting many of the book's photographs; the indefatigable work of Darlene De Vito Powers, who typed our manuscript through all its various stages; and the judicious editing of Stephen Ryan of Scarecrow Press.

Finally, with much love we acknowledge the support and encouragement of our parents and our families for all they have done for us through the years.

Introduction

*M*arilyn Monroe rose from total obscurity and an abject beginning to become a Hollywood star of a most compelling stature. Now, over forty years after her death in 1962, her stature is even more compelling. In his book *Goddess: The Secret Lives of Marilyn Monroe*, Anthony Summers puts forward a series of probing questions:

> Who was the woman who turned herself into "Marilyn Monroe"? She had a body, in truth, not unlike other female bodies. How did she make us notice her more than any other woman, in her time and on into the end of the century?[1]

It is our intention with this book to explore the ultimate effect of the powerful and lasting impact Marilyn Monroe has had on the world. We begin by first acknowledging the obvious fact that she was indeed the blondest of blondes, the sexiest of the Hollywood sex symbols. But that was hardly all she was: just another sexy Hollywood blonde from an apparently endless line of sexy Hollywood blondes. No, Marilyn stood out from the rest of the pack, partly because she had the ability to project both a lush sexuality and a palpable sense of innocence. Her drop-dead gorgeousness was laced with a liberal amount of vulnerability, which made her nonthreatening even when she was at her very naughtiest.

Yet this is only part of the reason Marilyn has attained the phenomenal status of an enduring cultural icon, shared by only a select few. In her study *Power and Allure: The Mediation of Sexual Difference in the Star Image of Mae West*, cultural critic Ramona Curry writes,

> I believe, in some stars coming to function as enduring cultural icons, long after the films and other texts that yielded their initial star image have

diminished in circulation . . . I myself would list Mae West, Marilyn Monroe, Marlene Dietrich, Judy Garland . . . as female stars who have attained the status as widely recognized cultural icons.[2]

While we fully endorse Curry on all this, we also believe that Marilyn's status as an enduring cultural icon is in a special class of its own. In fact, since her untimely death her legend has surpassed that of every other major Hollywood goddess—including even Jean Harlow, Greta Garbo, Rita Hayworth, and Ava Gardner—making her the greatest myth figure of them all. Two real clear indicators of her immense popularity are the following:

- The Marilyn Monroe Estate estimates that the many uses made of her "star" image take in between $50 million and $60 million per year.
- Since 1962, well over five hundred books have been devoted exclusively to her.

Yet another reason for Marilyn's singularly unique iconic standing is based on the fact that she has over time evolved into an extremely complex figure, capable of assuming "multiform meanings." Marilyn has by now acquired so many meanings that she and her life have become the grand subjects that inspire an astonishingly wide range of creative individuals.[3]

Marilyn has played her greatest, perhaps most immortal, role of all, that of the divine muse, to artists like Andy Warhol, Willem de Kooning, and Claes Oldenburg and to writers and thinkers such as Arthur Miller, Paddy Chayefsky, Garson Kanin, Norman Mailer, Truman Capote, Thomas Pynchon, Ayn Rand, Diana Trilling, Jean-Paul Sartre, Saul Bellow, Vladimir Nabokov, Gloria Steinem, and Joyce Carol Oates.

The central focus of this book will be an exploration of the meanings Marilyn has come to attain in the many theatrical, cinematic, televisual, dance, and operatic depictions of her. We will concentrate on those depictions we consider to best establish the book's thesis. This thesis is that the depiction of Marilyn onstage, on-screen, on television, and in opera clearly reveals that her ultimate standing as an enduring cultural icon has not simply continued; it has over time increased and intensified to über-mythical proportions.

Still, her journey to this place has not always been an easy one. As you will see, many of the earlier texts examined in this book do not shy away from the darker, unhappier aspects of her life. In some ways, the overall feeling created by such depictions is negative. But as more time passes, you will see some very interesting things happen. The attitude takes a decidedly upward turn. And just as the attitude changes, becoming more positive, there is also a change in the way Marilyn is ultimately represented. This sophisticated process, first established in the 1970s and further streamlined and refined through the 1980s, finally achieves the most perfect and complete positive expression of Marilyn Monroe in the 1990s and beyond.

Before we begin our journey from a place that admittedly descends into gray, abysmal negativity and unhappiness to a place of positive, rapturous transcendency, we should point out that we have chosen to arrange the contents of this book so that each entry is listed in chronological order. This enables us to observe that there is a very specific historical progression and evolution in the way that Marilyn is depicted, and it allows us to consider the ways in which the cultural trends and ideas of any one decade have influenced the content or style of a particular depiction. As the world changed, so did our perspective on Marilyn Monroe. This implies that there is a constantly shifting flexibility both to her image and to what we ultimately make of her. Much like a mirror, she gives us back a reflection of ourselves. For this reason, we have chosen to group all the depictions studied into the following four categories:

1. Marilyn Monroe as a character (explicitly referred to as Marilyn Monroe)
2. Marilyn Monroe as a roman à clef (depicting Marilyn as a thinly concealed fictional character)
3. Marilyn Monroe as a documentary subject (depicting Marilyn in the context of a nonfictional documentary)
4. Marilyn Monroe as a referent (works in which Marilyn is referred to or paid a visual tribute or homage)

A BRIEF HISTORY OF THE DEPICTION OF MARILYN MONROE

1950s

The 1950s was a decade overripe with plush possibility but also colossal conformity. Everything appeared big, bright, and so much bolder than life. Ike and Mamie were firmly ensconced in the White House, and in many ways everything seemed to be picture-perfectly right with America and therefore the entire world. But that is not the complete picture. Just beneath that shiny, Edenic surface, a far darker reality lurked. All that 1950s opulence and good, clean, wholesome conformity came with an exorbitantly high price tag attached. The Cold War and various forms of intellectual and cultural repression were but two of those high-ticket items.

There were—as there always are—exceptions to all this restrictive conformity. Faint glimmers of dissent against the decade's constraints and contradictions could be seen in the rebellious images projected by nonconformist actors like Montgomery Clift, Marlon Brando, and James Dean and in the literary output of writers Jack Kerouac and James Baldwin and the poet Allen Ginsberg.

And, of course, in the 1950s there was Marilyn Monroe. The decade began with her star-making appearances in two now classic 1950 movies, *The Asphalt Jungle* and *All About Eve*, and concluded with her brilliant performance as luscious lounge singer Sugar Kane in *Some Like It Hot* (1959). In between those cinematic high points, Marilyn would enjoy several others. Her ever-growing phenomenal appeal with the moviegoing public of the decade is clearly reflected in the success of many of her movies of the period, including *Niagara* (1953), *Gentlemen Prefer Blondes* (1953), *The Seven Year Itch* (1955), and *Bus Stop* (1956). On a more personal level, she would make celebrated marriages to great American hero Joe DiMaggio and great American playwright Arthur Miller.

Unfortunately, like the 1950s, beneath that beautiful, shiny surface of her life, there also lurked a far darker reality for Marilyn Monroe. Her marriages to DiMaggio and Miller ended in bitter divorce. Despite all her glamour and wealth, she suffered from stretches of insecurity and severe depression that only increased with time. In an effort to alleviate her inner demons, she would often turn to pills and alcohol for solace. The accumulative effects of this increasing substance abuse took a profound toll on both her private and her professional relationships.

All the depictions of Marilyn Monroe in the 1950s speak to the dualistic nature implicit in both the decade itself and the duality of her own sometimes troubled existence. In addition, the dualism in Marilyn's divided psyche was also the same dualism of the repressed 1950s with its image of woman as either Madonna or whore. And the dichotomy was even further complicated here because Marilyn could suggest both of these in her childlike innocence and her languid, lurid sensuality. In this respect, we see Hollywood's larger-than-life image of Marilyn as the ultimate sex symbol parodied in a 1954 episode of *I Love Lucy* and in both the 1955 play and 1957 movie versions of *Will Success Spoil Rock Hunter?* and infantilized and further eroticized in the 1957 movie *And God Created Woman*. We see the whole concept of the "Hollywood star culture" challenged and critiqued in the 1958 movie *The Goddess*.

1960s

The 1950s eventually gave way to the more idealistic energy and promise of the 1960s. This is perhaps best symbolized in the handsome young "Camelot" president John F. Kennedy and his glamorous and cultured wife Jackie moving into the White House at the start of the decade. (We will see later how JFK becomes illicitly linked to Marilyn Monroe in the future.)[4] While on the one hand the 1960s witnessed the beginning of the peace movement, civil rights, counterculture happenings, the women's movement, flower power, collective communes, LSD, free love, and even an overall (if somewhat naive) sense of political quietude, that is not the full picture. Because, on the other hand, the 1960s, like the 1950s, had a darker side. Along with the destructive war America waged in Vietnam, the decade also witnessed outbursts of violence, culminating in the shocking assassinations of John F. Kennedy, Martin Luther King Jr., Robert F. Kennedy, and Malcolm X. Not surprisingly, from out of the shining decade that began with so much promise, a growing culture of pessimism and despair gradually took hold as the decade progressed. This descent continued with such events as the rampages of the Weather people; the shootings at Kent State and Jackson State; the deaths of rock stars Jimi Hendrix, Janis Joplin, and Jim Morrison; and the slaying of young and beautiful actress Sharon Tate in 1969 by the deranged members of Charles Manson's "family." With her murder, Death and the Maiden became inextricably bound together forever in one haunting image. This metaphor is also a signifier for the young and beautiful Marilyn Monroe's own tragic death, for, totally worn down from a lifetime of exploitation, drugs, drink, and pain, Marilyn is found dead—nude, facedown on the bed, with one hand on the telephone receiver—in 1962.

In all the depictions of Marilyn in the 1960s, there is seen both the initial optimism and hope of the decade (reflected in Marilyn's own 1961 movie *The Misfits* and the theatrical 1962 romantic comedies *Venus at Large* and *Come on Strong*) and its later pessimism and despair (the 1964 play *After the Fall* and the 1967 movie *Valley of the Dolls*).

1970s

After all the political and social upheavals of the 1960s, the 1970s appear relatively tame by comparison. Then again, appearances can be deceiving, as many of the wilder ideas of the 1960s still remained in the 1970s, but those ideas became adapted and appropriated to fit a whole new time. Amazingly, even traces of the counterculture managed to find their way into the American mainstream. From that point on, even Richard Nixon's beloved Silent Majority was not quite so silent anymore. As for the fate of the once-high-and-mighty Nixon (who had been reelected president by the largest landslide since Roosevelt's reelection in 1936), even Nixon went through some major changes in the 1970s. The Watergate scandal and its subsequent cover-up eventually led to Nixon's fall from political grace and power forever.

On another front, the decade witnessed the end of the long and excessively bloody war in Vietnam. Still, the psychic scars the war left on the nation proved to be deep and long lasting. The aftermaths of Vietnam and Watergate helped bring about a series of disillusioning revelations exposing the numerous deceptions the government had perpetrated concerning these and other events. In the end, the final result of such negative revelations became transubstantiated into this deep-rooted distrust and suspicion of those in power. Thus, the culture of pessimism and despair that gradually took hold in the 1960s evolved into a culture of skepticism in the 1970s.

In the depictions of Marilyn Monroe in the 1970s, we still see the strong influence of the 1960s in terms of the newer frankness and permissiveness allowed in matters of content and style. The first attempt at a cinematic biographical portrait of Marilyn's life was made with the release of the soft-core pornographic movie *Goodbye, Norma Jean* in 1976. No less important is the way that the decade's cynicism found a means of expression in the depiction of her in the 1978 political thriller *Winter Kills.* This important thematic concern of Marilyn, projected into a landscape of political conspiracy and paranoia, eventually became a central component of her portrayal in many other depictions of future decades.

Finally, during the course of the 1970s, we also see the beginnings of the sophisticated and influential process of Marilyn's image being distilled and fine-tuned down to its purest, most powerful archetypal visualized essence. This occurs most noticeably in the 1975 theatrical production of *Kennedy's Children* and in director Ken Russell's dazzling 1975 movie version of the Who's rock opera *Tommy.*

1980s

America in the 1980s was a land awash in mind-boggling extravagance. Strongly influenced by the political and cultural ascendancy of Ronald and Nancy Reagan, the country took one long, hard detour to the extreme New Right. The Reagans—with their acutely elitist awareness of the phenomenal power of money and equally phenomenal power of the visual image—helped to bring about seemingly limitless fantasies of unlimited wealth and unlimited visual pleasure. All this opulent lavishness also found its way into the 1980s depictions of Marilyn Monroe. Most fittingly, in keeping with the times, three of these depictions took the form of rather ostentatious big-budget musical extravaganzas: the 1980 movie musical *Can't Stop the Music,* and the 1983 theatrical musicals *Marilyn!* and *Marilyn, An American Fable.*

Also noticeable in the decade is the carrying over of many of the ideas and concepts already exhibited in the past decade's depictions. Thematic concerns continue, such as Marilyn's having been sexually abused in childhood, her potent attraction to men, her pill and alcohol dependencies, and her exploitation initially by Hollywood and later, toward the end of her life, by powerful political figures. Most noticeable too, in the 1980s, is the ever-increasing emphasis placed on the sheer power of Marilyn's visual representation. If the ideological dominance of the Reagans' appreciation of the power of the image was but part of the reason for all of this happening, another reason was because by the 1980s all the formal aspects of Marilyn's depiction became so streamlined and codified in terms of her overall visual representation. In addition, in the 1980s, many of both the private and the public details of her life became so well known that they have now attained legendary proportions. Therefore, there is no real need to provide a lot of narrative detail. We are now more than capable of providing these details. But the meaning we might supply isn't the only possible meaning that Marilyn can assume. No, Marilyn is now capable of assuming many other meanings as well.

Paradoxically, however, as the content of Marilyn's depiction in the 1980s takes on boundless dimensions, the formal aspects of her depiction become simpler. In other words, as her content grows more complex and elusive, her form becomes more simple and direct. We will see examples of this with the 1980 TV movie *Marilyn, The Untold Story*, the 1982 play and 1985 movie versions of *Insignificance*, and the 1987 TV miniseries *Hoover vs. The Kennedys: The Second Civil War*. Along with everything else, we notice the darker, more negative aspects of her life beginning to get toned down in the 1980s. Although it cannot be said that these negative aspects ever totally disappear, they now are tempered with a more positive attitude. And with this fundamental attitude change, the Goddess, finally, makes her ascent.

1990s

As the gaudy, gilded era of the Reagans gave way to the younger, fresher perspectives of Bill and Hillary Clinton in the 1990s, Marilyn Monroe's star shone brighter and stronger than ever before. With the 1990s, we witness the many depictions of Marilyn, all coming together to form a kind of dazzling visual continuum. Further, the positive attitude of the 1980s is now completed, changing the way that she is depicted, which unites both the contextual and the formal aspects of her representation. Yet if the content of the depicted Marilyn is still much in evidence (encompassing the narrational, biographical, psychological, and philosophical), it is the formal aspects of her depiction that dominate. In the final analysis, what this does is to elevate Marilyn to this extraordinary figure. Having come to attain this position, Marilyn, like nature, is now timeless, eternal, always in fashion, forever classical, and in style.

In the 1990s, Marilyn's image was further formalized into specific poses, attitudes, and actions, all attesting to her unique, new condition. All the outward aspects of her depicted image are particularly well suited to remind us of her final transcendence. Appropriately, we then see Marilyn always depicted in her divine eternalness, with only slight variations, repeated again and again in the 1990s. But because she has now become an eternal goddess who is like nature, Marilyn is a goddess who is most fully accessible. She is not some aloof, forbidden bitch-goddess of exclusive detachment for the few. No, she is now a fully engaged, totally inclusive, democratized goddess for the many. Because of this, she is the Goddess of the People: a sublime pop deity in daily communion with her admirers. In addition, there is a performative dimension that is added to her image and that gives rise to a certain theatrical egalitarianism (which can even take on a melodramatic impulse). This causes a recurring element of self-reflectivity to arise in many of the works of the 1990s—as several of the characters being depicted are drawn to the art of performing—in Hollywood, the world of the theater, or simply as a means to enliven the banality and sordidness of their existence. Because of this new phenomenon of theatricality, we now see Marilyn as the sexy mannequin in the window of a fashionable New York shop winking at all the hot guys going by in *Can't Stop the Music* (1980); the eternally beautiful party guest in *Death Becomes Her* (1992); the shining fantasy that makes life bearable for a grief-stricken young mother in *Used People* (1992); a terminally ill, homeless man in *With Honors* (1994); a lonely, unhappy wife of a soldier in *Blue Sky* (1994); and a shapely waitress working at the cool, retro-style diner in *Pulp Fiction* (1994). Yes, Marilyn can be all these things for all people, forever bringing her magical and dramatic emotion and her healing presence to everyone as well as all her erotic warmth and beauty that always affect us like a burst of pure joy. Omniscient and omnipresent, Marilyn participates most actively in the lives of mortals so that there is now a little bit of Marilyn for and in everyone.

Millennium Marilyn

As images of the twentieth century fade away, the depicted Marilyn Monroe is prepared to explore a new beginning in a brand new millennium. Deflecting from the past, her depiction shows itself somewhat differently as it advances toward a site that initially appears to discard some of its previous philosophical, psychological, and novelistical tendencies. So how do we account for this? After the catastrophic (and still difficult-to-believe) attack on the World Trade Center on September 11, 2001, by fanatical political terrorists, combined with the baffling and delayed response of the administration of George W. Bush (such as his declaring war on the wrong country), America, along with much of the world, has shifted into a space where antireason and absurdity rule. Accordingly, with this development, there is a greater emphasis than ever placed on the complete validation of Marilyn's surface over her depth. By the same impulse, the artists of the new century have moved the depiction of Marilyn more toward the external, the elusive, the abstract, and finally the mythical, drawing her into a new twenty-first-century aesthetic of pure sight, sound, mystery, and color.

So we now see Marilyn being articulated into the full concentration of all that surrounds her: objects, color, decor, gestures, looks, poses, music, mise-en-scène, and the kinetic patterns of a world grown increasing baffling and absurd. This then is what Millennium Marilyn is all about, the elaborate visual patterning and dynamic juxtapositioning of sound, movement, and color over a more direct contextual meaning. New millennial depictions that reflect these twenty-first-century changes include those in which Marilyn is glimpsed in only a fleetingly brief scene or two (the comedy *Company Man* [2001], the TV miniseries *Jackie, Ethel, Joan: Women of Camelot* [2001], the TV movie *The Mystery of Natalie Wood* [2004]) or those depictions that replay ideas of the past in surprisingly new ways (the documentary *Marilyn Monroe: The Final Days* [2001]) and out-and-out satires (the spoof *Evil Hill* [2001]) or biographical and mythological reimaginings of her life (the TV miniseries *Blonde* [2001] and the play *American Iliad* [2001]).

Still, if several of these depictions of Marilyn shift away from the past, it is difficult to imagine that still other new forms and insights will not continue to evolve with time. For now, at least, a certain contextual reductionism prevails. If traces of the past still linger on, they have by and large become enshrined more in the realm of visual pleasure, legend, and myth. And so, temporarily disengaged from having to reflect any particular cultural space or Zeitgeist, the depicted Marilyn Monroe strays away from the power of immediate presence and is not secured by the presence of any one power. It is within this very disengagement that her depiction can ultimately explode the narrow limitations of Bushian antireason without doing any real serious damage to her stature as the preeminent enduring cultural icon of her time for all times.

NOTES

1. Anthony Summers, *Goddess: The Secret Lives of Marilyn Monroe* (New York: Macmillan, 1985), 4.
2. Ramona Curry, "Power and Allure: The Mediation of Sexual Difference in the Star Image of Mae West" (unpublished dissertation).

3. For a fascinating theory of the way in which Marilyn's multiform meanings operate on a political cultural level, see S. Paige Baty, *American Monroe: The Making of a Body Politic* (Berkeley: University of California Press, 1995).

4. The illicit knowledge of JFK's affair with Marilyn Monroe is perhaps best visually signified in the soft-core imagery highlighting the provocative, see-through gown she wore to sing "Happy Birthday, Mr. President" to him at Madison Square Garden in 1962.

Marilyn Monroe as a Character

(Explicitly Referred to as Marilyn Monroe)

Seven years after Marilyn Monroe's death in 1962, playwright John Guare became the first artist to depict her as a character in his play *Cop-Out* (1969) about supermacho cop Brett Arrow. By turns, Arrow can be brutal, fascistic, or primitive, and he's also into his job of tracking down Mr. Big or whatever pinko/commie he thinks is out to wreck America. He encounters Gardenia Gertie—a crippled old lady covered in blood. She pays him to track down the murderer of her cat Stockton and tells him of three possible suspects: her nephew, Gib; her niece, Larue; and her lover, William.

In good cop fashion, Arrow goes off to interrogate the suspects. Before doing so, however, he has a brief tryst with a young female protestor. Although Arrow treats her badly, she actually seems attracted to him. Eventually, Arrow finds his first suspect, the beautiful, brilliant socialite Larue, and sticks a lit cigarette into her neck. His treatment of Gardenia Gertie's nephew, playwright Gib, is no better. He calls him an "arto-faggot" and grinds his foot into Gib's hand.

During the course of the play, Arrow impregnates the protester and forces her to have an abortion. Then he breaks into Gib's play while it's being performed. In rapid succession, Arrow goes through the acting out the roles of all the American presidents. His leading lady is none other than Marilyn Monroe herself. She pops into Gib's play from out of nowhere as this extraordinary erotic goddess making love to the presidents, from wooden-toothed George Washington to slippery Richard Nixon. Having accomplished her task, Marilyn mimics her own death calling out for Bobby Kennedy on the telephone. Before she dies, Marilyn asks that her ashes be scattered among her beloved fans. Dressed as Uncle Sam, Arrow starts blowing her ashes out of an ashtray with a miniature fan. The play's action concludes with Gardenia Gertie confessing to killing Stockton

1

mainly because it made her feel young and beautiful and powerful again. She is then devoured by a pack of murderous alley cats, and, soon after, Arrow shoots his female protester to death.

In many respects, *Cop-Out* is a curious play that is quite prophetic in the way it uses the image of Marilyn Monroe. This surreal, absurdist, counterculture piece of theater has a complicated, stream-of-consciousness structure that smacks of its time, the late 1960s. This is most evident in its bold use of technical experimentation and social-political content. The play's antihero Brett Arrow is a fascistic cop, utterly opposed to anything he perceives of as being pinko/liberal. In this sense, he fits right in with the mood of Richard Nixon's beloved Silent Majority of the late 1960s and early 1970s.

The use of the female is also quite interesting, as the female protestor and Larue, as beautiful and desirable young women, though brutalized by Arrow, are both totally, absurdly infatuated with him. Diametrically opposed to them, there is the figure of Gardenia Gertie. At first, she appears to be a rather pathetic, broken-down, crippled, utterly sexless old lady. Then, in true absurdist fashion, she becomes the savage killer who butchered her own cat to make herself feel, perversely, young and beautiful and erotically powerful again.

The use of Marilyn is perhaps *Cop-Out's* most interesting use of all its female characters. She pops up in the midst of the play within a play as tempting as Aphrodite on her seashell. Her having slept with JFK and his brother Bobby is taken to its most ridiculously logical conclusion with Marilyn, the ultimate erotic goddess, sleeping with all the American presidents down through history:

> Marilyn Monroe (Gradually mounts in ecstasy): Oh, Woodrow, I feel so old. Oh, Calvin, say something. Harder, Harder, Harder, Harding. To think one day Herbert Hoover would be mine. Oh, FDR, your braces are cold against my legs. You don't tell me, Harry, you learned that from Bess. Oh, yes, Ike, you put me to sleep. Hold me, Daddy Ike. Oh, Jack. We're young. You and I are young. (Becoming an Old Lady) Bobby, answer the phone? (Gasps for breath. Desperate. Then bright and Marilyn again.) Hey, hey, LBJ where'd you learn to kiss that way? (Then as Old Lady.) Bobby? Answer the phone. . . . (Then Marilyn.) Ooooooo OO, Mr. Nixon. Just 'cos I'm dead doesn't mean you can treat me like that. Oooo OO. (Old Lady.) Bobby? Answer the phone![1]

In a scene such as this, Marilyn is depicted as a mythical heroine who, in death, transcends time and space to become the glamorous mistress of each and every one of the American presidents. But behind all the wild humor, such a scene also unexpectedly calls attention to her tragic and mysterious death and her plaintively calling out to Bobby Kennedy, which she supposedly did in her final, last hours.

In the end, what playwright John Guare has essentially done in *Cop-Out* is pick up on the darker mood and feeling of the late 1960s and filter them through his own distinctly personal dramatic vision. The end result is an often bizarre, absurdist drama in which Guare takes stylization and symbolism about just as far as they can possibly go. Symbolization and stylization are present in the play's depiction of Marilyn. She is transformed into the symbolic love goddess of every American president's erotic imagination. In this way, *Cop-Out* is a work that looks forward toward some of the more mature, more sophisticated, and more transcendent depictions of Marilyn that will come to proliferate particularly in the later 1980s and 1990s.

Curiously, the first of the six depictions of the 1970s featuring Marilyn Monroe as a character, the play *The Life and Death of Marilyn Monroe*, was performed not in America but in Glasgow, Scotland. And what is even more curious is that it wasn't even written in English but was based on a text written in German by playwright Gerlind Reinshagen. Playwright Anthony Vivis did the English translation for the Scottish production, which starred English actress Shirley Anne Field as Marilyn.

The Life and Death of Marilyn Monroe touched on all the major high points of Marilyn's life as she made her way out of obscurity, as the insecure, unhappy Norma Jean to the height of immortality as the world-famous Hollywood superstar Marilyn Monroe. Hollywood was presented in the play, with all its superlatives and hypocritical phoniness intact. *Variety* said of Field's performance, "Shirley Anne Field perfectly captures the voice, the face, the looks and the luminous smile of Miss Monroe." [June 15, 1971]

After the success of *The Life and Death of Marilyn Monroe*, a rash of short-lived plays purporting to be about the life and death of Marilyn came and went. One of the better received of these efforts was the 1975 Canadian radio play *Hey, Marilyn!* starring the vastly talented actress Beverly D'Angelo as Marilyn Monroe. In *Hey, Marilyn!*, D'Angelo, a talented singer, as well as actress, sang such clever songs as "I Can Do More," "Hi ya, Joe," and "Do It to Me, Daddy." In 1979, Cliff Jones adapted his radio play into a stage production starring actress Lenore Zann as Marilyn Monroe. *Hey, Marilyn!* as a stage play received only fair reviews from the critics. Zann, however, tended to fare much better herself in the critical department. Also failing to catch on with either the critics or the public was the 1975 off-off Broadway production *The Marilyn Project* by David Gerard. Here Marilyn is referred to simply as "Star." As in the 1973 off-off Broadway roman à clef depiction of her *The White Whore and the Bit Player* (discussed below), Marilyn's psyche is pictured in divided halves played by two different actresses, Joan MacIntosh and Elizabeth Le Compte. Unfortunately, playwright Gerard didn't employ the fascinating theatrical device as memorably as playwright Tom Eyen did in the 1973 play.

Here, it was just mere clever technique and not much more than that. The remaining two 1970s depictions of Marilyn Monroe as a character, *Tommy* (1975) and *Goodbye, Norma Jean* (1976), are, for different reasons, deserving of more detailed attention.

Tommy, directed by Ken Russell, begins in the closing months of World War II with the heroic Captain Walker leaving behind his wife, Nora, and his beloved England to fight the Germans. Not long thereafter, the pregnant Nora is notified that her husband has been killed. On VE Day, she gives birth to a son, Tommy. Five years later, still saddened by the loss of her husband, Nora meets and becomes romantically involved with oily camp instructor Frank Hobbs. He moves in with her and Tommy. While making love one night, Frank and Nora are surprised by an intruder entering the bedroom. Frank kills the intruder, who turns out to be Captain Walker. Tommy, witness to his father's brutal murder, becomes deaf, dumb, and blind over the traumatic experience.

Tommy grows up feeling neglected and unloved by his mother. In an attempt to assuage her guilt, Nora brings him to the Church of St. Marilyn Monroe to be cured. When this fails to revive his senses, Frank takes Tommy to the Acid Queen. Although none of this works, Tommy does make an important discovery: he's the number one Pinball Wizard of the World. Frank wastes little time in exploiting Tommy's newfound fame, which soon brings great affluence. But the guilt-ridden Nora ends up like Marilyn Monroe, turning to pills and alcohol to numb herself.

In their mission to cure Tommy, Frank and Nora next take him to the Doctor, who fails to cure him. However, when the drunken and drugged-out Nora pushes Tommy through her mirror, his senses are miraculously restored. He becomes the new Messiah, and hordes of converts flock to him to play pinball and re-create Tommy's traumatized state at the time of his miraculous conversion. Tommy's followers grow increasingly infuriated by the overbearing emphasis Frank puts on the profit margin, and they revolt, reject Tommy, and kill Frank and Nora. Tommy swims far off toward a distant shore and makes his way up a steep mountain. Standing on the mountaintop, he comes to the realization that although he may have lost his divinity, he is now finally free of all the good and all the evil that tormented him throughout his young life.

In filming *Tommy*, director Ken Russell begins and ends the action on a mysterious set of paradoxes. The movie opens with the sun setting and closes with the sun rising. Between these two paradoxes, there is much else that is not always easy to understand. Yet, for all these complexities, we can safely say that with *Tommy*, Russell has created a musical movie masterpiece. Using the Who's celebrated 1969 rock opera as his starting point, Russell has fashioned this source material into a powerful morality tale of sin–guilt–redemption. Most impressive are the many dazzling set pieces of musical numbers the director uses to tell Tommy's story. One of the most impressive of these comes when Nora takes Tommy to the Church of St. Marilyn Monroe to be cured. In and of itself, this remarkable sequence is most exciting with its shimmering, floating, thoroughly mesmerizing use of music combined with Russell's hallucinatory visual effects. What elevates the sequence to the level of true genius is the way Russell depicts Marilyn here. For the entire interior of the church is devoted to her life and times. There are large painted icons of her adorning the altar, walls, and stained-glass windows. The acolytes swing burning incense, filling the air with billowing clouds of smoke, which adds to the overall atmosphere of the scene. The incense-swinging acolytes all wear these Marilyn Monroe blonde wigs, masks, and pouty red lips as Russell's camera moves freely about throughout the hallucinatory action. Yet another interesting aspect of the sequence is the rhythmical flow of the editing, which fluidly cuts back and forth between the afflicted parishioners waiting to be cured, and the ecstatic Preacher flashing about a mirrored image of Marilyn for them to kiss.

Then, in the midst of all the phantasmagorical brilliance, the processional march begins with the acolytes slowly carrying the giant iconic statue of Marilyn down the aisle toward the altar. The ravishing cult statue replicates the famous iconographic scene from *The Seven Year Itch* when the air vent blows up her white skirt on the steamy, summer streets of New York. The famous scene was already loaded with a tremendous amount of meaning even before Russell decided to give it even more meaning in this cinematic context. In using Marilyn's image as he does, Russell is taking what is only implicit in plays like *Cop-Out* and *The White Whore and the Bit Player* (discussed below), where she is depicted as a kind of mythic goddess outside of time and space (and perhaps even all personal identity), and he makes it all extravagantly and sensationally explicit. For in *Tommy*, Marilyn Monroe is depicted the same way that the Catholic Church has traditionally depicted the iconographic images of saints for centuries. Her iconic representation has become deified, exalted, raised up to the lofty, high level of the immortal, the goddess-like, the divine.

Yet when Nora takes Tommy up to touch the icon of Marilyn in the hopes of curing him, something unexpected happens. Tommy's approach causes the giant statue to topple over, smashing into many pieces. Although the exact meaning of what occurs in the sequence is open to interpretation, one could view it as a referent to the fact that Marilyn has now been elevated to the level of an immortal goddess, making her a symbol of an unattainable perfect beauty to be worshipped and adored. And, although all of that perfection does give off an undeniably appealing magnetic aura, it is ultimately something that can only be worshipped and adored from afar but never, ever attained by mere mortals. Or, at least, not quite just yet, anyway.

The 1976 Australian import *Goodbye, Norma Jean* is the first biopic of Marilyn Monroe's life. The action begins in 1941; Norma Jean Baker is a beautiful blonde teenager living with foster parents because her mother Gladys has been confined to an insane asylum for life. Her foster mother treats her cruelly, and her lecherous foster father is always trying to take advantage of her. After he attempts to rape her, Norma Jean leaves and supports herself by getting a job at a munitions factory. What keeps her going are all her fantasies of one day becoming a famous Hollywood movie star. Her beauty and well-proportioned figure continue to attract the attention of all sorts of men no matter where she goes.

Fortunately for Norma Jean, one of the men she attracts is the decent Ralph Johnson, an army photographer who takes her picture and helps her win a beauty contest. It is through his pinup of her and her beauty contest win that Norma Jean is launched on a modeling career. Yet every step along the way, men continually take advantage of her. Things improve for her when she is taken on by Hollywood agent Irving Olbach, who takes her to a Hollywood party at the home of retired and ailing movie mogul Hal James. There she meets aging matinee idol Randy Palmer, who seduces her in the backseat of his Packard. Later, she is further exploited by a sleazy movie executive who expects her to perform sexual favors for a bit in a movie. To help cope with all this, Norma Jean turns to pills and alcohol for relief. At one point, to make ends meet, she even stars in a raunchy stag movie. After seeing her blue movie, Hal James steps back into her life to help groom her into a real movie star. He sets up an appointment for her with movie executive and notorious lesbian Ruth Zatimer. Ruth promises Norma Jean a screen test in exchange for sex. But when Ruth fails to get her the screen test, Norma Jean confronts her and the head of the studio, Sam Dunn, who retaliates by lashing out at Norma Jean.

Distraught over his rejection of her, she tries to kill herself by cutting her wrists. Fortunately, the now gravely ill Hal James focuses what's left of his life on making her a star. (Obviously, concurring with real life, he's the movie's Johnny Hyde character in Marilyn's life.) He employs a team of plastic surgeons, makeup artists, hairdressers, and dress designers to transform her into the glamorously beautiful future movie goddess, Marilyn Monroe. Although he dies just before she makes it, Hal James dies knowing that he has helped prove to everyone in Hollywood—and soon the entire world—that Marilyn Monroe is a force to be reckoned with.

In some ways, *Goodbye, Norma Jean* is comparable to movie star biopics of the past in the way that it alters and falsifies many of the biographical details of Marilyn Monroe's life. But what is not so comparable to past star biopics is the fact that this movie does not necessarily do this to glorify or glamorize

Marilyn's life in any way. No, this is done to eroticize her life to the hilt. In fact, so sexually loaded is most of the action that much of the time it feels as if we're watching her life turned into something of a soft-core pornographic movie masquerading as a star biopic.

In keeping with the movie's overall eroticized tone, the young Norma Jean has been totally eroticized and fetishized as well. The increased explicitness in this depiction of Marilyn's body has its effect on the narrative, which is structured by a series of seductions all based on the heroine's attempts to use her body to climb her way to the top of the ladder in Hollywood. And it is in these various sexual encounters the heroine experiences throughout the course of the narrative that her body even ends up getting reified into the mise-en-scène of the movie. As a result of this reification, her excessive sexuality and erotic display become invested with power and emotion. But at several points, this power and emotion take the negative form of anger, which Norma Jean mostly directs toward the men who take such advantage of her and exploit her. So, in her, we see a seemingly uncontrollable anger against society in general—and men in particular. But, interestingly, Norma Jean doesn't always seem so angry at the way men treat her. There are times when she gets downright depressed and even suicidal. Yet, no matter how depressed or how angry she might get, she always manages to perk right up, pick herself up, and go out and face all those hungry wolves all over again. At times, her abrupt mood swings give the action an unreal, schizoid quality. But in the final analysis, one must take all this with a grain of salt. For, in truth, it is too difficult to accept *Goodbye, Norma Jean* as being truly about the real life of Marilyn Monroe. Indeed, so much of the narrative displaces and eroticizes the heroine that the movie speaks much more of the hyperbolized excess that is the curious cinematic talent of its producer-director Larry Buchanan. Undoubtedly, the best thing of all about *Goodbye, Norma Jean* is actress Misty Rowe in the role of the young Norma Jean. She does a good job at capturing Marilyn's voice and mannerisms.

This Year's Blonde (1980) was the first 1980s depiction of Marilyn Monroe as a character. Presented as the first installment of a three-part miniseries, based on author Garson Kanin's (*Come on Strong*) novel *Moviola*, the movie focuses on Marilyn Monroe's special relationship with Hollywood agent Johnny Hyde. When he first encounters Marilyn Monroe in *This Year's Blonde*, she is nothing more than just another obscure, pretty, peroxided Hollywood starlet. But he perceives, at once, that this blonde starlet is not just any blonde. No, with his special assistance, she will become famous. He buys her contract from her agent and swiftly becomes her agent, lover, salvation, and something she never had, a loving father. But a little incident occurs that shows the absurd vanity of Hollywood. A makeup man notices a tiny bump on Marilyn's nose, which causes her to think her nose is grotesque. When Johnny introduces her to people at an important movie premiere, she attempts to hide her nose, which irritates him. Yet Johnny resolves it all by taking her to a plastic surgeon to remove the bump.

Johnny next builds up a portfolio of photographs with which he hopes to get Marilyn an important screen test. Eventually, he learns that she once posed for a sexy nude calendar. But she merely brushes off the incident and indeed later on in her career is able to make light of the whole thing. Meanwhile, Johnny continues to visit every major studio in Hollywood trying to sell Marilyn, but despite her beauty, he is unsuccessful in his valiant efforts—until one night when he takes Marilyn out dancing and meets director John Huston, who happens to be filming a new movie called *The Asphalt Jungle*. Johnny introduces Marilyn to Huston and asks him if there's anything in the new movie for her. Much to their astonishment, Huston says, there is. With the attaining of this important role, it is now the big time for Marilyn and her agent, Johnny Hyde. She goes on to make *The Asphalt Jungle* for Huston. On the night of the movie's premiere, Johnny is too ill to attend. But he encourages Marilyn to go on without him. Later when she returns home, she learns that Johnny has been rushed to the hospital, having suffered a massive heart attack. She immediately goes to be with him. This night becomes both a personal triumph of the highest exaltation of success for Marilyn and the blackest night of her life when she loses her lover, protector, and, most of all, creator, Johnny Hyde. But on a certain level, too, she's also aware that she has fully validated Johnny's belief in her potential. Hollywood superstardom is now hers forever.

In adapting Kanin's version of *This Year's Blonde* for television, James Lee makes some fascinating choices. He puts the main emphasis of the action on Johnny Hyde rather than Marilyn. This ends up making Johnny an incredibly proactive character, while Marilyn, for her part, is depicted as being more of a reactive character. So, because of this, it is Johnny Hyde we mostly find ourselves rooting for much of the movie. The second interesting choice Lee makes is to cut Kanin's original story in half. The tale Kanin tells on the page is an infinitely darker and more disturbing one than what is presented here. For in the book, we are taken beyond Marilyn's ensuing stardom and brought deep into all the amorality and high pressure typically associated with Hollywood. But in altering the narrative, the TV version of *This Year's Blonde* is a less pessimistic, more positive depiction of Marilyn. The reason that this all works as well as it does is chiefly because of Lloyd Bridges's playing of Johnny Hyde. In his capable hands, Johnny is, at once, completely credible and winning. We never doubt, for an instant, that he is the one and only man of real class and culture in all of Hollywood with a heart and, also, a wallet big enough to cultivate and bring forth the exquisite blossoming of Marilyn's unique hitherto unimaginable stardom. Although actress Constance Forslund may have the less showy, more passive role, she does manage to do some impressive things with her lovely and dignified portrayal of Marilyn Monroe.

If *This Year's Blonde* presents Marilyn Monroe at the start of her journey to mythic iconization, the 1980 movie musical *Can't Stop the Music* depicts her after having acquired full veneration. She is seen only briefly at the start of the movie when aspiring pop composer Jack Morell is roller-skating home to the Greenwich Village apartment he shares with his sexy roommate, ex-supermodel Samantha Morton. Jack skates by a posh Manhattan dress shop where mannequins of legendary Hollywood sex goddesses Jean Harlow, Betty Grable, and, of course, Marilyn Monroe are displayed in the window. Quite charmingly, the three beautiful blondes all come to life and smile at Jack.

After he plays his music at a disco to much success, Sam puts together a singing group—the Village People, consisting of a policeman, a construction worker, an Indian, a cowboy, a leather man, and a soldier—to make Jack's songs a hit. From that point, the movie basically becomes one extravagant production number after another, which include the Village People singing "YMCA," a Busby Berkely–like spoof, complete with scenes of musclemen and bodybuilders stripped down to their gym shorts (and beyond) wrestling, playing racquetball, pumping iron, and even diving into the Olympic-size swimming pool á la Esther Williams; an elaborate TV commercial in praise of the wonders of milk, culminating with the nude Sam in a gigantic champagne glass filled with milk; and a concluding over-the-top number set in San Francisco with the Village People dressed in Las Vegas–like sequined costumes.

Can't Stop the Music was intended by producer Allan Carr to cash in on the disco craze the same way his 1978 hit movie *Grease* had cashed in on the rock-and-roll craze. But in some ways, this outrageous movie was actually something of an anachronism. By 1980, the disco craze was pretty much on its last leg. Nevertheless, it must be admitted that the movie is still something of a curiosity piece, with its not-so-subtle gay overtones (each of the Village People signify a distinct and different fetishized gay fantasy archetype) and the way director Nancy Walker's camera always seems to turn into something of a dirty old man, fetishistically ogling leading lady Valerie Perrine's Jayne Mansfieldesque body. Almost as a reaction to all the outrageousness, Marilyn is used in a surprisingly simple, direct, and, therefore, most effective way. She appears as one of three mannequins displayed in the window of a posh New York shop. She is joined by Jean Harlow and Betty Grable. This makes the window display something of a triumvirate of three great blonde Hollywood pinup girls. Marilyn wears the famous white dress created for her by costume designer William Travilla for *Gentlemen Prefer Blondes*. We have already seen Travilla's costume being paid homage to in *Tommy*. And it can be stated that it is the iconic costume of choice (followed by her shocking pink *Gentlemen Prefer Blondes* gown and her "Happy Birthday, Mr. President" see-through gown) in the vast majority of the Marilyn Monroe depictions documented for this book.

In 1973, author Norman Mailer wrote the extremely unconventional and controversial biography about Marilyn Monroe titled *Marilyn*. In 1980, Mailer's book was adapted into a TV movie that attempted to encompass all the crucial incidents from her life. The string of episodes unfolds in the form of an extended chronological flashback, introduced at the opening by a scene in August 1962. Marilyn Monroe appears in this opening scene in a very bad way. Totally addicted to pills and alcohol, she has been fired off of her latest movie, *Something's Got to Give*, by her home studio, 20th Century-Fox. Unfazed about the future, she instead loses herself in the past. She remembers when she was little Norma Jean born to the unwed, unstable Gladys Baker. When her mother suffers a total catatonic breakdown, Norma Jean is sent to live in a series of orphanages and foster homes. The unhappy little girl often loses herself in fantasies of one day becoming a famous movie star. During World War II, she marries Jim Dougherty and, when he is drafted, gets a job at a parachute factory. One day she is spotted by a photographer, and soon she is bleaching her hair blonde, posing nude on red velvet drapery, and changing her name to Marilyn Monroe. Hollywood superagent Johnny Hyde makes her a star as her pill and alcohol dependencies intensify. In 1953, she marries baseball superstar Joe DiMaggio, but the marriage is short lived. After divorcing, Marilyn studies method acting at the Actors Studio in New York with Lee Strasberg. She also falls in love with married playwright Arthur Miller. After he divorces his wife, he and Marilyn marry and head back to Hollywood. Unfortunately, her addictions and her inability to carry a baby to term take a profound toll on her. Arthur writes *The Misfits* for her, but the filming of the movie marks the end of their marriage.

In 1962, Marilyn begins making *Something's Got to Give*. Her health is so bad that she holds up filming for days at a time. After she goes to New York to sing "Happy Birthday, Mr. President," to JFK, she is fired from the movie. Things go from bad to worse for her during the last weeks of her life. On August 5, 1962, she is found dead in her bed, nude, holding a telephone.

If the details of this TV movie's plot do sound familiar enough, it should first be pointed out that much of what made Mailer's book so controversial and unconventional has been either toned down or eliminated. One of the more fascinating aspects of the book is the way Mailer conceives of his heroine. He describes how Marilyn is first photographed to be a pinup girl while working in a parachute factory during World War II. This, in turn, ends up helping her discover the real focus of her life—it is in the camera's lens. She quickly realizes that when she gets in front of the camera, magic happens. In essence, the camera can even be said to become her great, magical lover that never fails or deserts her. This leads into her next realizing that the same magical love can also happen with the movie camera as well. Besides, being a mere pinup girl is indeterminate. But to be a great movie star, well, that is superdetermined. The only problem is that most of the movies Hollywood forces on her strip her of her existence, leaving her feeling empty inside. In an attempt to rebel against such shoddy treatment and to discover her true self and find personal enlightenment, Marilyn seriously studies acting. She no longer wants to be the debased Hollywood sexual object of lowbrow art. She longs to be the exalted subject of high art. With a particularly modernist twist, Marilyn Monroe wants to become an artist crossing over the border from the low to the high.

When the time came for *Marilyn*—a book about one of the most dazzling movie stars of the silver screen—to be filmed, like *This Year's Blonde*, it was also adapted for the small screen. But unlike *This Year's Blonde*, this version of Marilyn's life encompasses all her life, not part of it. George F. Custen explains why the biopic became a TV fixture from the 1970s on:

> TV seemingly—though this might not be the best word—democratizes fame, shrinks its contours. Second, by applying new, harder standards of scrutiny to the sacred lives of the "good" famous (e.g., extramarital lovers for Presidents Eisenhower, Kennedy, and Roosevelt, once taboo revelations about Rock Hudson and Rosemary Clooney), celebrities once constructed as "wholesome" are reconfigured with a tabloid point of view.[2]

As it turned out, however, it wasn't so much "a tabloid point of view" that gave writer Dalene Young her greatest challenge. No, her greatest challenge was how to translate Mailer's impressionistic and poetic prose into the stuff of a less controversial and a whole lot more conventional TV biopic. She achieves this by toning down the more erotic and poetic passages as well as Mailer's charges implicating the Kennedys in Marilyn's death. In place of the author's rich, lyrical prose, Young imposes on the material the more formulaic biopic structure, that old Hollywood standby the extended flashback. Custen points out that the extended flashback is always so favored by the makers of Hollywood biopics because it allows the star's life story to be told from a totally controlled, narrative vantage point.

Yet, even with this admittedly formulaic approach to the material, it is wonderful to be getting the first real attempt at depicting Marilyn's life in full. It is for this reason that *Marilyn, The Untold Story* becomes a seminal work. In addition, there are many other reasons for us to admire its achievement. True, Young may have toned down much of Mailer's more lyrical writing, but she's been wise enough to retain his presentation of the details of Marilyn's life. There's the young Norma Jean staring out, through tear-filled eyes, of her orphanage window down on all the movie activity happening on the back lot of RKO Pictures; the teenaged Norma Jean working in the parachute factory during World War II and, later, posing nude on red velvet drapery; the highly charged moment of Marilyn entertaining the troops in Korea with her sexy rendition of "Diamonds Are a Girl's Best Friend"; the filming of the iconic white skirt scene on the streets of New York in *The Seven Year Itch* and her emerging nude from the swimming pool in *Something's Got to Give*; and her singing of "Happy Birthday, Mr. President" to JFK.

Finally, it is in the re-creation of these famous scenes from Marilyn's life that the full impact of this movie resonates well beyond its individual creation; in many later works, the re-creation of such iconic scenes will become authoritative. As something of a primary canonical text, *Marilyn, The Untold Story* goes a long way toward consolidating and disseminating the fundamentals for what will become a unique new "visual vocabulary." It also draws on and absorbs a whole network of complex visual strategies, ultimately encompassing not only Mailer's book but also numerous other visual and descriptive resources chronicling the life and times of Marilyn, such as can be found in books about her, documentaries, newsreel footage, still photographs, and her own Hollywood movies. So rich is its capacity for this visual discourse that *Marilyn, The Untold Story* presents all this information in a single, transformed model for others to draw on in the future. Therefore, when future artists wish to depict Marilyn and the details of her life, this movie confirms their artistic approaches and aesthetic choices. Further, there is one other important thing that is most unqualifiedly in the movie's favor: the shapely, shimmering elegance of Catherine Hicks as Marilyn Monroe. The actress comes through with a star-making performance for which she received a Best Actress Emmy Award nomination for the prize that went that year to Vanessa Redgrave in *Playing for Time*.

In 1981, ballet superstar Celia Hulton played Marilyn Monroe in the ballet *Dances of Love and Death* in Edinburgh, Scotland. Costumed in Marilyn's famous white skirt from *The Seven Year Itch* and wearing high heels, Hulton was sensational as she danced her way through all the crucial incidents of Marilyn's life and eventual death. The dynamic choreography was strongly influenced by the innovative, avant-garde style of the legendary American dancer Isadora Duncan. There was then a concentration on these unconventional but deeply lyrical movements that emphasized the natural expression of Hulton's body and emotions. And, just as Isadora frequently turned to tragic and heroic themes in her visionary art, so too did Hulton's movements give way to a desperate abandonment as she re-created the tragedy of Marilyn's death. But Hulton not only danced the ballet most beautifully but also made a game stab at capturing the spirit of Marilyn.

Then, in 1982, there appeared at the Royal Court Theatre in London a text that qualifies as one of the very best ever of all depictions of Marilyn Monroe. *Insignificance*, by playwright Terry Johnson, presents Marilyn as one of the four mythical characters in this play of both the flesh and the spirit. Inspired by a knowledge that a personally inscribed photograph of Albert Einstein had been found among her possessions after her death, *Insignificance* has Marilyn sharing the stage with not only Einstein but with Senator Joe McCarthy and Joe DiMaggio as well. The action takes place in 1954 in the small, stuffy hotel room of Einstein, who awaits a meeting with McCarthy to assess his standing of patriotism, or does Einstein's highly eclectic mind have a communist, pinko taint? Einstein is busy doing his calculus when McCarthy calls on him in a most transparent simulation of friendliness, offering him some cordial advice on how he should act for his upcoming inquisition before the House Un-American Activities Committee (HUAC).

Now if Einstein's tiny New York hotel room represents, poetically, the physical universe that Einstein endlessly calculates, McCarthy represents total evil. True, he does at one point refer to Einstein as the True Child of the Universe, but then he also attempts to pressure him into not just denouncing communism but naming the names of the other communists as well. When Einstein says no, that he will ignore his subpoena before the HUAC and attend the Conference for World Peace instead, the outraged McCarthy shows his true colors. He not only threatens to have Einstein blacklisted but also threatens to destroy his life work of the physical structure of the universe itself, after which he departs.

Einstein falls fast asleep. He is pleasantly awakened by none other than Marilyn Monroe herself (who wears the famous *Seven Year Itch* white dress and dark glasses). She confesses that she felt an overwhelming compulsion to meet him, and she goes on to complain of the filming of her latest Hollywood movie, *The Seven Year Itch*:

> They fixed up a wind machine beneath a grating out on Fifty-third; I've been out there since before midnight having my skirt blown up around my goddamn ears.[3]

Marilyn and Einstein go on to speak wittily and with a few double entendres thrown in. She even launches into a charming demonstration of Einstein's theory of relativity, delighting him to no end. And, of course, being the sensual Goddess of Love and Beauty that she is, Marilyn next attempts to seduce the great man. Marilyn, while depicted as being very bright here, is the beauteous, sensuous, and deeply spiritualized body, and Einstein is the superlative mind—the rarest, most exquisite genius of the cosmos. At one point, Marilyn even cradles the pages of Einstein's calculus to her heavenly bosom as if she were holy Mother Earth herself cradling the whole of the universe.

But before there can be any such perfect blending of brains and beauty, the jealous Joe DiMaggio comes charging in with hopes of retrieving his wife. She manages to calm Joe down long enough to engage in a lively discourse on Einstein's theories of the physical universe. But Joe is not too happy, which so upsets Marilyn that she locks herself in the bathroom to get away from him. With Marilyn gone, Joe takes the opportunity to tell Einstein just how difficult life can be married to a glamorous Hollywood sex goddess. Einstein decides to take another room to allow the couple some privacy. Joe ends up falling asleep, and Marilyn quietly sobs over all the ocean of pain in her life and mind.

Later, Marilyn awakens bedraggled and alone; McCarthy returns. He is immediately struck by her resemblance to whom else? Marilyn Monroe. But, being who and what he is, McCarthy doesn't really believe she is Marilyn. He accuses her of being a call girl, merely imitating the star. When Einstein returns, Marilyn urges him to stand up for himself and throw the foul McCarthy out. Then, later, she even offers her sexual favors to McCarthy in exchange for his not destroying Einstein's life's work. McCarthy responds to her offer by beating her savagely. As she collapses, Joe returns and gets into a heated argument with McCarthy. Marilyn intercedes and encourages her husband to let McCarthy go on his way. Joe then attempts to reconcile with his wife, but she tells him to call his lawyer—the marriage is over. Joe accepts his medicine like a man and departs. Marilyn climbs back into bed, as both she and the bedclothes are now covered in blood. The brutal beating McCarthy gave her has caused her to miscarry the baby she was carrying. After she has had a chance to clean herself up, Einstein returns. He tells her of the profound guilt he feels over his part in the development of the Bomb, and he talks of his concern for the future of mankind. Then, all of a sudden, there is a great flash of blinding white light and an enormous explosion and a great wind. Clearly, Einstein has imagined the worst—a nuclear explosion. Luckily, it was only a passing thought, just Einstein's own private thought, and the effects disappear in an instant. But in that instant, Hiroshima and Nagasaki are powerfully evoked. In an attempt to try and calm him down again, Marilyn reads to Einstein some of the banal stage directions from the latest Hollywood movie she is making. And so, a universe begins and ends, then begins again in one convulsive white, hot flash. . . .

In the imagining of this meeting of four great historical figures, Terry Johnson has managed to mix in so many layers of meaning and cosmic psychology that each of his principal characters becomes mythical and powerfully charismatic: Albert Einstein, Senator Joseph McCarthy, Joe DiMaggio, and, of course, Marilyn Monroe. Johnson uses Marilyn here in a way similar to the way she was used in *The White Whore and the Bit Player* and *Tommy*. The main emphasis is on her status as an iconic figure. The figures of Einstein, McCarthy, and DiMaggio are used similarly. The major difference, however, is that the basic dynamic of the play consists of the way in which each one of the male figures interweaves and is radiated back by the shiny, glamorous mirror of Monroe. She is the golden sun around which the men revolve for warmth and illumination. But if Marilyn is the golden sun, she is also the very heart and soul of the play. And if she is the soul, Einstein is the mind and DiMaggio the physical body. But more specifically, he represents the body tormented and in the symbol of Everyman. As such, he is the body seemingly kept in a perpetual state of agitation over his failure and inability to attain, contain, and neutralize completely the perfect, unattainable beauty symbolized in Marilyn Monroe.

At the start of the play, we have the great man, the groundbreaking genius of the new era, Einstein, eternally scribbling away in a gallant attempt to comprehend the physical universe. His astute penetration into such lofty matters attest to his preferring to reside in the world of his own private devising rather than the infinitely more chaotic one outside himself. Thus, when Marilyn makes her appearance, she suddenly pulls Einstein out of his private, interior reverie and makes him fully aware that he is now indeed with someone who is something special. Thus, the stage has been set for that mythical and magical coming together of Beauty and the Brain. Elevated to such a dramaturgical position, Marilyn makes evident the fact that she is much more than just a beauteous distraction on the great man's illuminative and esoteric thoughts. She is also something of a kindred spirit.

As undoubtedly the most brilliant man in the universe, what better way is there for the Eternal Goddess of Grace and Beauty to show her heartfelt appreciation to him than to give herself to him? It is even possible in this dramatic context to speak of Marilyn as opening up a new interspace between the Dionysian force of her vitality and eroticism and the Apollonian delight of Einstein's visions and dreams. Yet, besides just this dynamic new interplay between these two great cosmic forces, the nature of her engaging conversation shows that she is in possession of a finely tuned mind to complement her endlessly desired body. She also displays a lively spirit such as when she stands up for Einstein against the evil machinations of McCarthy, whose mission it is to torment and even destroy the eternal mind–body–soul triumvirate of Einstein–DiMaggio–Monroe. McCarthy then signifies the repressive, soul-destroying banality of the 1950s. In his dealings with Marilyn, all he can do is lash out and destroy her. The full ramifications of his destructiveness come when he savagely beats her, causing her to suffer a bloody miscarriage. With the killing of the baby in her womb, McCarthy becomes the transmogrification of the Agent of Death robbing Marilyn of the Divine Child evidently charged with the power to pull her out of her private pain and confusion.

When DiMaggio makes his grand entrance into the play, he sets in motion a whole other dramatic adventure. He is mad with desire for Marilyn, yet he is completely mystified that she will not do what he wants, behaving as both a loyal and faithful wife to him as well as his own personal domestic goddess. When he proclaims that he wants her to give up making movies and Hollywood to play the role of the traditional wife, she derides him for being a stupid man. But, actually, Marilyn is wrong about this. And in making this accusation against Joe, she indulges in a bit of existential reductionism. Not only is Joe not stupid, but for much of the play he exhibits this true cunning, peasant intelligence. He is permeated here with the most powerfully instinctual existential tensions both to survive and to thrive against all the odds. And when he steps out on the stage, he brings much to distinguish himself, and in a real, specific sense, he is as extraordinary in his own right as Marilyn is in hers.

In *Insignificance*, Joe becomes a very likable and sympathetic character. Behind all his macho swaggering and braggadocio and behind even all his petty jealousies, he truly does love and care about Marilyn. He alone seems to understand the baffling paradox that she, along with everyone else, simply cannot. Hollywood, with all its wealth and glamour and fame, along with all its lurid sex and drugs and booze, is destroying her even as she so desperately needs Hollywood and all the adoring masses it provides for her. In light of this, it is ironic that despite the commanding love Joe has for her, Marilyn cannot reciprocate. As a mythical Hollywood movie goddess, she is destined to be worshipped and adored not by just one mere man alone—no matter how exalted his station. Despite everything she does, she believes that she has found the magical way to make her life bearable in the fulfillment of her dreams of Hollywood stardom and the attainment of the love of the masses. In this twofold path, she believes she can, finally, achieve for herself the self-justification and self-redemption she seeks. The fullest expression of Joe's understanding comes when he agrees to divorce Marilyn as she requests. In his own way, Joe clearly understands everything about Marilyn. And so, if it is Marilyn's true destiny to be loved by all of mankind, then, it is Joe's true destiny to understand and go on loving her forever despite everything. And it is for precisely this reason that he more than proves his right to the title of Great American Hero. Gifted actress Judy Davis played Marilyn Monroe in the play's London premiere, impressing both the critics and the public. One such member of the public who was most especially impressed was movie director Nicolas Roeg. He quickly purchased the screen rights to transform the play into a movie starring his wife, Theresa Russell, as Marilyn Monroe in 1985.

In keeping with the Reagan 1980s obsession with extravagant opulence and excessive luxury, two big, splashy theatrical productions based on Marilyn Monroe's life appeared in 1983. The first of these musical extravaganzas, *Marilyn!*, opened at the Delphi Theatre in London, and it turned out to be the slightly better received of the two. The second musical, *Marilyn, An American Fable*, opened at the Minskoff Theatre on Broadway six months later.

British actress Stephanie Lawrence played the role of Marilyn Monroe in the London musical. The musical was influenced by the 1978 Tim Rice/ Andrew Lloyd Webber smash hit, rock opera *Evita*. Of course, it can be argued that poor Stephanie Lawrence was not quite as lucky and didn't have a hit show like *Evita* to showcase her musical gifts. But who knows? Maybe if Rice and Lloyd Webber had turned their attention to Marilyn Monroe rather than *Evita*, things would have turned out very differently indeed for the lovely Lawrence. Still, as things did turn out in 1983, although *Marilyn!* was basically thrashed by the critics, Lawrence nonetheless came out of it smelling like an English rose.

Much the same thing that happened to Lawrence also happened with the Broadway musical *Marilyn, An American Fable* and the performance of leading lady Alyson Reed as Marilyn Monroe. When the show opened, the majority of the critics didn't much care for the fact that it ignored so many of the richer complexities of Marilyn's real life. In place of rich complexity, there was, instead, as Benedict Nightingale of *The New York Times* aptly put it, ". . . a saga about a fluttering innocent who wants nothing more than to be very, very famous and is, understandably, disillusioned when the beastly Hollywood moguls give her commercial scripts and actually expect her to memorize them." [November 27, 1983]

Still, if the play did open to poor reviews, Alyson Reed worked hard to catch Marilyn's spirit. The critical response to her flawless performance in this profoundly flawed production was duly noted. Clive Barnes in the *New York Post* said of her,

> This is the transmogrification of the ugly duckling Norma Jean into that swan of Hollywood, Marilyn Monroe. The transformation is sensational and Alyson Reed playing Marilyn complete with kiss, curl, pout and breathy voice, handles it all with aplomb. The famous still poses are almost all there and Miss Reed freezes into them with commanding authority. [November 21, 1983]

If Lawrence and Reed gave first-rate performances in less than first-rate vehicles, Karen MacDonald surpassed them both playing Marilyn Monroe in

Norman Mailer's play *Strawhead*, which premiered at the Provincetown Summer Theater of Provincetown, Massachusetts, in the summer of 1983. As good as Mailer's 1980 *Marilyn, The Untold Story* is, *Strawhead*, based on his 1980 imaginary memoir of Marilyn, *Of Women and Their Elegance*, surpasses it. The full daring of *Strawhead* is that it enlarges the imaginative scope and adds layers of meaning only hinted at in the TV movie. And in the end, it achieves the authenticity of a fully developed work of art. It does what all great art must do: it makes Marilyn's story a part of our own.

Strawhead begins with Marilyn sitting at her dressing table remembering her flamboyant acting teacher, Mr. Charles, who always expounded on the fact that everyone has two souls inside of them. His words, in turn, make her think of her horrific childhood. (And it is this childhood that becomes an amorphous, unseen component of the play, often unconsciously influencing Marilyn's thoughts and feelings of unresolved anguish and plunging her into dark despair.) After Mr. Charles vanishes, photographer Milton Greene appears. He gives Marilyn a sexy black sweater to wear as he photographs her. In front of Milton's camera, she is magical. She works a similar magic when she later appears in a skintight gold lamé gown, the shoulder strap of which breaks, exposing her breast.

As her relationship with Milton deepens, he helps Marilyn get out of her contract with 20th Century-Fox and to form her own company, Marilyn Monroe Productions. While this is happening, Milton's sophisticated wife, Amy, teaches her all about elegance. Eventually, Marilyn moves into the Greene's home, and Milton and Amy work hard to refine and educate her. She is given books of history to read. Unfortunately, her paranoia gets the better of her when Milton arranges to have Edward R. Murrow interview her with the Greenes on his TV program *Person to Person*. Soon after, she leaves their home and moves to a suite in the Waldorf Towers. While there, she remembers many painful memories from her life, and she comes to rely more and more on pills and alcohol to cope. Besides her painful childhood, one of her darkest memories is of a strange night of sex and drugs she once experienced that ended with her discovery of a black Doberman pinscher with its throat slit.

Away from the Greenes, Marilyn begins a serious relationship with playwright Arthur Miller, driving a further wedge between her and them. Still, she does win a lucrative, new contract from 20th Century-Fox, and Milton acquires *The Prince and the Showgirl* for her to make with Laurence Olivier as her leading man and director. She also studies acting with Lee Strasberg at the Actors Studio. When Lee denigrates Olivier to Marilyn, she begins to grow skeptical of Olivier. And later, when Arthur and Marilyn go to England to make *The Prince and the Showgirl*, she and Olivier clash over her new method acting style and the fact she has brought along Lee's wife, Paula, as her drama coach. When the movie is finished, she ends her relationship with Milton and Amy.

The Prince and the Showgirl fails at the box office, and after Marilyn plays Roslyn in *The Misfits*, she and Arthur divorce. She grows more and more confused and depressed, as her dependency on pills and alcohol grows out of control and 20th Century-Fox fires her from *Something's Got to Give*. About the only real bright spot left in her life is when she runs into Milton and he makes a date to visit her in the fall of 1962. But, of course, she never even makes it through the summer of 1962.

We have previously looked at the way in which Mailer's *Marilyn, The Untold Story* created a "visual discourse" that had overtones that took it far beyond its original context. With *Strawhead*, these overtones have become wedded to a richly layered theatrical text that projects Marilyn and her life onto an epic scale. With *Strawhead*, Mailer is given a chance to enlarge the scope and deepen the meaning of Marilyn until she becomes a towering, theatrical figure. Mailer's intent is made clear with the play's opening. Mr. Charles, Marilyn's acting teacher, appears to explain to her his theory of everyone having two different personalities. This raising of the question of a divided psyche serves to illuminate the troubled dualism of Marilyn's own mind and soul.

No sooner does Mr. Charles vanish than does Milton Greene appear. He has come to photograph her, and the two of them feel an instant rapport. When he gives her a sexy black sweater to wear, he grows nervous when she uninhibitedly changes into it in front of him. Besides establishing the basic characteristics of Marilyn and Milton for us, this opening scene also introduces us to the special way that color is employed to heighten dramatic power. When she first appears, Marilyn dresses like a typical Hollywood starlet, wearing a clingy red blouse and skintight green slacks. But when the garishness of her attire offends Milton's masterful photographer's eye, he has her change into the deep black sweater. With this simple change of costume, Milton's black sweater connects Marilyn to sultry sophistication and a subtle, understated elegance. This sophisticated effect gets canceled out in the very next scene when she makes an appearance at the Photoplay Awards. Dressed in a flashy skintight gold lamé gown, she's a gaudy golden spectacle. When her shoulder strap breaks, exposing her breast, she is angrily denounced by Joan Crawford. With this angry denouncement of Marilyn, Crawford is at once transformed into a mad version of Snow White's jealous and narcissistic stepmother, the Evil Queen ("Mirror, mirror on the wall, who is the fairest of them all?"). This instantly marks the notorious "Mommie Dearest" as one of the more terrifying figures in *Strawhead*. With thick eyebrows; big, broad shoulders; and stern condemnation, Crawford—like McCarthy in *Insignificance*— signifies all the dark, oppressive forces of the 1950s and also a certain banal Hollywood hypocrisy.

Fortunately, all of Crawford's nastiness gives way to the warmth and Audrey Hepburn–like elegance of Milton's wife, Amy. While Milton assists in helping Marilyn set up her own production company, both he and Amy help transform her into a woman of elegance. It is toward this end that Milton arranges for famous society dressmaker Norman Norwell (whose well-heeled clientele fully appreciate the *tres* snob appeal of his lavish, all-out glamorous high-fashion creations) to design for her a whole new wardrobe entirely in the color white (with all its rich symbolic association to purity, truth, innocence, and the divine), reflecting Marilyn's personal evolution into the world of true elegance and sophistication. Milton goes on to add another layer of meaning to her connection to white when he tells her that he wants her to star in a movie with the only actor who is truly worthy of being her leading man: the incomparable Charlie Chaplin. With Chaplin all in black and Marilyn all in her stylish, Norman Norwellesque white, Milton understands that the cinematic pairing of these two great Hollywood legends would combine to form the perfect light–dark duality necessary for the perpetual continuation of the eternal Hollywood Life Force. This visually striking strategy also works to define the legendary Chaplin in terms of his mutual exclusivity to Joan Crawford's Evil Queen, thus conceptualizing him as the play's most unlikely Prince Charming figure. Mailer's use of Chaplin in such a dramatic context is most inspired. For Chaplin is truly Marilyn's only male star equivalent.

Marilyn's association with the colors black, white, and red continues throughout the play. She longs to make a movie about Jean Harlow. Harlow was always associated with extreme whiteness. And this association of Harlow and white continues when Milton presents Marilyn with a white ermine fur like Harlow wore in the 1930s. Then later, Marilyn gets to associate herself with the purity and innocence of whiteness again when she wears a stunning white gown while filming *The Prince and the Showgirl* in England. Since she more or less becomes like a heroine from out of a Henry James novel in this section of the play, her pristine whiteness is dramatically apopros. Like Daisy Miller or Isabel Archer in *Portrait of a Lady*, she is very much the innocent American girl from the New World, confronting the more sophisticated and even more jaded wiles of the Old World. Mailer's characterization of Marilyn in the England segment becomes a theatrical tour de force.

In the scene when Milton presents Marilyn with the black sweater, black signifies the sultry, sophisticated side of her personality. But black can also take on a more negative, deeply unsettling association. This happens when she discovers the murdered body of Romulus the black Doberman pinscher. After engaging in much drinking, drugging, and wanton sex, Marilyn discovers Romulus, with his throat slit, lying in a pool of blood. The nightmarish image of the black dog, lying in his own red blood, appears to her throughout the play as a constant premonition of dread and foreboding. The recurrence of red and its association with blood and pain and death then becomes another strong image in the play. For red in this scene is the color of the dead dog's blood, signifying the color of death and suffering from then on. This is also the sad meaning of red when Amy asks Marilyn about her painful monthly periods and then expresses her horror over the fact that Marilyn has had as many as twelve abortions performed on her. As the excruciating pain of her period causes her to double over in agony, we almost imagine that she is going to bleed to death before us. Mailer takes us so deep into her pain-wracked body that we become totally absorbed in her suffering.

Again and again in the play, Mailer continues to plunge us deeper and deeper into Marilyn's heart and soul by showing us the way she feels and thinks. He makes us see the world through her eyes. And all throughout the play's three hours' length, there is so much going on inside of Marilyn. For instance, as a part of the Greene's refinement of Marilyn, she is given books of history to read. She finds herself drawn to biographies of sensual historical women like the empress Josephine, Marie Antoinette, Madame Du Barry, and Emma Hamilton. And in addition to the role these historical women in her books play in Marilyn's life, the role the men of her time play is equally significant. Indeed, so familiar have we become with this aspect of her life that all Mailer has to do is have only the slightest reference to a man and we instantly understand. Traces of men and the effects they have had on her are everywhere, which actually isn't always a good thing for Marilyn. Besides all her unwanted pregnancies, there is the unspeakable treatment she would receive at the start of her career. To Hollywood, she was initially looked on as little more than a whore. But then, as her star began to rise, the treatment she received did somewhat improve. It was in her efforts to escape such shoddy treatment that she went to New York and formed Marilyn Monroe Productions with Milton.

The play examines Marilyn's powerful attraction to Arthur Miller as being tied into her need for respect. That such a great man (she even compares him to President Lincoln) could love her redeems and validates her. Thus, having married Arthur Miller, formed her own production company, and received the most glowing reviews of her entire acting career for her playing of Cherie in *Bus Stop*, Marilyn heads for England to make *The Prince and the Showgirl* with Olivier. But when her pill and alcohol abuse make her unable to memorize her lines, Olivier becomes so enraged that he shouts at her just to say the line and look sexy for the camera. Rather than encourage her, Olivier's reductio ad absurdum of Marilyn has quite the opposite effect. She turns and runs from him and his insulting words. For, in effect, his scorn renders her meaningless. And what he fails to understand is that she is no longer just some meaningless Hollywood starlet doomed to suffer such disrespectful treatment from him or anyone else anymore. No, she is no longer the "Strawhead" that that Hollywood Philistine Zanuck once called her. She has fought long and hard to be taken seriously as an actress. She has studied method acting with Lee Strasberg in order to attain a higher level of artistic consciousness for herself. She has earned the right to star in a movie opposite Laurence Olivier under the auspices of her own production company—Marilyn Monroe Productions. She is a mythical star at the top of her game. And now she only wants nothing more than to be respected and photographed in a beautiful white gown, with exquisite refinement and elegant grace, like a refined heroine in an exquisite novel by Henry James.

After her disastrous experience with Olivier making *The Prince and the Showgirl*, Marilyn's life unravels at an alarming rate. Her relationship with Milton and Amy falls apart. Marilyn Monroe Productions is dissolved. Her inability to carry a baby to term plunges her into deeper depression and disappointment. Predictably, her marriage to Arthur ends in bitter divorce. After unsuccessful love affairs with Frank Sinatra and the Kennedys, she dies on August 5, 1962. But Mailer concludes *Strawhead* with Marilyn triumphant, all in white and wrapped in her Jean Harlowesque white ermine, sitting in front of her mirror sipping vodka. As she continues to gaze at herself in the mirror, Charlie Chaplin appears. When she notices him, she is transfixed from sad and depressed to total, rapturous delight. Charlie most graciously presents her with the gift of a single rose, and they greet one another in an enchanting mime, after which they exit the stage together hand in hand. At last, Marilyn has found her most perfect companion and ideal leading man whose enduring fame and myth creation is surely equal to her own. Among all Hollywood stars, they become the greatest stars of all.

Mention must now be made of the performance of Karen MacDonald as Marilyn Monroe in *Strawhead*. This lovely and powerful actress has had a long and fruitful artistic affiliation with the American Repertory Theater of Cambridge, Massachusetts. Her acting in *Strawhead* was such that she shattered even her own past superlatives with her awesome tribute to Marilyn Monroe. Mailer's daughter Kate Mailer would later star in a production of *Strawhead* in New York at Marilyn's own alma mater, the Actors Studio, in 1986.

Marilyn Monroe is paid tribute to in the opening credits of the 1984–1985 season of TV's popular *Saturday Night Live*. As all the various cast members of the show are introduced in a lively filmic montage of famous New York landmarks (that is, the Statue of Liberty, the Empire State Building, Yankee Stadium, the Chrysler Building), Julia Louis-Dreyfus makes a most memorable appearance. Dressed as Marilyn in *The Seven Year Itch*, she struggles to stop her billowing white dress from blowing up too high as she is projected as a fleeting image floating high above the legendary New York skyline. Her presence in this televisual context has a lyrical dreaminess about it. For just as fleetingly as she first appeared, she next vanishes, and the diaphanous vision of the Goddess triumphant in her favorite city in the world—New York City— is over. Or the diaphanous vision is over until the opening credits of *Saturday Night Live* would appear again the next week.

From out of the midst of the gaudy spectacle that was the Reagan 1980s and almost as if from out of a chrysalis, two distinctive artists emerge. The first of these artists, pop sensation Madonna, virtually takes the world by storm all during the course of the 1980s. The second artist is, for lack of a better word, that female impersonator par excellence, Jimmy James. Both Madonna and James did much to challenge the reactionary impulse that defined much of the Reagan era, as both artists also greatly assisted in Marilyn Monroe's final ascension, helping her soar into full transcendence.

Now a large part of Reagan's electoral victory was based on his close alliance with the increasingly powerful New Right that had emerged in the latter part of the 1970s. Made up predominantly of religious extremists, a large part of the New Right's political agenda was to crush down all laws supporting gay rights legislation. And so, as the New Right did its worst, Ronald and Nancy Reagan ushered in an era of total extravagance. Debra Silverman observes,

> There was a deeper correspondence between the political program of the Reagan White House and the emergence of an aristocratic culture . . . the reactionary politics born of the first Reagan inauguration: a style aggressively dedicated to the cult of visible wealth and distinction, and to the illusion that they were well earned; a style of unabashed opulence, whose mixture of hedonism, spitefulness, and social repudiation are captured in the slogan "Living well is the best revenge."[4]

Lest we not forget, it is also during the 1980s that the AIDS epidemic shifted into high gear. But for the most part, Reagan and his administration met pain and deprivation with denial. Yet if Reagan's response to AIDS was mostly ineffectual, the response of the New Right was another matter entirely. Film historian Barbara Klinger comments that

> from the perspective of the New Right, AIDS was a just punishment visited on all the unjust, a revenge on homosexuality and the sexual revolution. At the same time, its presence ratified the New Right's pro-family platform, the return to "traditional values."[5]

As stated, both Madonna and James worked overtime in the 1980s to counter both Reagan and the New Right as they also, simultaneously, served Marilyn

Monroe very well in their mission. By all accounts, Madonna's obsession with Marilyn started at the beginning of her own recording career. On some level, Madonna felt a powerful connection to Marilyn and all that she endured at the hands of the Hollywood of the 1950s. In an interview, she once said of the period, "In those days, you were really a slave to the whole Hollywood machinery, and unless you had the strength to pull yourself out of it you were just trapped."[6] With thoughts such as those running through her mind, when the time came for Madonna to make the video for her 1985 hit song "Material Girl" (and could there be a better anthem for the Reagan 1980s?), she turned to Marilyn Monroe for her creative inspiration. And, more specifically, it was from Marilyn's famous rendition of "Diamonds Are a Girl's Best Friend" from *Gentlemen Prefer Blondes* that Madonna got the idea for her Grand Design.

To begin, for the set of the video, Madonna wanted everything from suspended chandeliers to a large staircase and a bevy of good-looking, tuxedo-clad chorus boys. When the topic of her costume arose, there again Madonna knew what she wanted. Her gown had to be an exact copy of the one Travilla designed for Monroe to wear in director Howard Hawks's musical masterpiece. Madonna's costume was then fashioned into an exact replica of Marilyn's: a shocking pink, shoulderless gown, with a simplicity and bold elegance in design. Madonna also wore a profusion of sparkly diamonds. Although the finished video ends up paying a postmodern tribute to the 1953 movie, there is one major difference between the two. The image that Marilyn always projected was one of sensual warmth and endlessly welcoming invitation, while Madonna projects a much tougher, more calculating quality in the video. Where Marilyn is all soft, curvy allure, Madonna is hard-edged, disdainful, challenging. This aspect of her reinterpretation of Marilyn got even stronger and more pronounced throughout the decade as Madonna used her newfound wealth and fame to combat the Reagan administration and the out-and-out bigotry of the New Right.

Jimmy James also took up the struggle against AIDS, Reagan, and the New Right in a big way. He offered an incarnation of Marilyn Monroe that was different from but every bit as significant as Madonna's reinterpretation. On first encountering James, we cannot help but be struck by his face, which appears to be round, simple, and even blank and empty of appearance. But, as we continue looking, we realize the error of our first impression. For James creates his mysterious art out of his own body, face, and voice and even his very own soul. If there are many shining jewels finale in James's impersonation crown of creation, the most dazzling jewel of all was his extraordinary Marilyn Monroe. Whenever James assumed the role of Marilyn, he glowed with this spooky, otherworldly conviction and passion. And movement for movement, gesture for gesture, and note for perfect note, Jimmy James *was* Marilyn Monroe for much of the 1980s and 1990s, proving that he truly belongs to the world's great artists.

Another important depiction of Marilyn Monroe happens in 1985 with director Nicolas Roeg's movie version of *Insignificance*. Roeg managed to accomplish this transfer from one medium to another so as to remain faithful to Johnson's original theatrical vision while also remaining true to his own strikingly cinematic vision. As a director, Roeg was influenced by famous French New Wave director Alain Resnais, and the master moviemaker's influence on Roeg's style is considerable. It can be seen in the very way Roeg has structured the narrative of *Insignificance*. True, much of the action still takes place in a New York hotel room in 1953, only now that action is just part of a more elliptical and epical story. For much of the time, the action does not unfold as straightforwardly as it did on stage. Now, it is broken up, interspersed and interrupted by either brief flashes of mysteriously ambiguous scenes or much longer sequences that depict painful events from the lives of the characters.

This is not meant to imply that Roeg's movie is without its share of joyous memories. For instance, there's Einstein, as a boy genius back in the Germany of 1890, performing his amazing scientific experiments in his bedroom. Also, there's Joe DiMaggio, as a boy in 1921, playing baseball with his schoolboy chums in a back lot. Still, these joyous memories aside, much of what does get remembered by the characters becomes painful and difficult. Without doubt, this helps explain a certain feeling of remoteness such negative memories might evoke. These darker memories include Einstein remembering the horrific time in 1933 when a group of Nazi thugs destroyed his beloved sailboat. Then, there are a whole series of disturbing memories that haunt Marilyn. It is in the depiction of these scenes from her life that the full impact of the 1980 TV movie *Marilyn, The Untold Story* can be felt. Roeg makes excellent use of that depiction's unique "visual discourse" to help flesh out and add more dimension to his complex, cinematic portrait of Marilyn. He puts us deep inside her memories so that we experience her painful reminiscences along with her.

Along with all these sequences from the past of Marilyn and the other characters, Roeg also intersperses throughout the narrative brief flashes of scenes that are used much more symbolically and stylized, arranging these images more rhythmically and/or contrapuntally than in a straightforward or naturalistic manner. These include scenes of a golden watch endlessly falling through space and Hiroshima after being bombed. If we don't always get the full complexity of Roeg's layered imagery, we remain absorbed in the rich succession of hypnotic images flickering across the screen just as we also do in the superb performance of Theresa Russell as Marilyn Monroe.

If Marilyn Monroe's relationship with the Kennedys was only obliquely hinted at in *Marilyn, The Untold Story*, in the 1987 TV miniseries *Hoover vs. The Kennedys: The Second Civil War*, her connection to them comes out in a very big way. The miniseries begins in July 1960 with JFK becoming the Democratic candidate for President against Republican Richard Nixon. At the same time, JFK is carrying on a passionate love affair with Marilyn. Additionally, he shows his support of Martin Luther King Jr. and the civil rights movement, all of which makes the blood of the powerful head of the FBI, J. Edgar Hoover, begin to boil. After JFK is elected president, he appoints his brother Bobby as attorney general, and Hoover's blood further boils. As both Kennedy brothers become more deeply involved with MLK, Hoover's blood then comes to full boil. When Bobby later dares to question Hoover on the FBI's record on civil rights and its lack of action against organized crime, Hoover's blood boils over. He becomes more determined than ever to annihilate the Kennedys and all they represent. From then on, Hoover goes out of his way to dig up all the dirt he possibly can on JFK's romantic involvements with Marilyn and gangster moll Judith Campbell, who is simultaneously carrying on with Mafia kingpin Sam Giancana. Equally busy, albeit on a loftier front, MLK takes an even stronger stand on civil rights, which causes Hoover to denigrate him and his cause even further. And in his continued efforts to denigrate JFK, Hoover shows RFK explicit photographic evidence of his brother's involvement with Campbell. Furious over Hoover's great coup, RFK urges JFK to break off with Campbell.

Not long after she performs at the president's birthday party at Madison Square Garden, Marilyn is more or less passed onto RFK. With this development, Hoover next turns his full attention on gathering evidence of this new affair. When she is found dead in 1962, RFK is badly shaken up by the loss. He next increases his show of support of civil rights, which naturally infuriates Hoover to no end. When JFK is assassinated in 1963, Vice President Lyndon B. Johnson becomes president, and RFK falls into a deep depression. In 1964, LBJ is reelected President. But in 1968, LBJ decides not to run for reelection, RFK decides to run for president, and MLK is assassinated. Later in the year, RFK is also assassinated. Through it all, Hoover remains ensconced in full power. At the conclusion of the miniseries, he prepares to align himself with the new incoming President Richard Nixon.

As all this would indicate, *Hoover vs. the Kennedys: The Second Civil War* offers us a depiction of America as this totally out-of-control madhouse. But the madman running the show is not the president. No, apparently, he is J. Edgar Hoover. This is so much so that all the oppressive aspects of the social order are projected onto the scary figure of Hoover. Delirious with power, driven by sadism, and paranoid of ever losing control, Hoover is constantly patrolling the rigid borders of morality for all who dare to transgress. He's therefore completely obsessed with all the president's many mistresses. And of all the president's affairs, it is the one he is conducting with Marilyn Monroe that most captures Hoover's ever-fevered imagination. Not a single one of the president's romantic trysts with her goes unnoticed and undocumented. With this move, the miniseries combines the realm of the private (sexuality, romance, adultery in high places) with the realm of the public (political paranoia, clandestine espionage activities, protofascistic power plays) until the two realms become one and the private is spoken of in a public narrative voice. The realms of the private and the public also get collapsed into the figure of Marilyn Monroe, although, in this depiction, Marilyn's immense sensuality doesn't take on any negative connotations. Instead, it is the far more blatant sexuality of Judith Campbell that assumes that dubious position. Campbell is the one who bears the trace of the bad girl. When she's not gracing the bed of the president, she's getting it on with Sam Giancana. Her desire may be single, but it's double-edged. And, it is through this double-edged desire that the prospect of political scandal is manifested.

If, on the one hand, JFK's indiscretions make him extremely vulnerable to Hoover, on the other these same indiscretions also give his younger brother Bobby many a sleepless night. It is left to him to neutralize and contain his brother's two main mistresses. In the case of Campbell, this is relatively easy. She is treated much like some anonymous Hollywood bit player and relegated to the movie's periphery. But in the case of a star of Marilyn's magnitude, such a cavalier approach is out of the question. After all, she is a dazzling Hollywood superstar. She lives in the world of the fantastic where everything is possible. Therefore, as befitting her exalted station, she must be treated accordingly. Besides, Bobby Kennedy fully understands his brother's desire for her. The full import of this desirability and Marilyn's total stardom is signified in three key scenes in the miniseries. In the first, she's like a seductive siren out of a Greek myth beckoning the president into taking a steamy shower with her. While Marilyn's romp in the shower signifies her total desirability, the scene in which she sings "Happy Birthday, Mr. President" signifies the zenith of her transcendent superstardom. Heather Thomas nicely re-creates the famous scene in the miniseries. But the full beauty of her portrayal of Marilyn is that as excellent as she is at projecting the titillating side of Marilyn's star image, she's equally good at projecting Marilyn's warmth and vulnerability. These aspects of Marilyn's personality come into play when Bobby Kennedy visits to deliver the message that the president is ending his relationship with her, which leads into his making love to her. And in such a scene, Marilyn grows more complex, she becomes more enriched, as she embraces her new lover—the attorney general of the United States. Now she is the Eternal Feminine.

And Thomas plays the scene just as we imagine Marilyn must have: with a refined eroticism. The actress makes Marilyn both beautiful and eloquent at the same time, allowing her beauty to do the real communicating.

Now in the 1987 animated short film *Rendezvous in Montreal*, the sophisticated computer technology of the 1980s is employed to re-create Marilyn Monroe and Humphrey Bogart in a mythical meeting in Montreal. At first, Bogie finds himself stuck in the hereafter feeling utterly bored and depressed. To alleviate his dark mood, he thinks of Marilyn, and he next calls on her to accompany him back to earth. When she accepts his invitation, Bogie is practically beside himself with excitement, although when she does first appear to him, she's nothing more than a disembodied golden head of marble with silvery hair, which disappoints him to no end. Later when Bogie meets her in a bar in Montreal, he remains disappointed that she is still made of marble and not the alluring flesh he desires. But being Bogie, all that it takes is his sending her a simple kiss, and Marilyn is finally awakened by him.

This enchanting little movie, created by husband and wife computer animators Daniel Thalmann and Nadia Magnenot Thalmann, features often-remarkable computer animation to re-create Marilyn and Bogie and puts them together as the stars of the same movie. While the faces of the stars do occasionally have a stiff, doll-like feel, the Thalmanns still deserve accolades for their creation of this stylish new way to depict Marilyn. For with this depiction, they succeed in grafting yet another layer of representational meaning onto our continually evolving perception of Marilyn Monroe as they take her to the very edge of the margins of imagination. Within this computerized pictorial context, we can also focus attention on the new imaginal terrain of the coming epoch and some of the possible new ways in which she might well be imagined in the future. However, it is perhaps only inevitable that she, who lived so much of her life in the very crux of the technological matrix of photography and motion pictures, should now be prepared for such a radical, new representation.

A most bizarre tribute to Marilyn Monroe occurred in 1988 with performance artist Peter Stack portraying her in *Dead Marilyn*. This depiction is, hands down, one of the most controversial and problematic of all the depictions chronicled in this study. Stack puts himself as the figure of Marilyn Monroe at the narrative center, depicting her in such a controversial way that the representatives of the Marilyn Monroe estate condemned Stack and his performance as nothing less than an unholy sacrilege to her memory.

So what did this depiction of Marilyn contain to so incite the Marilyn Monroe estate? Well, the action began with the view of a dark and shadowy graveyard. Then, a blast of jarring music was sounded, like a cosmic storm about to break out over the entire universe. That theatrical flourish was followed by the exceedingly haunting image of Marilyn rising up from the grave, which had so prematurely claimed her. Much to the spleen of the Marilyn Monroe estate, Stack's Marilyn looked like some sort of a desolate vampire. The effect of this was grotesquely ghoulish. For, although Marilyn was wearing one of her famous slinky, revealing gowns, her breasts protruded most obscenely, like two overripened cantaloupes. Additionally, her lustrous platinum hair had become a dull, tangled mass of brillo-like kink. Her eyes were darkly shadowed in crudely applied gobs of thick mascara, and they even glowed with a spooky, supernatural intensity. Stack did attempt to defend all this by admitting that he fully realized how purposely shocking his performance was: "The reason is because I'm in it for shock value, to get the point across quickly. If the anger weren't so tightly focused, it might be missed."[7]

Shock value or not, and even if we cannot say we completely condone everything about this performance with all its perverse excesses, Stack was clearly getting at some real, hard truths. Although the work is in decidedly bad taste, the fact of the matter remains that for much of her life Marilyn was used, abused, and exploited by powerful men. This mistreatment resulted in her feeling a smoldering inner rage toward those who had wronged her. This thematic concern will be taken up and more fully developed in the 1990s. Thus, in its own way, the outrageous *Dead Marilyn* is getting at something important—almost in spite of itself.

As in *Hoover vs. the Kennedys*, the involvement of Marilyn Monroe with the Kennedys is taken up once again in director Larry Buchanan's 1989 movie *Goodnight, Sweet Marilyn*. In many ways, this is a strange movie. Much of its strangeness is because about 75 percent of the narrative is nothing more than a pastiche of Buchanan's 1976 *Goodbye, Norma Jean*. The main action of the 1989 movie takes place on the last day and night of Marilyn's life. But the woman we are presented with is not the luminous Goddess of Love of *Gentlemen Prefer Blondes* and *The Seven Year Itch*. No, this is the later Marilyn after she's been knocked around, strung out, and beaten down one time too many. She's so sadly, neurotically, tragically drained of any signs of life that it becomes painful to have to see her this way. And Paula Lane as Marilyn plays the role for all it's worth. With her pale white skin, her dark sunken eyes, and her pale gold hair, she's a ghostly presence: the Sex Goddess as Seductive Specter.

Because the main action of *Goodnight, Sweet Marilyn* takes place in Marilyn's small, cramped bedroom, the movie creates a claustrophobic sense of life and fate happening on a deserted movie set or abandoned back lot. This makes Marilyn seem trapped in a predetermined drama and that her doom is a forgone conclusion. And because she's so trapped in the claustrophobic mise-en-scène only further adds to the ominousness of her predicament. For much of the movie, Marilyn is confined to her bed (which will ultimately become her death bed), and she is mercilessly questioned by two of the most sinister-looking CIA agents in movie history. Before interrogating her, they shoot her full of drugs to make her talk. And talk she does, revealing to them the story of her life. These extensive scenes consist of most of the footage from *Goodbye, Norma Jean*. The contrast between the vibrant and feisty Misty Rowe as Norma Jean juxtaposed against Lane in the new footage is most shocking in terms of what life has done to poor Marilyn. There's a scene in which Lane wears a slinky black gown in anticipation of her dinner date with RFK. But, sadly, instead of the romantic interlude she has so meticulously set the stage for with him, the two creepy and intrusive CIA agents show up to do their worst. As one of them questions the barely conscious Marilyn, the other removes all traces of her involvement with the Kennedys. So this is the "real" purpose of their visit: to obliterate this whole part of her life. The agent who relentlessly questions Marilyn puts forth a series of probing questions about a supposed press conference she has planned as a means of announcing her involvements with the Kennedys to the world.

What Buchanan is doing is taking all the revelations made in a documentary such as *The Last Days of Marilyn Monroe* and then giving them a more imaginative and considerably darker artistic spin. An example of this is the fact that in the movie there is not one but three separate attempts made to kill Marilyn. So not for the last time is her ideality depicted as being linked to death. Besides just linking Marilyn to death, this movie also makes her something of a harbinger of her own death until she even becomes like her own memento mori. Nothing can stop the overpowering sense of inevitability in the way that the narrative moves slowly and steadily toward the death of Marilyn. The movie is so seeped in death that death even comes to her, as stated, on three separate occasions. After she is almost drowned to death in her own swimming pool, she is revived by the two CIA agents to be questioned relentlessly by them. And after they've finished with her, they administer a powerful overdose to kill her yet again. Still she somehow miraculously survives, only finally to be given a fatal suppository by her friend and one-time lover Mesquite. Although before he does succeed in killing her, Marilyn is visited by the ghost of her mother Gladys (amazingly acted by Phyllis Coates, the original Lois Lane in TV's *Superman* of the 1950s). If Marilyn looks like a ghost in this movie, Gladys is the real thing, calling out to her daughter from beyond the grave to join her in death.

Despite Gladys and the efforts of these men, it is clear that Marilyn can never be completely destroyed. No matter how hard they all try to make a dead body out of her, she remains resistant to her own total destruction. A part of her will always live on. And even though the movie's ending has an apocalyptic quality with its unsettling depiction of the Goddess reduced to a female corpse, the very last image we are presented with is of Marilyn Monroe transcendent: she's alive again and singing a sensuous torch song. Buchanan bathes her in a soft, golden-toned visionary glow. This not only suggests the divine but also is befitting the ascension and rebirth of the Goddess in the 1980s.

Marilyn Monroe plays a role in the 1989 cosmic sex comedy *Another Chance*, which tells the story of trashy, womanizing TV soap opera star John Ripley. Early in the narrative, John finds himself becoming thoroughly obsessed with international supermodel Jackie. So taken is he with her that he even brings her to meet his family on their idyllic farm. But just as their relationship looks as if it will take, Jackie catches John cheating on her with a mysterious woman. As a result, she breaks off the relationship.

Without Jackie, John's life falls completely apart. He ends up losing his job on the soap opera, and soon the only job he can find is working as a celebrity impostor impersonating who else?—John Ripley. It is while performing with a group of other actors that he meets, among others, Marilyn Monroe, Humphrey Bogart, and Clark Gable. And when Bogie starts harassing Marilyn, John steps in to protect her honor, only to be shot to death by the gun-toting Bogie. In Heaven, the dead John appears before St. Peter to be judged. But before he is damned to Hell for the horrendous way he treated women, John pleads with St. Peter for another chance at life. Amazingly, John is granted his second chance. A changed man, he wins Jackie's trust again and her hand in marriage. Although he is even tempted by the same mysterious woman, whom it turns out is a sexy she-devil, John resists her to start a new life with Jackie on his family's farm.

Now, traditionally, the number three has always been considered the most positive number in symbolism, religion, mythology, legend, fairy tales, and folklore. In religion, there is the doctrine of the Holy Trinity: the Father, the Son, and the Holy Spirit. And three is a much-repeated number in the Bible. There are the three supreme virtues of Faith, Hope, and Charity; the Holy Family consists of three: Jesus, Mary, and Joseph; and there are the three Magi, the three denials of Christ by Peter, the three crosses at Golgotha, and the Resurrection after three days. Further, three became the number of perfect harmony for Pythagoras, of completeness for Aristotle—with its beginning, middle, and end—and three is important in many fairy tales and in folklore.

Three is also well represented in *Another Chance*. Since the movie is laden with all sorts of comical cosmic implications, this makes perfect sense. To begin, John Ripley spends most of his time doing three things: acting in a cheesy TV soap opera, starring in even cheesier TV commercials, and, when he's not doing those two things, keeping busy seducing every beautiful woman he can. There are then always three women surrounding this seducer. The woman he is presently seducing, the woman he has seduced, and the woman he will soon seduce. Taken together, three women form a perfect Aristotelian beginning, middle, and end. It is for his callous treatment of these women he loves and leaves that John will have to be judged by St. Peter in Heaven not once but on three separate occasions for his sins against womanhood. John will also have three separate encounters with Marilyn Monroe. First, when he watches her perform a scene from *Some Like It Hot*; second, when he comes to her aid after the psychotic Humphrey Bogart most aggressively hits on her; and, third, when she comforts John after Bogie shoots him down. It could be argued that in his coming to the defense of Marilyn as he does, John proves that there is a part of him that is definitely redeemable. But actually, he's already proven that in his love for Jackie and when he pleads with St. Peter in Heaven for another chance at life and love on earth, all of which makes him a more appealing character than he was at the beginning of the movie.

The 1990 Italian sex comedy (with an English sound track) *Bye, Bye Baby* also features a womanizing man (Paolo), who, much like John Ripley, treats women despicably. The movie opens with the heroine, Sandra (a successful Milanese doctor), having a knock-down, drag-out-fight with Paolo, who happens to be her philandering husband. As the acrimonious couple battle one another in the background of the frame, their harsh words are almost completely drowned out by a television set placed in the foreground. Marilyn Monroe appears on TV singing "Bye, Bye Baby" from the movie *Gentlemen Prefer Blondes*. The lyrics of the song and the seductive image of Marilyn act as a kind of ironic counterpoint to all the disruptive physical and emotional carnage Sandra and Paolo wreck on one another. The song is further used to equally good effect as composer Manuel Desica's instrumental variations of the melody are played all throughout the movie. Sometimes, the song takes on a muted, wistful quality as Sandra learns to adjust to her new life without her husband. Or it can become an enticing burst of hopefulness as she begins a new love affair with handsome fellow doctor Marcello.

The budding relationship of Sandra and Marcello is contrasted with Paolo's romantic entanglement with sexy billiards player Lisa. And even though Lisa is a woman of apparently voracious erotic appetite, Paolo keeps going back to seduce his ex-wife (over all her protestations). This series of highly manipulative seductions is generally accompanied by these conspicuously artificial movie set rainstorms. Along with the continuous use of the song "Bye, Bye Baby" throughout the movie and the exaggerated falsity of these rainstorm scenes, there is an overall melodramatic extravagance to much of the action. This prevailing sense of the artificial continues on in the look of the superstylized lush imagery of the movie's settings. The principals play out their overwrought scenes against glittery backdrops of posh hotels, elegant restaurants, luxury resorts, and palatial Italianate villas that fill the screen with phantasmagoric flights of pure fancy, drenched in bejeweled rainbow colors. The movie's high-as-a-kite visuals aside, the most ironic use of the artificial comes at the very end, when we are surprised to learn that the voice we heard coming out of Marilyn Monroe's mouth at the beginning of the movie wasn't even her own. No, it was instead Liza Ross impersonating Marilyn. For the record, her rendition of Marilyn is good enough to make style, at least momentarily, its own reward.

The 1991 episode of the cult British TV sitcom *Red Dwarf* titled "Meltdown" is, after the movie *Slaughterhouse-Five*, Marilyn Monroe's second appearance in the fantastic world of science fiction. Produced by the BBC, the program is set on the spacecraft mining ship the *Red Dwarf*. All its crewmembers have been killed off except for David Lister. His only company is the hologram of a former colleague, the always irritating Rimmer; the mutated ship's Cat; the naive android Kryten; and a speaking computer image named Holly. Each week the crew of the *Red Dwarf* find themselves in outlandishly otherworldly misadventures as they journey from one far-off galaxy to another.

In the "Meltdown" episode, the crew journeys to the planet Waxworld, which is made up of nothing more than a giant theme park. The inhabitants of Waxworld, the Waxdroids, have all broken free of their original programming and are presently engaged in a ruthless civil war against the exceedingly evil Waxdroid Adolph Hitler and his fellow Nazi henchmen. Hitler and his crew call themselves the Army of Darkness. This Waxdroid Axis consists of Caligula, Stalin, Mussolini, Rasputin, the Boston Strangler, and so on. In opposition to the Army of Darkness, there are the Forces of Good, exalted members of which include Elvis Presley, President Abraham Lincoln, Gandhi, Mother Theresa, Queen Victoria, and, Marilyn Monroe. As the Army of Darkness plots to transform the whole of Waxworld into a space of total anxiety and nightmarish catastrophe for all, the Forces of Good pray for a miracle to save them and their entire planet from impending chaos.

This movement toward the miraculous happens with the arrival of the unlikely presence of the motley crew of the *Red Dwarf* into Waxworld. Rising to the demands of the momentous occasion, Rimmer assumes the position of the supreme commander of the Forces of Good. This conspicuously theatrical— and, therefore, in a way conspicuously unreal—quality reaches the very height of the surrealistically ridiculous when he prepares all the "good" Waxdroids to do battle against the evil ones. Among Rimmer's army trainees is the perfectly coiffed and impeccably made-up Marilyn Monroe. She wears her scandalous, skintight scarlet dress from *Niagara* with a militant pair of black army boots. But, actually, in this particular context, her sexy combat attire achieves a sort of illogical logic of its own. (Even a Waxdroid version of Marilyn Monroe eager to go off to fight the good fight must still signify glamorous Hollywood star above all!)

Writer Robert "Bob" Slatzer made claims of a long love affair and a secret marriage to Marilyn Monroe in the 1950s. While many doubt the veracity of his claim, there is something irresistibly appealing and quite moving about the man's lifelong devotion to Marilyn. The 1991 TV movie *Marilyn and Me* tells the story of this relationship. The movie opens in August 1962 with Bob getting a telephone call from columnist Walter Winchell informing him that Marilyn has died. This makes Bob remember when he first met her when she was Norma Jean in the 1940s in Hollywood and on their first date she lured him to a deserted beach to make love in the moonlight. But directly after, Marilyn grows cool and elusive toward him. Not too long after, she shows up at his door and announces she is moving in with him. Initially, things seem to go well. Bob introduces her to Walter Winchell and takes her to a Jean Harlow movie. Seeing the glamorous Harlow on the silver screen makes Norma Jean decide to dye her own hair golden blonde and pose nude on red velvet drapery to further her career in Hollywood.

When 20th Century-Fox offers her a contract, she becomes Marilyn Monroe and ends her relationship with Bob. Understandably upset, Bob leaves Hollywood and moves back home to Ohio to work as a newspaper reporter. But when Marilyn calls him to resume their affair, Bob is lured by her back out to Hollywood again. At the same time, superagent Johnny Hyde becomes extremely interested in Marilyn. He vows to make her a star. Although Bob proposes to her, she turns him down, preferring to become involved with the powerful Johnny instead. After Bob takes her to Mexico to have an abortion, he then takes her back to live with him after Johnny dies and his vindictive widow has her put out of the house. But she eventually leaves Bob again when she becomes involved with Joe DiMaggio. Yet, while having problems making the movie *Niagara*, she calls Bob to join her. When Joe learns of her involvement with Bob, he breaks off with her. Darryl F. Zanuck intercedes, informing her that he wants her back with Joe. In defiance of Zanuck, she marries Bob instead. But in the end, Zanuck gets his way. Marilyn's marriage to Bob is soon annulled. She marries Joe, but their marriage doesn't last even a full year. After their divorce, she attempts to reconcile with Bob. But, worn out from all the ups and downs of their complex relationship, Bob resists her this time.

As to whether what is depicted in this movie actually occurred is open to some debate. But not so debatable is how affecting much of it proves to be. When the hero first meets Marilyn, he's a struggling scriptwriter and she a struggling Hollywood starlet. But for all of that, it soon becomes apparent she is already light-years ahead of him. This becomes perfectly evident on the night of their very first date. All dressed up in his finest suit, Bob brings her a dozen of white roses (her favorite flower), and he takes her out to a posh restaurant for dinner. He's like Tom Sawyer dressed in his Sunday best to go call on Miss Becky. But, much to Bob's amazement, he soon discovers that his beautiful date has more on her mind than just dining. She lures him to a deserted moonlit beach where she wastes precious little time at all in convincing him to undress and go skinny-dipping with her. And with this—and right before Bob's unbelieving eyes—Norma Jean transforms from the sweet, childlike girl next door to an alluring, immortal goddess.

Understandably enough, Bob then goes from being Twain's Tom Sawyer to a character more along the lines of Philip Roth's Alexander Portnoy. And as wonderful as their date appears to go, Norma Jean astonishes Bob yet again when he takes her home. Before taking her leave of him, she transforms yet again from a warm and alluring goddess of love to a cold, unfeeling young woman who informs him that in the morning she may no longer even like him. Yet, not long after, Norma Jean appears on his doorstep with suitcase in hand and moves in with him. From there on, the movie becomes something of an emotional and erotic roller-coaster ride as Norma Jean, the struggling movie starlet, gradually evolves into Marilyn Monroe, the supreme object of Bob's and every man's affection.

Very often, Bob's steadfastness is no small feat, for as Marilyn's career goes from good to great, she also goes through a series of different men. Besides Johnny Hyde and various other Hollywood types, there is, of course, Joe DiMaggio. Yet, through it all, she always finds her way back to Bob. And through it all, Bob patiently waits until she catches him completely off guard and marries him. After the couple head off to Mexico for a quickie marriage, they return to Hollywood to confront a none-too-happy Darryl Zanuck. At first, Zanuck hides his profound displeasure over his newest star's marital status. He is shown handling the two newlyweds in such a way as to make us understand exactly how he got to where he did in Hollywood. For although he feigns happiness for Marilyn, he is soon preying on all her insecurities when he reminds her of the possible damage her new marriage will have on her career. And his evil little ploy does work brilliantly in the end. After less than four days of marriage to Bob, Marilyn agrees to an annulment and marries Joe DiMaggio, which definitely does meet with Zanuck's wholehearted approval. After that marriage falls apart, she attempts to rekindle the flame with Bob. Only this time around, he refuses the alluring bait. Instead, he sends her on her way, which, as it turns out, is also out of his life forever.

Now if we might initially feel skeptical over the truthfulness of *Marilyn and Me*, that feeling quickly disappears as Jesse Dabson as Bob and Susan Griffiths as Marilyn Monroe soon turn skepticism into pure inspiration. Dabson combines an easygoing masculinity with just the right amount of wondrous innocence to never be anything less than winning. Equally impressive is Griffiths's portrayal of a mercurial Marilyn Monroe.

Marilyn Monroe makes her second appearance in a miniseries about the Kennedy family with *A Woman Named Jackie* (1991). The action begins in the 1980s with Jackie waiting in a New York hospital, accompanied by her son John, for her daughter Caroline to give birth. On this auspicious occasion, she reflects back on the events of her life. She remembers the miserable marriage of her parents, Black Jack and Janice Lee Bouvier, which led to divorce and her mother marrying Hugh Auchincloss. Although Jackie and her younger sister Lee were then surrounded by great wealth and splendor, they were heirs to none of it. This led to their mother's constant stressing on them of the importance of their one day marrying wealthy men.

Jackie strikes the jackpot when she marries the handsome and fabulously wealthy congressman from Massachusetts, John Fitzgerald Kennedy. But their marriage is not without its problems, most of which are brought on by his constant womanizing. However, when Jackie gives birth to daughter Caroline, the marriage does appear to be running more smoothly. This sense of smoothness continues when JFK announces his run for the presidency. Jackie's beauty, grace, and impeccable style become great assets to her husband when he is elected president. Unbeknownst to her during this whole period, he is also busy conducting a passionate affair with Marilyn Monroe.

As the First Lady of America, the country begins its love affair with Jackie. In her own right, she is as glamorous and charismatic as any Hollywood movie star or the princess of a fairy tale. Her fairy-tale existence does darken when she becomes aware of her husband's affair with Marilyn. But, actually, Jackie isn't the only one to find out about it. So, too, does J. Edgar Hoover. When JFK finally breaks off with Marilyn, his brother Bobby steps in. But when Bobby also breaks off with her, Marilyn, in a fit of despair, takes her own life. Still upset over JFK's affair with Marilyn, Jackie goes off on a cruise on the yacht of Greek billionaire Aristotle Onassis. She returns home to accompany JFK to Dallas on the day of November 22, 1963.

In the aftermath of JFK's assassination, Jackie is canonized by the American people to the level of complete and perfect sainthood. But she soon realizes that with sainthood there comes a profound loss of privacy for both herself and her children. When Bobby Kennedy is later assassinated, Jackie leaves America. Toward this end, she marries Onassis. As Mrs. Aristotle Onassis, Jackie lives out her most extravagant fantasies of conspicuous consumption. However, with time her marriage grows strained. She moves back to New York, as Onassis spends his days with his true love, opera diva Maria Callas. Although he plans to divorce Jackie, Onassis dies, leaving her a wealthy widow.

She moves to New York to live in grand style off her mother lode of the Onassis fortune. The miniseries concludes with Caroline giving birth to Jackie's first grandchild—Rose.

A Woman Named Jackie offers us Jackie's life as a lush, melodramatic TV miniseries. For the purpose of this study, we will concentrate only on Jackie in relation to Marilyn. Both women were, of course, great legends and icons in their own comparative ways. But, it must be remembered, Jackie was born into high society, and she was born regally beautiful. Still there were some psychic traumas when her parents divorced, the result of Black Jack's notorious gambling and womanizing. During World War II, her mother married the superrich Hugh Auchincloss. An important point to consider in this is that with her mother's marriage, Jackie and her sister Lee, while raised with all the culture and accoutrements of great wealth, were not heirs themselves to any of it. Therefore, it is imperative that Jackie and Lee marry men of extreme wealth. In attempting to achieve her mother's goal for her, Jackie experienced much insecurity about money. She eventually became completely obsessed with the desire to acquire more and more money and all the refined luxuries that it could buy for her. This reaches its shocking apotheosis in the film with her second marriage to the superrich Aristotle Onassis.

Now Marilyn Monroe, the second major woman in JFK's life in the miniseries, is depicted on an entirely different status level than Jackie. She is born poor and illegitimate to a mad mother into a family marked by hereditary insanity and misery. Still, like Jackie, Marilyn is born exquisitely lovely. And, like Jackie, she is ambitious (although her ambition is not totally for wealth), desiring to eclipse the terrible scenario of her birth and rearing and to transform herself into the successful movie star, Marilyn Monroe. It becomes her stardom that gives her access to President Kennedy. And it is her beauty and charisma that attracts him and that leads him to embark on a tumultuous, impassioned affair. Unfortunately for Marilyn, it is only one of his many affairs, though his most notable one to date, and while Jackie is the queen of the White House, Marilyn is the queen of JFK's mistresses. But Marilyn, in her passion, falls deliriously in love with the president. She has delusional fantasies of his divorcing Jackie and marrying her. Indeed, at one point, she even has the audacity to call Jackie at the White House. The miniseries depicts this juicy conversation between the two disparate women, concluding with Marilyn calling Jackie a bitch. But, actually, although cool and supremely detached in her treatment of Marilyn, to her credit, Jackie is not really all that much of a bitch toward her husband's most illustrious mistress. Perhaps, realizing that her position as First Lady is unassailable by any of her husband's mistresses, including even his most beautiful and notable mistress, Jackie can afford to be generous and display a bit of the aristocratic noblesse oblige toward her

Hollywood rival, which she does with a certain aplomb in this televisual context.

Bob Slater's lifelong obsession with Marilyn Monroe in *Marilyn and Me* is infinitely easier to comprehend than the lifelong, obsessive quest for youth and beauty controlling the lives of the hysterical characters in the 1992 screen comedy *Death Becomes Her*. In this wildly over-the-top parody, fading and aging star Madeline Ashton double-crosses her old friend and wannabe writer Helen Sharp when she steals her famous plastic surgeon fiancé, Dr. Ernest Manville, away from her. After losing Ernest, Helen becomes obscenely fat and suffers a complete breakdown. Seven years pass in which time Madeline becomes an old Hollywood has-been and Ernest a raging alcoholic. Intending to gloat over Helen's pathetic state, Madeline attends a posh book party for Helen's novel *Forever Young*. In her skintight scarlet red gown, forever young is exactly how Helen does look. Frantic to outdo her gorgeous rival, Madeline visits the same mysterious Beverly Hills cult priestess that Helen had, to get a magic potion that guarantees eternal youth. She also warns Madeline that it also grants eternal life, whatever the condition of the drinker's body. While Madeline is off acquiring eternal youth, Helen busies herself with seducing Ernest and convincing him to kill Madeline off so that they can be together forever. Their plan badly misfires and ends with the women practically ripping one another to shreds. After Ernest repairs all the damage the two women have inflicted on each other, they try to force him to drink the magic potion and join them in a perverse eternal triangle. They bring him to a mansion where a great ball is under way of the long-lived. Marilyn Monroe is among the guests. Ernest eventually manages to make his escape. At his funeral some years later, Madeline and Helen get into a catfight and pull each other down the steps of the church, shattering themselves to pieces.

Death Becomes Her is a gorgeous movie that begins with a big bang and ends with a whiny whimper. At the beginning, Meryl Streep as Madeline Ashton is singing her head off on a Broadway stage; at the conclusion, both she and Goldie Hawn, as Helen Sharp, have lost their heads on the steps of a church. Director Robert Zemeckis unleashes a barrage of mind-boggling special effects and some wildly over-the-top performances from his two leading ladies in this wickedly dark comic send-up of Hollywood and America's unending obsession with the pursuit of eternal youth and immortality.

A perhaps less spectacular but by no means less special effect is seen when Marilyn Monroe is glimpsed as a guest at the great ball of the long-lived. She is most iconically clad in her shocking pink, Travilla-designed gown from *Gentlemen Prefer Blondes*. She converses socially with an elite circle of other immortals, such as Andy Warhol, James Dean, Elvis Presley, and Greta Garbo. Yet, even taking into account much of the movie's dark comic attitude, the idea of immortality Marilyn signifies is light-years away from the grasping, vindictive immortality Madeline and Helen so frantically covet for themselves, as at this stage in the juncture of the development of how she is depicted, the image of immortality Marilyn projects is much closer to the sort associated with Ernest when he is eulogized by his saintly minister as a great man at the end of the movie.

As in *Death Becomes Her*, the triangular relationship of two beautiful blondes pitted against one another in competition for the affection of a genial enough man is also the theme of the 1992 *Madame Montand and Mrs. Miller*. Produced by the BBC, this television play imagines the meeting of the great French actress Simone Signoret and Marilyn Monroe when they both have their hair done by the same hairdresser. The question that gets posited by the text becomes, Isn't it bad enough Simone Signoret had to share her husband, Yves Montand, with Marilyn, and now must she also have to share her hairdresser as well?

The action begins in 1960 with Montand busy filming the movie *Let's Make Love* in Hollywood opposite Marilyn as his leading lady. He and Simone reside in a suite at the Beverly Hills Hotel. Across the hall from the Montands, Marilyn and Arthur Miller reside in another suite. One day Marilyn and Simone have their roots touched up by Patti, the same hairdresser who used to dye Jean Harlow's hair platinum in the 1930s. And in the process, the two women become close friends. After she expresses her admiration for Simone's brilliant performance as Alice Aisgill in the movie *Room at the Top*, which she predicts will win her the Best Actress Oscar, Marilyn bemoans the fact that she never gets offered to play great movie roles like Alice Aisgill. But Simone points out that Marilyn Monroe is a great star while she herself is only an actress married to the great star Yves Montand.

Later when Simone wins the Oscar for *Room at the Top*, Marilyn salutes her, although she grows secretly envious of her friend's success. Still later, Marilyn becomes depressed and restless when Arthur leaves her to work on her next movie, *The Misfits*. When she refuses to appear on the set of *Let's Make Love*, Simone goes to her and convinces her to return to work. She also promises that Montand will help Marilyn with the difficulties she is having with her role. Shortly thereafter, Marilyn becomes romantically involved with her friend Simone's husband. Several years pass, and a now greatly aged Simone looks back on the whole episode of Marilyn's affair with her husband and professes to having forgiven her for what happened back then. However, she does confess that the pain it caused her still remains even if she has tried to hide it from the world.

Written by Sue Glover, *Madame Montand and Mrs. Miller* presents a portrait of Simone Signoret as a world-weary, complex femme du monde and also as something of a mirror image of Marilyn Monroe. Yet as the narrative unfolds, there are important differences that get established between the two women. Although it is true that Simone is most definitely a beautiful woman of expansive sensuality, she is still, first and foremost, a great actress who even goes on to win an Oscar. Yet Simone tells Marilyn she prefers to see herself as the faithful wife of a great international star—Yves Montand. In essence, Simone possesses much that Marilyn never will have. For sadly, even despite all her wealth, glamour, and fame, Marilyn suffers from much uncertainty and remains profoundly insecure about herself and her talent.

Now, it should perhaps be pointed out that this text is clearly based on the dramatic premise that the action should be interpreted from the point of view of Simone Signoret. Although both she and Marilyn are depicted as embodying a lush, movie-star sexuality, it is only the lush movie-star sexuality of Simone that can ever possibly be truly contained within both the narrative and the patriarchal structures. Only she is able to sublimate her potentially dangerous sexuality into this acceptable discipline of her rigorous art. For her efforts, she has gone on to score several theatrical triumphs on the stage in Paris and has starred in many celebrated movies. And, most important, she has also achieved a happy ten-year marriage to Montand and found fulfillment in motherhood.

In direct contrast to Simone Signoret, there is Marilyn Monroe. She is different from Simone and, therefore, dangerous. She seriously doubts her acting ability, cannot keep a husband, and is unable to give birth to a child. Further, there seems to be no way that her rampant sexuality (as it is depicted here) can be as successfully contained as Simone's can be. A powerful example of this occurs when she carries on her illicit love affair with Montand. Not only are she and Montand already married to others, but also Marilyn's sexuality will eventually become so overwhelming and excessive that it will ultimately prove too destructive for him to handle.

When the news of the affair between Marilyn and Montand makes worldwide headlines, Simone, being the great actress that she is, manages to put up a brave front and patiently waits for his inevitable return. In her heart, Simone, of course, realizes (as did Jackie Kennedy) that Montand will eventually become much too overwhelmed with Marilyn's excessive sexuality, which will leave him no other choice but to return back home to the peaceful serenity of his patient and loving wife just as JFK returned to Jackie. Yes, Simone can even afford to be diplomatic and treat her younger rival with a maternalistic compassion. For example, when Marilyn holes herself up in her hotel suite, refusing to go to the movie set because she feels so unattractive, Simone goes to comfort her. In such a scene, Simone exhibits the age-old wisdom of the Continent itself. In her 1978 autobiography *Nostalgia Isn't What It Used to*

Be, Simone continues to display this same sophisticated, Old World sensibility when she puts forth the rhetorical question, "Can *you* think of many men who wouldn't have responded to Marilyn's charm?"[8] For all that, however, the Simone we see at the end of the movie isn't quite so magnanimous. She's grown old and fat and even stopped dyeing her hair blonde, letting it go almost completely gray:

> I was going to change the color—but no! Who cares! Let them see the gray, the lines, and the fat. I am Signoret—this is me—I am alive. . . . And if the hurt hasn't healed—well, no one must know. No one.[9]

And so, we are left with a pensive final image of Simone burying deeply inside herself all her pain, hurt, and humiliation from the prying eyes of the world. The bitter tears she may still cry are strictly a private affair. No longer a cinematic love goddess, in her prime, Simone turns her full power to the act of aging. And as Catherine David observes, in Simone Signoret's hands aging becomes a weapon; there is even "an act of defiance made out of it."[10]

As in *Death Becomes Her,* the immortality of Marilyn is again signified in the 1993 movie *Netherworld.* This depiction projects her into the eerie context of a macabre horror-fantasy movie for the first time. The hero of the movie, Corey Thornton, is surprised to discover that his estranged late father has left him a great mansion in Louisiana. When he arrives at his new home, he falls in love with beautiful young Dianne Palmer, whose mysterious and domineering mother oversees the property. Dianne makes a point of warning Corey never to go near the town's decadent brothel. But he soon finds himself powerfully drawn to the place with its main attraction of the gravely beautiful Delores, who, besides turning tricks, possesses supernatural powers. Along with Delores, Marilyn Monroe also works in one of the brothel's more exclusive suites. Corey becomes thoroughly obsessed with Delores. He eventually comes to learn that his father was himself deeply involved with her and the brothel, which holds all sorts of strange secrets and hideous creatures. He also learns that his father has plans of returning from the dead. One night while waiting for his assignation with Delores, Corey encounters Marilyn, who tells him that it is up to him to help his father's return back to the living. Totally baffled by her words, Corey meets with Delores. She seduces him, then puts him under a spell so that he can make contact with his dead father. When Corey realizes that his father plans to inhabit his body, a brutal fight breaks out between them. But aided by a change of heart in Delores and the power of the true love of Dianne, Corey wins the battle. He returns back to the living, and his father's corrupt soul gets trapped in the body of a caged parrot.

If the star attraction of the brothel in *Netherworld* is Delores, she's also the High Priestess of this rather bizarre bird cult, and the brothel is a dark void that leads directly to the Netherworld and, ultimately, total damnation. With this, the movie then becomes the perverse dramatization of a quasi-psychoanalytical scenario—the unexpected surfacing of the invisible, chaotic forces of instinct or the unconscious, all signified in the mysterious figure of Delores. But in opposition to Delores, there is the figure of Marilyn Monroe as the prostitute as Sacred Whore. In her white-on-white brothel suite, her body seems to purify and immolate itself every time she gives herself to a man. Because she is a great star, and even though she is portrayed as a prostitute here, her immense erotic energy gets transformed from whoring into another kind of greatness. She becomes a link between rationality and irrationality, between visibility and invisibility, between mortality and immortality. And it is for this reason that she appears even more enigmatic and mysterious rather than horrific or frightening as does the scheming Delores. Most amazingly, this is so even when Marilyn tells Corey of how she has returned from the dead to become a signifier of her own immortality. Or, in other words, the invisible (death) is made the alluringly visible (life) in the figure of the reincarnated Marilyn Monroe in *Netherworld*.

Marilyn Monroe is still alive and fairly well in the 1993 feature film *Calendar Girl*. The movie is a period comedy and coming-of-age saga in which three graduating high school seniors head to California to meet the calendar girl of their dreams—Marilyn Monroe. The three friends—Jerry, Roy, and Ned—become hopelessly smitten with Marilyn as boys when they first see her famous nude calendar. After their graduation, Roy enlists in the army, so the boys decide to drive out to Hollywood to find Marilyn. In Hollywood, they stay with Roy's aging hipster Uncle Harry. Soon they're parking outside Marilyn's home on Helena Drive in hopes of getting a glimpse of their beloved calendar girl. Eventually, they pursue her to a nude beach. But instead of finding Marilyn, the boys themselves are found by the Gallo Brothers, two car repo thugs for whom Roy used to work and whose convertible he has taken to drive out to California. They successfully outsmart the Gallos. With the thugs out of the way, they then read of Marilyn's great love of animals and decide to haul a two-ton heifer to her Brentwood home. Roy even manages to slip inside to see Marilyn, but she refuses to go out with him on a date. Later that night, Roy gets a phone call from her. She tells him she cannot sleep and wants him to take her out on a drive. Roy nobly passes his date onto Ned, who winds up staying out all night walking the beach with Marilyn and cherishing the memory forever.

The action of *Calendar Girl* takes place during the last months of Marilyn's life. Because we know this period was not always an easy one for her, our knowledge of this colors the overall tone of the narrative. In other words, what could have all too easily been just another horny youth comedy becomes something more. True, there may be something excessively juvenile and even vulgar about the three boys with their obsessive and fetishistic sexual fantasies centered around the elusive figure of Marilyn. But it is their youthful idealization of her that ennobles them in our minds. Even more, it is crucial to remember that Hollywood movie narration and mise-en-scène has traditionally been organized around the creation of the figure of the woman as being aligned with lavish spectacle, expansive space, and, of course, the alluring image. In her classic article "Visual Pleasures and Narrative Cinema," Laura Mulvey points out that the woman is usually associated with the alluring surface of the image, and, therefore, it is relatively easy for her to become the passive fixation and obsession of the more active male spectatorial desires of voyeurism and fetishism. This scenario can often make the male the active mover of the narrative, while the female becomes associated more with the space of passive subjectivity. Yet the space that Marilyn occupies in *Calendar Girl* also becomes the movie's center. If the three boys and their various antics do move the narrative along, the focus of this movement is all toward Marilyn. Her presence gets articulated in the movie in three separate ways. She is a major component of the voice-over narration of Ned. Then she exists in the scrapbook he keeps of her. Additionally, images of her proliferate in the form of the extensive scenes from all her movies that the boys are endlessly watching.

When the three boys start their vigil outside her home waiting to meet her, Marilyn's presence is experienced mostly in the brief glimpses they manage to catch of her almost from the edge of the frame. What this emphasis on the movie's slippery frame line does is create a mysterious border between the realm of the mortal (the boys) and the immortal (Marilyn). As the presence of Marilyn slips in and out of the frame, she plays a captivating game of now-you-see-her-now-you-don't with the boys. And with her slipping in and out of the frame line as she does, she represents a connection between the mortal and the immortal, the visible and the invisible, the attainable and the unattainable. This strategy keeps the boys in a constant state of suspense. Although Marilyn may be the Goddess hunted, she is also the Goddess of the hunt, forever keeping the boys in wild pursuit of her—that is, until she unexpectedly stops long enough for them to catch up with her. Now, some critics of the movie have complained that in letting the boys fulfill their dream of meeting Marilyn, the filmmakers make a big mistake. But one could also argue that in having the boys fulfill their dream, the movie is tapping into the spirit of the times. For, as stated, what the 1990s were all about was Marilyn's depiction as a fully accessible Goddess of the People. And, as such, it is only fitting that she makes herself amenable to the fulfilling of the boys' dreams.

The 1993 play *Body*, first presented at The Players Ring of Portsmouth, New Hampshire, is of interest in that the action is set in the basement of the Los Angeles City Morgue on the morning of August 5, 1962. It is within this setting that (as in *Calendar Girl*) three LA street kids encounter the (now) lifeless body of Marilyn Monroe. Yet playwright David J. Mauriello manages to avoid any possible charges of salaciousness or sensationalism that such a situation could easily have. The three teenage characters of the play—Tim, Gonzo, and Gus— are ultimately made to become our stand-ins as they successfully navigate their way through all the emotional and psychological land mines that are woven into this metaphysical psychodrama. As the narrative unfolds, Mauriello uses the figure of Marilyn Monroe as a dramatic symbol through which the boys discover many deep truths. In keeping with this symbolism, *Body* partakes of the use of heightened imagery and theatrical stylization. These qualities are manifested in the language the boys speak to communicate their innermost thoughts to one another. Still, at the edges of these passages of the poetic stage language, there is also an internal form of ritualization being played out. This representation of the ritualistic triggers off a rippling effect during the course of the narrative that can turn toward ceremonies of shock and menace. These rituals reach their culmination when the boys encounter the body of Marilyn Monroe.

At the start of the second act, the boys slowly approach Marilyn's nude body, which has been laid out on a marble slab (strongly suggestive of some paganistic sacrificial altar). And, as we also saw happen with the concluding scene of the movie *Goodnight, Sweet Marilyn*, Marilyn is once again bathed in a golden-toned, celestial light. This dramatic moment suffuses the scene with an even greater sense of heightened imagery and theatrical stylization. Further, the moment, which is initially disturbing, forces each of the boys to experience the tragedy of Marilyn's death in his own way. In so doing, each characterization increases in complexity. For the pragmatically orientated Gus and Gonzo, there is a profound sense of unreality and disbelief about the whole experience. To them, seeing is not believing or knowing. For this reason, they long to touch and make some sort of physical contact with her. After Gus runs his fingers through Marilyn's hair, the boys discuss what has occurred. And as is typical, it is left to Tim to translate for the other two boys the meaning of their experience:

> Gonzo: What's it feel like?
> Gus: Hair.
> Gonzo: Sure it feels like hair . . . but what does it *feel* like?
> Gus: Not dead, I know what you mean, not dead, like she's acting.
> Gonzo: In a movie.
> Gus: I can see why guys went crazy, like . . . having an . . . angel, an angel
> letting you fuck her . . . a white angel with golden blonde hair.[11]

But if Marilyn signifies "a white angel with golden blonde hair" to Gus, she is also a signifier for the archetypal heroine of many fairy tales for the boys.

This mythical subfoundation of the play is composed of a modernistic reimagining of such classic fairy tales as *Snow White* and *Sleeping Beauty*. Benefiting from the glamour and fame of her achievement of Hollywood stardom, Marilyn's role is analogous to the poor young woman of so many fairy tales who is transformed by some magical, otherworldly means into a beautiful princess or golden goddess. It is for this reason that the boys come to imagine that they, too, can somehow reawaken her from death with the power of a kiss. With this fairy-tale projection of all their longing and desire onto her, they actually believe their kiss has the magical, healing power to awaken and recover not just Marilyn but also themselves. Like the princes who come to kiss Snow White and Sleeping Beauty, Tim, Gus, and Gonzo hope to restore order and integrity back onto the memory of Marilyn's life, their own lives, and perhaps even ours as well.

Susan Griffiths (*Legends, Marilyn and Me, Pulp Fiction*) appears as Marilyn Monroe in the 1993 "Goodbye Norma Jean" (not to be confused with the 1976 movie of the same title) episode of the sci-fi TV show *Quantum Leap.* Director Christopher Humbler cleverly reworks themes from Joseph L. Mankiewicz's 1950 classic *All About Eve* into "Goodbye Norma Jean." Now it is Marilyn who plays the Margo Channing–like role, and Liz Vassey plays Barbara Whitmore, the conniving Eve Harrington–like figure. In place of the backstage world of Broadway there is, instead, the equally treacherous (if considerably less witty and erudite) world of Hollywood moviemaking. The quality of the narrative soon becomes instantly associated with the antirealism and absurdity implicit within Hollywood at its most venal. Here much of that Hollywood venality is collapsed into the figure of Barbara as she first worms her way into Marilyn Monroe's good graces and then even goes so far as to attempt to take Marilyn's place. But, eventually, through the assistance of *Quantum Leap*'s hero, Sam (played by actor Scott Bakula, so good playing Joe DiMaggio in the 1983 Broadway musical *Marilyn, An American Fable*), Marilyn does come to see the true reality behind all her younger rival's duplicitness. When Sam encourages her to attend rehearsals for her final movie, *The Misfits*, looking ever radiant and stunning, Marilyn is at first, surprised to see Barbara dancing most seductively with her own legendary leading man Clark Gable. Moving in with a breathy sigh, nonchalant toss of the head, and artificial smile (similar to all the artificial smiles Barbara gave her all during the episode), Marilyn quickly pushes the pushy upstart out of the way to assume her place as Gable's rightful leading lady.

In 1993, the New York City Opera presented the premiere of the opera *Marilyn*, with music by Ezra Laderman and a libretto written by the poet and playwright Norman Rosten. Actually, Rosten based his libretto on his excellent 1973 memoir *Marilyn, The Untold Story*. Rosten's book offers a lyrical portrait of

Marilyn. The narrative follows the period of her life from her divorce from Joe DiMaggio and to her marriage to Arthur Miller, their subsequent divorce, and, finally, her tragic death in 1962. And in Rosten's depiction of Marilyn, we see the symbol of Death and the Maiden coming together, as the book is written with a sad, almost lugubrious beauty. Yet in adapting his memoir into the opera *Marilyn*, Rosten has made several odd creative choices. He structures the operatic text as a series of vignettes from the perspective of Marilyn's life in 1962. These vignettes are presented in the form of that old Hollywood standby the extended flashback. In melodramatic accordance, the opera's cast consists of Marilyn and such generic characters as the Psychiatrist, the Senator (who vaguely resembles RFK), two lecherous Hollywood moguls, and, in what is unquestionably Rosten's oddest choice of all, one generic ex-husband named Rick. In the creation of this composite character, he literally collapses all three of Marilyn's husbands into one two-dimensional figure.

What of the music supplied by composer Ezra Laderman? Did it help matters any? Unfortunately, the answer to this question is in the negative. For with the music there was also a generic approach taken rather than a daring or original one. Opera critic Mark Swed of *Opera News* said of the score,

> Laderman's music is more voyeuristic than veristic, its rhythmic squareness and comfortable lack of personality, whether bright jazz or academic atonal expressionism, never seeming to fit Marilyn Monroe.[12]

Putting aside the matter of Laderman's music and Rosten's libretto, another reason for the failure of this opera to catch on has to do with the fact that *Marilyn* concludes on a negative note of total despair with a final depiction of Marilyn left as a lifeless corpse on stage. Now, by concluding this way, Laderman and Rosten do root their opera firmly within the codified tradition of many famous nineteenth-century operas that also perpetuate either the death or the total domestication of the female heroine/victim at the conclusion.

Yet, in placing their depiction of the operatic Marilyn within this tradition, Laderman and Rosten may be displaying their knowledge of opera history, but they are also demonstrating that they are out of step with the 1990s. For, as we argue, the 1990s are not about Marilyn as tragic victim any longer. No, what the decade is about is her exaltation as the transcendent Goddess of the People. Fortunately, the critical response to the beautiful and talented soprano Kathryn Gamberoni in the role of Marilyn Monroe was infinitely more positive. In *Opera News*, Swed described her performance as "terrific," and Edward Rothstein of the *New York Times* felt that the diva's "lyric soprano had more impact because of the very able impersonation that was behind it." [October 8, 1993, C3]

The 1994 TV movie *Marilyn and Bobby: Her Final Affair* also looks at Marilyn Monroe's doomed relationship with Robert F. Kennedy. In the early part of 1962, RFK as attorney general is kept busy investigating the criminal activities of Jimmy Hoffa and Sam Giancana. To retaliate, Hoffa employs a surveillance team to get all the dirt it can on RFK—and, most specifically, on his romantic involvement with Marilyn. Hoffa's indefatigable surveillance men duly record all the couple's lovemaking on tape. Later, they even find Marilyn's secret diary, which fully documents the details of her involvement with both Kennedys. Along with Hoffa, J. Edgar Hoover's FBI is also shadowing the couple, collecting evidence of their affair. All during this period, Marilyn is also continually calling in sick at 20th Century-Fox, which disrupts the making of *Something's Got to Give*. To retaliate, the studio fires her. Making matters even worse, RFK refuses to help her and then, on his brother's advice, abruptly ends his relationship with her. Marilyn plunges into despair and turns to pills and alcohol and even threatens to hold a press conference to tell all about her involvement with the Kennedys.

On the night of August 4, 1962, a totally drugged-out Marilyn calls Peter Lawford to say good-bye to him and the Kennedy brothers. RFK then orders his men to go to her house to confiscate her secret diary. Although Lawford, who is also at the house, calls an ambulance to take the dying Marilyn to the hospital, FBI agents order that the ambulance take her back home to die of an overdose. RFK flees Los Angeles in a helicopter as Marilyn's nude body lies dead in her bed and her diary mysteriously disappears forever.

Marilyn and Bobby: Her Final Affair is like a classic "whodunit," only in reverse. The movie depicts the dynamics of the ill-fated love affair between Marilyn and RFK as being enigmatic and somewhat elusive. This enigmatic quality then gets carried over into the narrative, in which the murder of the heroine happens at the end of the movie rather than at the beginning. Because of this break with tradition, the identity of her murderer or murderers is not revealed. There is then no final revelation of the truth, no solution to the mystery. Justice is not served. This lack of narrative closure leaves us hanging, feeling anxious and even upset. We cannot help but find ourselves wondering, Who killed Marilyn Monroe? We replay the movie over again in our minds, attempting to figure out the solution to the mystery. We consider all the possible suspects: who could have committed the crime?

There is a wealth of suspicious characters to choose from. One of the most suspicious of all is Jimmy Hoffa. So determined is he in his hatred of the Kennedys that he is prepared to do whatever it takes to destroy them. Not only does he have Marilyn's home and telephone bugged, he even orders a hit on RFK and seriously contemplates having Marilyn herself killed. In comparison to Hoffa, J. Edgar Hoover seems far more levelheaded and rational in his behavior. Although he does typically misuse his authority to do all he can to torment the Kennedys, he is depicted nowhere near as ruthless as Hoffa. Still another major suspect is Mafia kingpin Sam Giancana. But amazingly, even his behavior is more preferable than Hoover's foul misconduct.

If the combined efforts of these three suspicious characters do much to threaten Marilyn's physical well-being, the antics of the Kennedy brothers wreak much havoc on her emotional, mental, and spiritual well-being. Not helping the matter any is the treatment she typically receives at the hands of the Hollywood studio bosses who seem to go out of their way to humiliate and mistreat her at every turn. JFK's treatment of her is no less cruel. When finished with Marilyn, he casually passes her onto his younger brother. But the whole matter backfires on the president as Marilyn and RFK find themselves truly attracted to one another. And as the relationship between RFK and Marilyn heats up, Hoffa increases his constant surveillance of them. The couple does not disappoint. With evidence firmly in hand, Hoover wastes little time in bringing it to JFK's attention. The president summons his brother to the White House and orders him to break off his relationship with Marilyn. RFK meets with Marilyn and tells her that his breaking off with her is nothing personal; it's only politics. But highly indignant over the choice of words he uses, Marilyn becomes furious.

She lashes out at the Kennedys, bitterly complaining that they have used her, treated her as if she were meat. She threatens that she will get her revenge on them. With her outburst, we get a side of Marilyn that we have never seen before. Before our eyes, she is transfigured from the Goddess of Love into an Avenging Angel yielding a fiery sword to strike down all who have ever wronged her.

But this role is only a short-lived one for Marilyn to play. Her angry reaction marks her as a very dangerous woman. After all, when a powerful man dismisses her, she is meant to disappear, not challenge his authority. With this one act of defiance, Marilyn totally violates her boundaries and transgresses against the patriarchal superstructure. For her gross indiscretion, she must be punished. The form that Marilyn's punishment takes is to be her total destruction. Too many powerful men can no longer afford to have her around anymore. The movie's depiction of her death is disturbing. It is a night full of strange noises, terrible sounds, uncanny incidents, and ominous sights. Screams are heard on the wind; sleep is broken and impossible to sustain; the skies grow dark, and gloomy, threatening chaotic happenings. On this, the last night of Marilyn's life, the hypersignifying mise-en-scène becomes that of a Hollywood horror movie. The sanctity of her home is soon invaded by a virtual army of strange men who intend her great harm.

Through it all, Marilyn is depicted as alone, nude, and totally vulnerable. Paradoxically, there's a look of serenity and resignation about her. In a series of classically arranged and beautifully lit, tableau-like compositions, her iconic nude body is most seductively arranged, thrusting us as viewers into the role of voyeur. Yet this body that possesses all the attributes of movie-star sexiness is soon to become a body drained of all life. So, *Marilyn and Bobby: Her Final Affair* concludes on a final note of ambiguity. Marilyn is dead. Her nude body lies across her bed, with her hand on her telephone. And like so much else in the movie, this final composition creates a mysterious effect. True, she is now dead, and the patriarchal order has been (temporarily) restored, but Marilyn's translucent female flesh still defiantly gives off the glowing aura of life itself. Or perhaps it is eternal life that is conveyed.

Writer-director Quentin Tarantino paid unique cinematic homage to the immensely popular "pulp" crime stories of the 1930s and 1940s as well as to Marilyn Monroe in his 1994 sleeper smash hit *Pulp Fiction*. Featuring flavorful dialogue, an eccentric cast of characters, and spectacular use of visual design, the movie also exhibits Tarantino's excellence at directing his actors and his exciting use of period music. All these details blend together in the standout set piece of the movie that takes place in the 1950s theme Jackrabbit Slim's restaurant scene. Presented in lurid, primary colors, the walls of the restaurant are adorned with posters from 1950s B movies. The booths the restaurant's patrons sit in are made up of the glistening bodies of 1950s cars; all the restaurant's large picture windows don't look out onto the outside street, but instead black-and-white movies of the 1950s are projected behind them; and the wait-staff consists of such 1950s icons as Marilyn Monroe, James Dean, Donna Reed, Mamie Van Duren, and Elvis Presley.

Tarantino's use of Marilyn Monroe in this sequence is also most inspired. Not only is she being used as an ultimate symbol of the nostalgic 1950s, but she also serves as a bridge that connects the 1950s to the 1990s. In the movie, Marilyn wears the iconic *Seven Year Itch* white dress that she now wears in the majority of all the depictions of her. But Tarantino is also smart enough not to use her as simply just another one of the restaurant's run-of-the-mill waitresses. Therefore, she is additionally the trophy girl who presents the movie's characters Mia and Vincent with a dancing prize. Then, in the midst of all the wild action, Marilyn, for no real apparent reason, stops to stand over an air vent. Suddenly, the bustling sounds of a subway car fills the place, making everything shake and rattle. As the train rushes by, her skirt billows up around her waist to a thunderous outburst of applause after which Marilyn bows in appreciation.

Marilyn Monroe's connection to an American president figures into the plot of the 1996 comedy *My Fellow Americans*, which tells of two former presidents who detest one another but are forced to travel together to attend a state funeral. Jack Lemmon plays money-grubbing former Republican President

Russell Kramer, and James Garner plays womanizing former Democratic President Matt Douglas. When a defense contract kickback backfires, current President William Haney, rather than be exposed himself, has President Kramer framed for the crime. After a bomb explodes on the helicopter carrying the two former presidents, they decide to set out for Kramer's Presidential Library in Ohio to get some documents that will clear him of the crime. While on a train, they have a memorable encounter with Elvis Presley and Marilyn Monroe. After experiencing a whole series of other wild, cross-country adventures, the two ex-presidents mend their differences and decide to run for reelection on the same ticket.

My Fellow Americans features the use of Elvis Presley and Marilyn Monroe as fellow passengers that Presidents Kramer and Douglas encounter on the train taking them across America. Both Elvis and Marilyn are iconically dressed in pure white. Elvis wears a sequined white Las Vegas–style jumpsuit complete with an ermine-trimmed cape, while Marilyn wears her favored *Seven Year Itch* white dress. When the womanizing President Douglas spots Marilyn, he instantly reverts into his Don Juan guise. And since seduction has always been his main game, he promptly attempts to seduce Marilyn. And this cinematic use of Marilyn Monroe becomes almost like a narrative coda to the way she was used back in the 1969 play *Cop-Out*, where her sexuality made her the signifier of the sexual fantasy of every one of the American presidents down through history. So then, what's one more president more or less?

The 1996 cable TV movie *Norma Jean and Marilyn* opens on a closure. The time is August 5, 1962, and the first words heard are of a radio announcer pronouncing Marilyn Monroe's death. From there, the narrative jumps back to when Norma Jean (Ashley Judd) is just starting off her career as a model with lofty dreams of one day becoming a great star in Hollywood. She also gets involved with a young struggling actor named Eddie. Still, while pursuing her dreams, Norma Jean can't stop herself from remembering the details of her unhappy childhood. After her mother, Gladys, is institutionalized, she goes from one horrible foster home to another where she is exposed to much abuse. Yet, despite her painful memories, Norma Jean's attention stays relentlessly focused on the attainment of her dream. Toward this end, she bleaches her hair blonde, gets romantically involved with Hollywood superagent Johnny Hyde, and poses nude on red velvet drapery. She also comes to rely more and more on pills and alcohol. Although Johnny's health deteriorates at an alarming rate, he does succeed at securing her a contract at 20th Century-Fox. When Darryl Zanuck criticizes her appearance, Norma Jean subjects herself to painful plastic surgery. After the operation, Norma Jean disappears, and Marilyn Monroe (Mira Sorvino) takes her place. But one day Norma Jean reappears and remains a significant presence from then on. Marilyn's two dueling alter egos get into a series of highly dramatic conversations and frequently melodramatic, bitter confrontations for the rest of the movie, which chronicles all the now familiar highs and lows of her life. The movie concludes with the chilling image of both the Marilyn and the Norma Jean sides of her psyche dead and locked in each other's arms.

Norma Jean and Marilyn picks up on many of the same thematic concerns first introduced in the 1973 play *The White Whore and the Bit Player*. Whereas playwright Tom Eyen used the dramatic device in his play mainly for its symbolic and mythical implications, in this movie the emphasis is placed more on the psychological implications of the split. With this in mind, we would now like to read the movie through the screen of Freud's highly influential essay *The Uncanny*.

It is in *The Uncanny* that Freud takes up the figure of "the double," which he argues is created in the child as a kind of psychic insurance against the destruction of the ego and can also be used as "an energetic denial of the power of death." In this way, the double is invented by the child as a preservation against the ultimate extinction of the self, which connects the double to the narcissism of the child. But later, Freud contends that "when the narcissistic stage is surmounted, the double reverses its original aspect."[13] When this occurs, the double is completely out of place and unwanted.

In *Norma Jean and Marilyn*, this aspect of the double occurs in the scene when Marilyn literally kills off the double—signified by the Norma Jean part of her personality—by running her over with her automobile. And, of course, when the heroine is successfully transformed into Marilyn Monroe, on some level the Norma Jean part of herself is no more. For a while, too, everything seems to go exactly as planned with Marilyn undergoing the long, painful process of being transformed into a Hollywood movie star. After having achieved her goal, what need has she any longer of the ungreat Norma Jean? The only problem with all this is that the Norma Jean part of her doesn't see it that way. And therein lies the great conflict of the movie, which gets fully articulated in the increasingly heated conversations and arguments that continually erupt between the two halves of Marilyn's divided psyche. After Marilyn has difficulty performing a scene from Ibsen's theatrical masterpiece *A Doll's House* on a stage, she flees the scene, only to be confronted by Norma Jean, who categorically refuses to listen to her complaints. Instead, she demands that Marilyn push herself even harder until she becomes as great a stage actress as Geraldine Page. The scene also firmly establishes the distinct contrast between the two sides of Marilyn's personality. While Marilyn is usually confused, highly emotional, and overly sensitive to other people's criticism of her, Norma Jean couldn't care less what others think of her. Her only concern is that the Marilyn Monroe part of herself becomes a great, dramatic actress.

Another strong Freudian influence in the movie is the role that Marilyn's dreams and fantasies play in the narrative. This is established at the start when the action opens with the dream of the teenage Norma Jean being completely nude in church and continues when Marilyn tells her psychiatrist of a recurring dream she has about her estranged father. In the dream, she is dressed as a prostitute, complete with a dark wig and dark glasses. She meets a mysterious older man and agrees to go to a hotel room and have sex with him. Directly after the sex act, Marilyn angrily rips off her wig and reveals to him that she is his long-lost daughter, Norma Jean. In Freudian terms, this dream becomes an angry acting out of the Electra complex in which the daughter harbors profoundly unresolved desires for sexual gratification with the father.

Still, as angry as Norma Jean gets toward the father in the dream, it seems that the real object of all her scorn is mostly directed toward the Marilyn part of herself. For example, at the end of the movie, Norma Jean screams at the totally distraught Marilyn, reminding her of how worthless she is and that no man—not even her own father—has ever really loved her. The deeply unsettling power and dramatic intensity of this devastating diatribe of one part of the psyche pitted so fiercely against the other owes much of its forcefulness to the powerful performances of the movie's leading ladies—Ashley Judd and Mira Sorvino. For the most part, Judd plays Norma Jean as a coal's bed of excitement and dark-toned allure. This Norma Jean is much hungrier for fame than we can ever remember and willing to do just about anything she has to do to achieve it. But her ruthless ambition grows to such monumental dimensions that she must invent her alter ego Marilyn Monroe to win the world's love and affection and achieve that fame. Because, unlike Norma Jean, Marilyn is soft, weak, and vulnerable beyond belief. Sorvino plays her with an ethereal fragility and delicacy here. She may be Everyman's erotic fantasy, but she's also something of a lost angel.

The 1997 Broadway comedy *Jackie: An American Life*, by playwright Gip Hoope, seems to be the work of a loose, off-the-bat kind of theatrical sensibility. It is an abandoned, wildly imaginative theatrical creation based on the celebrated life and times of Jacqueline Kennedy Onassis that plays much like the miniseries *A Woman Named Jackie*, only reimagined and replayed as an elaborate vaudevillian comedy. Amazingly, Hoope manages to skip most drollfully over most of the major events of the heroine's life like a stone tossed across rippling water. And so as the nonstop narrative sails from one iconic scene to another, the play relies quite a bit on satire and cartoonlike imagery to tell Jackie's story. For instance, at the beginning, Jackie's possessions are being auctioned off after her death at Sotheby's Auction House. (A half-used box of steel-wool pads, a dirty sponge, and one used rubber glove fetch millions of dollars.) Then, directly following the insane auction scene, all the bidders are led offstage like a herd of mindless sheep heading for the slaughter. It is at this point that the elegant Jackie makes her grand appearance. Looking like the petted darling of the international jet set, she sits at the top of a majestic staircase like a true dream of celebrity, surrounded by a theatrical marvel of a set that opens up into an aesthetically ethereal vista of a series of receding classical porticoes that seem illusionistically to go on and on forever.

The play's sense of satire and imaginative design remain pleasing throughout as the playwright continues to come up with scene after scene of theatrical (and often bitingly acerbic) exactitude. Among these many scenes are the one in which Marilyn Monroe makes a brief cameo appearance (as she now always seems to be in any depiction about a member of the Kennedys) at the lavish Hollywood fund-raiser for JFK given by Frank Sinatra and the members of his Rat Pack. In the midst of all the attendant hoopla, Marilyn surrealistically ascends from the shimmery depths of Sinatra's swimming pool (into which an extremely drunken Shirley MacLaine keeps pouring out bottles of vodka) looking as irresistibly alluring as Venus rising up from the sea foam. Immediately following her ascent, she and JFK begin their ritualistic dance of erotic seduction:

> Marilyn: Then, let's make it official business!
> JFK: How's that?
> Marilyn: I have a check for twenty-five-thousand-dollars for your campaign. That's official business . . . right?
> JFK: That's very generous of you, Marilyn.
> Marilyn: Now, all you have to do is find it.[14]

In 1998, playwright Robert Brustein's play *Nobody Dies on Friday* premiered at the American Repertory Theatre of Cambridge, Massachusetts. The work focuses on the complex relationship Marilyn Monroe shared with her acting teacher, Lee Strasberg; his wife, Paula; and their two children, Susan and John. On New Year's Day 1960, Marilyn has had way too much champagne to drink the night before at the New Year's Eve party given by Lee and Paula. Because she is in no state to go home alone, Marilyn sleeps in nineteen-year-old John's bedroom at the Strasberg's apartment overlooking Central Park. As Marilyn sleeps in John's bed, he must spend the night on the sofa in the living room. While busy tidying up, Paula accidentally wakes John up. Mother and son soon get into a heated discussion over the fact Marilyn has had another fight with Arthur Miller. The rebellious John is resentful of Marilyn's disruptive presence in their home. But Paula and twenty-one-year-old actress Susan are much more protective of her.

The agitated Lee enters and joins his family, complaining of not being able to find the obituary page of the *New York Times*, to which John replies,

"Famous people wait to make the Sunday paper. Nobody dies on Friday because nobody reads the *Times* on Saturday,"[15] which gives the play its evocative title. This leads into a discussion about Lee's teaching of method acting. John criticizes the way he believes Lee doesn't properly prepare actors to act. He is particularly critical of his father's handling of Marilyn. But Lee vehemently defends the frailty of Marilyn's psychological state. When the now awakened Marilyn calls out for Lee from John's bedroom, he goes to her. After Lee returns, he and John get into a bitter confrontation of the directionlessness of the young man's life. Completely fed up with his father's antagonism toward him, John convinces Susan to go out with him. Lee and Paula then discuss Marilyn, and Paula criticizes her husband for his indifference to their own children. Lee gets so upset that his nose begins bleeding. But even with his bleeding nose, he, ever at Marilyn's beck and call, rushes in to comfort her again.

Lee spends most of the day either comforting Marilyn or arguing with his family until he receives a telephone call from director Elia Kazan informing him that he has been rejected as the artistic director of the new theater company being formed at Lincoln Center. This causes Lee to grow angry toward everyone, except for Marilyn, of course. It finally takes her overdosing on pills before he snaps out of his foul state of mind. While Paula resuscitates the unconscious Marilyn, Lee and John attempt to resolve their differences. Their resolution proves only temporary, but Lee does make big plans to direct Marilyn as prostitute Sadie Thompson in a TV production of *Rain*. The action concludes with the Strasberg family all going to Marilyn when she summons them, that is, all except John.

On the surface, the Strasberg family appears to be the model of the perfect 1950s nuclear family. There's the industrious father, Lee; the stay-at-home mother, Paula; Susan, the lovely ingenue daughter and aspiring actress; and John, the handsome son and heir apparent. Yet once we get below that surface, things grow a lot more complicated. Lee can be overbearing and unfeeling; Paula harbors all sorts of secret resentments toward her husband; Susan, despite her intelligence, beauty, and talent, is as insecure as Marilyn and abuses pills, too; and John fails at everything he ever attempts and has a severe drinking problem and even Marilyn Monroe–like suicidal tendencies.

Despite this dysfunction, Lee and Paula Strasberg are viewed by Marilyn as the perfect parents she never had. This is why she resorts back to infantile behavior, holing herself up in John's bedroom, never once leaving her bed, and demanding that the family wait on her hand and foot. Since she is not ever seen in the play and only her voice is heard, her physical absence ends up creating an unexpected and overwhelming unseen presence. And with this characterization of Marilyn as a presence into an absence, her figure ends up perplexing and dismaying the Strasbergs as she exemplifies the dislocation of the signifier and referent. Because of this, her "presence" becomes totally dependent on the references the Strasbergs make of her, and this, in turn, confines her to a theatrically verbal existence predicated on their perception of her. The reason this works as well as it does is primarily because the theatrical is so very much a part of all the Strasbergs' lives.

Still, for all the family's theatricalism, John still cannot help but resent the unseen but always dominating presence of Marilyn. Yet beneath all his resentment of her there lies a more potent rage against the father. The disgust that John feels toward the father eventually extends from beyond him alone to dominate the overall tone of the entire play. This occurrence can perhaps be explained as the family nexus of the American middle class of the 1950s become dysfunctional. In *Nobody Dies on Friday*, the father no longer seems to know best about anything or anyone anymore. And with this loss of the traditional father, there quickly follows a loss of identity for all the other characters. Therefore, the theme of individual loss of identity—carried principally in the character of John—comes to organize all the play's central conflicts.

At one point, Paula struggles to explain to Lee how difficult it is for John to be the son of Lee Strasberg. But what she has left out of her explanation is that being Lee Strasberg's wife isn't exactly an easy role to play either. It is only Susan who Lee seems to have any strong affection toward. But even she feels the need to transform herself into a pale imitation of Marilyn Monroe. She dyes her dull brown hair a dazzling platinum blonde and resorts to taking upper and downer pills à la Marilyn.

For Paula, John, and Susan, the space that is traditionally reserved for the father must be designated as empty. Yet what is not there for any of them is overflowing to the brim with love and understanding for Marilyn, the brightest and most glamorous Hollywood star by far whose orbit has ever come within proximity of Lee. Another invisible but highly charged presence in the play is the doomed figure of 1950s rebellious icon James Dean, another of Lee's celebrated acting students. Paula grows sad while looking at a photograph of Dean, and Lee alludes to him on several occasions. Not having Dean around anymore means that all of Lee's creative attention must now be focused entirely on the cultivation and stimulation of the acting genius of Marilyn Monroe. Lee believes that he can even take all the horrors of her oppressive past and transform them into the unique dramatic technique and theatrical vocabulary of a new art form. Under his expert tutelage, destruction will become creation. He proclaims to the members of his family,

> Marilyn's instrument may be a little rough right now. She has no technical training yet. She can easily be thrown off. When she's uncertain, she freezes.

. . . But she acts with instinctual truth. With my help she could be another Eleonora Duse. Another Jeanne Eagles. In fact, that's one of the parts I'm going to direct her in—Sadie Thompson in *Rain*.

With this reference to the seductive figure of Sadie Thompson of *Rain*, Sadie, like Marilyn's physical presence and James Dean's tragic life, becomes another unseen yet powerfully evocative presence. Created by Somerset Maugham, Sadie Thompson is a prostitute whose lucrative career is cut short when she runs afoul of the sternly patriarchal Reverend Alfred Davidson, who first condemns Sadie's immorality and then converts her to become the very model of the perfect Christian woman. But after converting her, he brutally rapes her and, to repent, kills himself by cutting his own throat. In some ways, the sad, twisted story of Sadie Thompson and Reverend Davidson even rather perversely mirrors the development of the relationship of Lee to Marilyn. And if Reverend Davidson could transform a whore into a paragon of Christian virtue, then why cannot Lee Strasberg transform a glamorous Hollywood sex goddess into a divine actress of the American theater such as Jeanne Eagles, Pauline Lord, or Laurette Taylor? What Brustein seems to be doing is collapsing all of Lee's hopes and dreams into the amorphous, unseen figure of Marilyn. This, in turn, gives a sad, metaphorical dimension to much of the action.

Despite Lee's lofty goal, John continues to persist in his skepticism of Marilyn's ability to ever become a great stage actress, which would seem to make him the one member of the Strasberg family who might understand the full extent of her difficulties. Still, there is perhaps no real way that John—or anyone else for that matter—can ever fully comprehend the mystery of Marilyn. About the best that he or any of the play's other characters can do is inscribe on her a theatrical language of their own devising in which her absence is turned into some sort of a presence. Bit by bit and piece by piece, the four characters attempt to verbally construct Marilyn Monroe. And so, in this process, Marilyn becomes the blank tabula rasa on which all their (and our) perceptions and fantasies can be projected. And, most amazingly, she seems capable of containing all the meanings the Strasbergs (and we) inscribe on her.

Marilyn Monroe makes a brief cameolike appearance in the 1998 cable TV movie *The Rat Pack*. In the early 1960s, Frank Sinatra becomes increasingly fascinated with the charismatic Democratic presidential candidate John F. Kennedy. Using his connection to Kennedy's brother-in-law, Peter Lawford, Sinatra makes his way into the secluded confines of JFK's inner circle. In addition to himself, Sinatra brings along the other members of his illustrious and infamous Hollywood–Las Vegas Rat Pack: Dean Martin, Sammy Davis Jr., and Joey Bishop. Sinatra then puts all his considerable clout into getting JFK elected president. Along the way, he also introduces JFK to Marilyn and Judith

Campbell. In little time at all, JFK is busy conducting love affairs with both women.

When JFK becomes president, Sinatra is initially in a state of euphoria. This continues when the love of his life, Ava Gardner, visits him. But after the couple argues, Ava walks out, and Sinatra falls into a foul mood. His mood brightens somewhat when JFK announces he will stay with him when he visits California. Sinatra even has a new addition added to his home in anticipation of JFK's visit. But when Bobby Kennedy intervenes, he convinces his brother to distance himself from Sinatra. JFK goes to California but stays instead at the home of the Republican Bing Crosby. Sinatra blames Peter Lawford for the betrayal and cuts him dead. The members of the Rat Pack all drift apart, Marilyn is found dead in 1962, and JFK is assassinated in 1963; the legendary "Camelot" era of the early 1960s comes to a bitter ending.

Right from the start of the movie, it is firmly established that the members of the Rat Pack live by their own male code by which their wives are treated one way and their mistresses another. Rat Pack wives are placed high on pedestals to be worshipped and adored. Wives can be continually cheated on, lied to, and patronized, but they *must* always be catered to and indulged to the utmost. With Rat Pack mistresses, the matter grows more complicated. In the case of a mistress like Judith Campbell, who once again bears the onus of the Eternal Whore, the mistress can be easily disposed of when she outlives her usefulness. But, in the case of a mistress that truly matters, a whole other set of operatives is in order. In *The Rat Pack*, both Marilyn and Ava Gardner are depicted as such mistresses.

Since we have already witnessed Marilyn just so classified in the 1987 TV miniseries *Hoover vs. the Kennedys*, we are quite familiar with the iconographic terrain. Now, the fact that both she and Ava Gardner are beautiful and highly successful Hollywood superstars sets them far apart and high above Judith Campbell and her more common ilk. Marilyn and Gardner have attained such an exalted station and grandeur that they are forever young, forever beautiful, forever in love. For Sinatra and company, Marilyn and Gardner are viewed as being the most dazzling objects of desire. They are also viewed as such by the rampant capitalistic economy of Hollywood. To Hollywood, they are worth millions upon millions of dollars. Because Hollywood perceives each of these stars as total merchandise, Hollywood must bestow on each the monetary gains to which her exalted cinematic status commands. And with such monetary gains comes a certain freedom. It is for this reason that neither Marilyn nor Gardner truly does *need* the Rat Pack men in quite the same way that the Rat Pack's indulged wives need them. It is also for this reason that Gardner is entitled to display such imperious, exalted movie star behavior toward Sinatra, even leaving him sexually unsatisfied in his bed when she feels he isn't paying her proper attention. And it is for this same reason that, even though she is escorted by Joe DiMaggio for the evening, Marilyn can still so brazenly flirt with JFK. True, Marilyn's love for Joe and Arthur Miller may have faded away. However, since she holds the notion of life as a movie, all that is of importance to her is that she shows her love to her president and to all her adoring fans in the great movie palaces of the world.

The 1999 screen comedy *The Underground Comedy Movie* is an artistically exhausted affair consisting of an unrelated series of unrealistic vignettes built around such supposedly provocative subjects as masturbation, defecation, urination, sadomasochism, voyeurism, and even necrophilia. Marilyn Monroe, unfortunately, gets pulled into this sorry affair at the beginning and end of the movie. Talented actress Gena Lee Nolin (who should have known better) appears as Marilyn Monroe reenacting *The Seven Year Itch* subway scene on a flimsy, artificial-looking movie set. As the rushing breeze causes her white skirt to blow high into the air, Nolin responds by emitting a series of ever increasing squeals of such orgasmic delight that the scene quickly aligns itself with the doctrine of soft-core pornographical excess. This alignment with the pornographic erupts full force in Marilyn's second appearance in the movie. Once again, Nolin re-creates the famous scene from *The Seven Year Itch*. Only now she is joined by two horny old winos that frantically masturbate while lecherously gazing on her beauteous form. Thus, Marilyn's depicted image is sadly brought down to such an all-time outré low that it can only improve from here. And, fortunately, it does improve.

Playwright Jim Tommaney's play *The Final Hours of Norma Jeane* (1999) received its premiere at Edge Theatre of South Beach, Florida. Ostensibly about the last hours of Marilyn Monroe's life, the action starts off simply with what at first appears to be a richly textured realism. At the beginning, Marilyn is being guarded in her home by Secret Service men Lars and Rick on the orders of their commander in chief, and her not so clandestine lover, President John F. Kennedy. The men soon introduce us to the fact that this night is a "locked-box" routine. This means that the security around Marilyn is particularly heightened because she has grown increasingly demanding of JFK to visit her. Along with the shift in Marilyn's mood, the richly textured realism gives way to a more complex mixture of theatrical extravagance and hallucinatory stylization. When this happens, all the conspiracy theories about her death blossom into blood-red blooms, and her fate becomes a matter of the utmost concern. It is also at this point that the language the characters speak becomes a rich verbal interplay of literary, historical, and mythological references.

Accordingly, this same dramatic delineation affects the depiction of Marilyn, as fact and fantasy, sex and power, myth and history, and life and death all cojoin to contextualize her into the embodiment of the living Goddess. For in the play, she signifies the eternal Goddess who dwells in every woman but is most fully incarnated in Marilyn Monroe. Understandably, both Lars and Rick are utterly entranced by this sensuous and mythical Goddess in their midst. And she, in her impassioned longing for JFK, improvises erotic games with the men, using the heightened artifices of myth and epic history to satisfy her desires. She is at her most imaginative with the alpha male, Rick, when she assumes the role of Catherine the Great:

> Marilyn: Yes. The Empress.
> Rick: Risen from lowly beginnings.
> Marilyn: Yes.
> Rick: To command an empire. Like you.
> Marilyn: Like me.
> Rick: The Empress tires of courtiers who lick her boots.
> Marilyn: They are tedious.
> Rick: She is bored by the shallowness of court manners.
> Marilyn: The powdered wigs and foppish manners annoy her.
> Rick: She seeks comfort in the arms of . . .?
> Marilyn: A rough stableman.[16]

It is in the last half of the play that two things happen in confluence to change the status of Marilyn being in charge of her predicament and set in motion the steps toward her downfall. She makes an indiscreet telephone call to the White House threatening to reveal her affair with the president to the media. With the introduction of this new dynamic, something decisive takes place. This something is heavy with the cold-blooded impetus to have Marilyn "terminated" as it is known in CIA/FBI parlance.

In a last, desperate attempt to divert Rick and Lars from their deadly task, like the fabled Scheherazade, Marilyn decides to entertain the men with her many amazing stories. But when she is finally forced to realize that they will not be deterred, she decides to be the one to choose the form her death shall take: a lethal overdose of her barbiturates. And so, the divine Marilyn is back in charge once again even, as in this sad case, of the directing of her final, desperate act. After she has purified herself in a ritualistic, scented bath, Rick brings Marilyn her pills to take. But before dying, she curses Rick and Lars and JFK and all the Kennedys and even the future of America. A kind of perverse satisfaction follows her searing condemnation of America and its eventual fate. And the dreamlike quality of so much of the play—carried along by the all-encompassing, sensuous flow of the rhythmic dialogue—suddenly shifts into the hard-edged didacticism and harsher truths of social-political-philosophical agenda. Such a shift supercharges Marilyn with a final, destructive power. All at once, the dream vision of the narrative ceases, plunging us into the nightmare reality of the same dark abyss to which Marilyn has been so cruelly doomed. So, yes, in the end, *The Final Hours of Norma Jeane* is a true tragic statement of life and the cruel irony of fate, but the play nonetheless asserts the final personal triumph and grandeur of its legendary heroine—Marilyn Monroe.

The legendary Lena Horne once described Dorothy Dandridge as "the black Marilyn Monroe," and Horne's description is fully articulated in the 1999 cable TV movie *Introducing Dorothy Dandridge*. The movie once again employs the extended chronological flashback format to tell the dramatic tale of Dorothy Dandridge's tempestuous life. In the 1930s, Dorothy is part of a singing act performing at the famous Cotton Club in Harlem, where she meets and becomes romantically involved with Harold Nicholas of the Tap-Dancing Nicholas Brothers. Against the wishes of her mother's sexually abusive lesbian lover Auntie, she marries him. But soon after giving birth to a severely brain-damaged daughter, Harold deserts them both. While attending a posh Hollywood party, Dorothy hides under a grand piano with Marilyn Monroe and Ava Gardner and later meets her future agent and eventual lover, Earl Mills, at the same swanky party. Despite many forms of racial discrimination and other personal indignities, Earl expertly guides Dorothy's career. Her biggest break comes, however, when director Otto Preminger announces he will make a Hollywood movie with an all-black cast as a contemporary version of Bizet's great opera *Carmen* to be called *Carmen Jones*. Dorothy wins the role of the sexy Carmen, and she is a sensation. She becomes the first black woman in history to be nominated for the Best Actress Oscar, begins a torrid love affair with the married Preminger, and inspires Darryl Zanuck to go ahead with his big plans to transform her into the first true black leading lady in Hollywood. On Preminger's advice and against the judgment of Earl, she turns down Zanuck's offer, effectively killing off her Hollywood career. And later, when Preminger refuses to divorce his wife, her relationship with him meets as dismal a fate as her movie career.

Without Earl, Preminger, or Hollywood, Dorothy flounders. Her life further deteriorates when she becomes dependent on pills and alcohol and makes a second disastrous marriage to the sadistic Jack Dennison, who bankrupts her, forcing her to have to relinquish all parental custody of her daughter. Amidst all this sorrow, Earl reenters her life. With his love and assistance, Dorothy plans a career comeback and prepares to regain custody of her daughter. Unfortunately, before any of this happens, she is found dead in the nude.

As this would indicate, there are several strong parallels between the life of Dorothy Dandridge as it is presented in this televisual depiction and the life of Marilyn Monroe, although the difficulties of Dorothy's life are further exacerbated by the fact that she is a black woman who met with much racial discrimination as she pursued her career. When Earl books her into a restricted hotel on a singing engagement, she complains to him of not being allowed to use the front entrance or the bathroom facilities. And later, in the Hollywood of the 1940s and 1950s, the only roles that are offered to her to play as an actress are either "maids or whores." Then, almost as if by magic, the once-in-a-lifetime role of Carmen comes her way. When Otto Preminger makes his grand entrance into the movie, he becomes, at once, its Johnny Hyde–like figure capable of launching the heroine into stardom.

But if Preminger is a Johnny Hyde–like figure, responsible for launching Dorothy's star into the big time, he is also the one most responsible for later plunging her rising star into almost total obscurity. This happens when he first advises Dorothy to defy Darryl Zanuck's plan to make her a big star in Hollywood. Most amazingly, Zanuck—so often depicted as a thorn in Marilyn's side—is depicted as being relatively decent in this context. And also, quite decent is the figure of Earl Mills. In his love and real devotion to Dorothy (and even in his understandable jealousy when she becomes entangled in Preminger's nefarious web), he assumes something like the role that Joe DiMaggio usually plays in many of the Marilyn Monroe depictions documented in this book.

When we first see Dorothy hiding under the grand piano with Marilyn Monroe and Ava Gardner at the party, we immediately get the association. By Dandridge being in such exalted cinematic company, we are made aware that this is also her rightful place in the Hollywood hierarchy. When later in the movie she becomes visibly shaken after hearing of Marilyn's death, the news both saddens her and fills her with a profound sense of dread and foreboding for her own situation. And her response is, of course, the correct one for her to have. For Marilyn's death is depicted here as being a strong precursor of her own soon-to-come death.

In addition to the many depictions of Marilyn Monroe as a character in the performing arts of the 1990s, there was also a proliferation of the use of her image in commercial photography. Numerous artists, photographers, actresses, and supermodels have paid postmodern photographic homage to Marilyn in this way.[17] What unites all these two-dimensional depictions of Marilyn can immediately be perceived in the mimetic and the diegetic aspects of this imagery. Although the mimetic depiction does not usually require any mediation on the part of the spectator (its meaning is quickly perceived), the diegetic depiction is often in need of some sort of mediation (since what is conveyed is not always so readily apparent).

Examples of both of these components can be seen in the photospread. Figure 15, photographer Toni Parras's image of Naia Kelly (from Jim Tommaney's play *The Final Hours of Norma Jeane*), is an excellent example of a mimetic depiction. The direct mimetic connection is established at once to the famous photograph taken of Marilyn Monroe by photographer Eve Arnold in 1961. Parras meticulously re-creates every detail of the original source right down to the curvaceous ornamentation adorning the back of the chair on which the actress sits. There is also the extended arm of the hairdresser unexpectedly entering the smooth photographic frame in a last-minute attempt to perfect Marilyn's sleek blonde hair. Anchored by such a strong and direct visual channel to the 1961 original source, the meaning of this type of photographic tribute is quickly perceived and appreciated by the viewer for both its physical exactitude and its nostalgia-inducing accuracy.

Figure 17, Miguel Starcevich's photograph of model Nana Kazari (2004), is an example of the diegetic depiction, conveying more of an elusive, not-so-readily-apparent meaning. Here, the smooth photographic frame is less determined, more dreamlike in nature, as reality is first observed and then subtly transmuted and transformed. The model sits at her dressing table rather dreamily applying her shiny lipstick (there are even traces of the worshipful Hollywood glamour close-up in the chiaroscuro effect that Starcevich uses to light her face) as her reflection shimmers before us in her makeup mirror. In essence, she is twice framed, becoming a frame within the frame. The fact that her mirror throws back an image of her looking at herself suggests a more complex relationship between her and us. This not only provides her with a pure mode of losing herself in her mirror, but it also provides us with a privileged spectatorial perspective of which she herself isn't even aware. Starcevich's command of modern photographic technique is on full display, further adding to the overall impact of the viewing experience as Kazari strikes her decidedly Marilyn Monroesque pose for both the edification of the camera and us.

The first depiction of Marilyn as a character of the new millennium is the 2000 comedy *Company Man*. The movie's protagonist, Allen Quimp, is an underachieving high school grammar teacher constantly tormented by his shrewish wife, Daisy, to make something more of himself. In an attempt to get Daisy off his back, Allen tells her he is a CIA operative. At first, she refuses to believe him, but when he accidentally helps a Russian ballet dancer defect, she writes a book about their lives. As a way of getting Allen off its back, the CIA sends him off to Cuba, with Daisy following him as Fidel Castro plans to take the country over. Allen is soon recruited to overthrow Castro. He attempts to humiliate Castro by sending him a special CIA-manufactured shampoo as a gift from Marilyn Monroe to make all his body hair fall out. When nothing comes of anything he does, Allen and Daisy make their escape while the Bay of Pigs invasion is being waged. Daisy's book, *Mrs. Spy, That's I*, becomes a huge best-seller, and Allen prepares to set off for Vietnam, where the CIA naively believes he couldn't possibly do any harm.

Company Man begins by poking fun at the absurd and destructive American-sponsored Bay of Pigs invasion of Cuba in the 1960s and concludes with the country's disastrous involvement in Vietnam. For all that, however, the narrative proceeds along by these wild fits and starts, often recklessly discarding anything that even vaguely resembles a rational or cohesive plot. Much more in this movie's favor is the way Marilyn Monroe is depicted in terms of stylization, color, and visual design. The focus is more on her fantastic, mythical, and larger-than-life dimensions over any kind of toned-up realism. Her one scene begins with a close-up of her feet resting on a pillow as her toenails are being painted bright red. The camera slowly ascends, revealing her smooth, shapely limbs as Marilyn is heard seductively speaking into the telephone. Her breathy words appear to be synchronized with the gliding, upward movement of the camera, which momentarily lingers across the glittery gold lamé of her skintight gown. As the movement of the camera comes to an end, there is a close-up of Marilyn's face. While her hairdresser brushes her golden hair, she verbally seduces Castro into using the shampoo she is sending him. Yet, in this outlandish scene, there is such a fantastic seductiveness about it all that we are immediately pulled into the luxurious, seductive beauty of the frame and briefly forget about the movie's wobbly plot for a while.

The 2000 spoof *Evil Hill* features the character of Dr. Evil from the 1999 hit comedy *Austin Powers*. Since the events of *Evil Hill* happen years before, he is called simply Mr. Evil here. He is, rather improbably, the proprietor of a charming children's bookshop in Bavaria. One day, he is ecstatic with joy when Marilyn Monroe comes into the shop. The next day, he accidentally runs into her again and clumsily spills red soda pop all over her white dress. Apologizing profusely, he manages to summon up the courage to ask her out on a date. Much to his amazement, she accepts. The next day, he goes to visit her at her hotel, and she informs him she can no longer see him. When he presses her to tell him why, she confesses that her new boyfriend is with her. Mr. Evil loses his temper and pushes his way into her hotel room, only to discover that her boyfriend is none other than President Kennedy. After two burly Secret Service agents throw him out, the embittered Mr. Evil is fast on his way to becoming the evil Dr. Evil.

Evil Hill takes the character of Dr. Evil as a young man and improbably projects him into the plotline of the 1999 Julia Roberts movie *Notting Hill*. When Marilyn Monroe walks into his shop, she wears her famous *Seven Year Itch* white dress, and Mr. Evil can barely contain his excitement. He is immediately smitten with her, as was the Beast with Beauty, and he offers her his gracious assistance. In this meeting of Marilyn and Mr. Evil, as well as in the movie's opening scene when Mr. Evil's red balloon is popped by some bratty kids in the street, we can see how the movie is organized primarily around three motifs—color coding, outlandish situations, and humorous stretches of bizarre dialogue. Pushing at the very limits of reality, the movie's attention-getting antireality is conveyed in its casually funny talk and the way that director Ryan Schifrin plays around with the stylized use of color. Freed from the traditional moorings of the depictions of Marilyn of the past (in which red usually signified the power of negation), the color red is used in this movie as an indicator of hope and an image of happiness. Being such a strong visual storyteller, the director knows how to get the most out of such wild juxtapositions of color. In the scene in the brightly colored bookshop, Marilyn is the personification of the beautiful-in-nature transformed into the embodiment of the glamorous movie goddess. As she glides about the bookshop, like a vision in white, the ugly Mr. Evil grows giddy, utterly defenseless against her intoxicating sensuality.

Later, while still floating on air after their first encounter, Mr. Evil accidentally bumps into Marilyn and spills red soda pop all down the front of her dress. This segues into the witty cinematic montage of their first date. The next morning, still walking on air from the romantic night before, Mr. Evil brings a bouquet of bright flowers to present to Marilyn. In this scene, the color red is once again being tweaked in a humorous way as Mr. Evil follows the red carpeting up to her hotel room as if it were the Yellow Brick Road leading him to the utopian Land of Oz. Unfortunately, when he arrives at his destination, he finds Marilyn cool and aloof. When she next informs him that JFK is her new boyfriend, Mr. Evil wonders how he can possibly compete with the powerful president. Actually, he later answers his own question. To compete with the most powerful man in the world, Mr. Evil must transform himself into the exact opposite: the most evil man in the world.

America's obsession with Marilyn Monroe's connection to the super-rich and superpowerful Kennedy family enters into the new millennium with the TV miniseries *Jackie, Ethel, Joan: Women of Camelot* (2001). And in keeping with the new century's use of her, Marilyn is presented only briefly, and the main emphasis is placed on the deployment of the stylized use of color and mythical symbolism over any kind of reality or in-depth character development of her portrayal. The action begins in 1960 with John F. Kennedy being elected president. Each of the Kennedy wives responds to his win in such a way as to delineate each of their individual personalities. Jackie is slightly annoyed, Ethel expresses a pragmatic cynicism, and Joan is full of optimism for the family's seemingly limitless future. The relationship of the three women then goes through many ups and downs as they respond to the pressures of being Kennedy wives. Inevitably, the constant philandering of their husbands takes a great toll on each of them. When Joan tells Jackie about Ted's constant cheating, Jackie does what she can to placate her. Still, despite Jackie's comforting of Joan, she herself gets extremely upset over JFK's indiscreet affair with Marilyn Monroe. And Ethel also looks with displeasure at her own husband's later involvement with Marilyn. The situation with Marilyn comes to a head when she sings "Happy Birthday, Mr. President" to JFK at Madison Square Garden and Jackie threatens to divorce him. Yet she, along with the rest of the world, is saddened by the tragic news of Marilyn's death. And later, Jackie manages to rally behind her husband during the Cuban missile crisis. And she is also with him in Dallas when he is assassinated in 1963.

In 1968, encouraged by Ethel, RFK runs for president but gets assassinated. His death means something different for each Kennedy woman. Ethel goes into a state of perpetual mourning, Jackie decides to marry Onassis and leave America, and Joan stands ever faithful behind her husband, although her resolve is badly tested when he is involved in the drowning death of the young woman Mary Jo Kopechne at Chappaquiddick. In the aftermath of Chappaquiddick, Joan starts drinking heavily and turns to Alcoholics Anonymous to recover. Newly sober, she decides to divorce Ted, only to reunite with him for the sake of his campaign. Despite her support, Ted loses his bid to be president, after which Joan leaves him forever.

In *Jackie, Ethel, Joan: Women of Camelot*, the figure of Ethel Kennedy is depicted like some mythical fertility goddess: she's a political Earth Mother with a hungry baby forever at her milk-laden breast, a total life-giving, Democratic life force. When faced with life's adversities, Ethel always utters a terse, "It's God's will!" She signifies the height of the commonsensical. And she also signifies the mortal body in all its glory as well as all its agony. While Ethel signifies the body in the triumvirate of Kennedy women, Jackie signifies the mind. She's the society girl as cultural heroine. To a certain extent, she is as she was depicted in *A Woman Named Jackie* since a part of her still craves money and social status above all else.

As for Joan, she is a signifier for the soul, juxtaposed against Jackie as mind and Ethel as body. This representation (of Joan as soul) becomes emblematic of the function on which the action of this miniseries turns. Clearly, no longer encumbered by the confines of verisimilitude, the narrative unfolds in a space of the excessively theatrical, the mythical, the symbolic, and the melodramatic over the real. This can be best seen in the way Ethel responds to Marilyn Monroe. Possessing neither Jackie's culture and elegance nor Joan's physical beauty and sublime spirituality, Ethel views Marilyn as a divisive threat when she first encounters her at a most erotically charged party given by Peter Lawford. After having had too much champagne to drink, Marilyn theatrically flirts with RFK under the ever watchful and suspicious gaze of Ethel. This makes her, at once, an object of envy and hatred for Ethel.

But later, after she's thought about the matter, Ethel realizes there's actually no real need for her to worry too much about Marilyn Monroe. Although it is true that Marilyn signifies the desired and pleasurable female body, in the end that is all that she can ever signify. Because of her inability to produce a baby, Marilyn can never signify the maternal body (as Ethel so extravagantly can). Consequently, there is no real place for a childless woman within either the nexus of the Kennedy family or the patriarchal superstructure, both of which view motherhood as a woman's most sacred calling. Fittingly, Jackie's response to Marilyn is deeper and more complicated than Ethel's. Initially, she feels distrust of her husband's most famous and glamorous mistress. Not long after Marilyn sings "Happy Birthday, Mr. President," Jackie urges him to end the affair. Now, a large part of Jackie's response can be linked directly to her being so conscious of what is or is not appropriate in terms of acceptable behavior in the private and public realms. After all, appearances for Jackie must be kept up at all costs. Still, despite her disapproving of Marilyn, Jackie's disapproval gets tempered with a certain degree of empathy and compassion. It is in this expression of compassion for Marilyn that Jackie becomes a more appealing figure than she's usually depicted as being.

The new-millennial use of theatrical artifice and color coding is employed in the two scenes in which Marilyn appears. And in both, there is very much an aspect of her playing out a very specific role on stagelike spaces of spectacle. That this role playing is to be taken as being explicitly theatrical is made evident in the first of these scenes when Marilyn meets RFK at Peter Lawford's hedonistic party. Marilyn is dressed in a flashy electric blue dress, giving her a powerful, high-keyed visual impact. Yet, since the sequence is meant to depict the start of Marilyn's newest love affair, the blueness of her dress also suggests an optimistic hopefulness. In the second of Marilyn's scenes, she sings "Happy Birthday" to the president. Wrapped in white ermine and clad in her revealing Jean Louis white gown, she "appears to be wearing nothing but crystal beads speckled over her luscious flesh."[18] Stylization and color coding combine together as the extreme whiteness of her appearance takes on an otherworldly, ghostly quality.

Two other texts of 2001, the TV miniseries *Blonde* and the play *American Iliad*, provide good examples of the artists of the new millennium striving more toward the realm of the mythical over realism in their depiction of Marilyn Monroe. Based on Joyce Carol Oates's fine 1999 novel, *Blonde* presents Marilyn's life deconstructed and then reconstructed into a new mythical mode. At the start, the illegitimate Norma Jean is raised by her beloved grandmother Della. When Della dies, she is sent to live with her exciting but emotionally unstable mother, Gladys. After Gladys suffers a complete mental breakdown and sets their apartment on fire, Norma Jean must live in an orphanage. She is eventually placed with foster parents, Warren and Elsie Pirig, but complications arise as Norma Jean grows into a voluptuous young woman, attracting the attention of various men (including even her own stepfather). Her stepmother intervenes by marrying her off to a respectable young man, Bucky Glazer. When Bucky goes off to fight in World War II, the lonely Norma Jean cuts her wrists. To alleviate her loneliness, she gets a job at a munitions factory where she is discovered by photographer Otto Ose. He turns her into a pinup model and introduces her to Hollywood superagent I. F. Shinn, who makes her a star.

Under Shinn's expert guidance, Norma Jean becomes Marilyn Monroe. Soon she is involved with Cass, the bisexual son of Charlie Chaplin, and his companion Eddie G., the son of Edward G. Robinson. After Marilyn gets pregnant, she has an abortion, ends her relationship with Cass and Eddie G., and marries the Athlete (Joe DiMaggio). Her new husband's jealous nature leads to their soon divorcing, after which Marilyn goes to New York to study acting with Lee Strasberg. There she meets the Playwright (Arthur Miller). From that point, *Blonde* follows the similar narrative trajectory of most of the other biopics of Marilyn, until concluding with her singing of "Happy Birthday, Mr. President" to JFK at Madison Square Garden.

In his review in the *New York Review of Books* of Oates's novel, critic Luc Sante analyzes the author's powerful attraction to her subject:

> The subject is a natural for her, combining many of her recurrent themes: the innocence and darkness of the postwar decade, the construction of great myths, the sexuality and autonomy and exploitation of women. She wanted to give a voice and a material care to this elusive being (Marilyn Monroe). [June 15, 2000]

In both Oates's novel and this televisual adaptation, we cannot help but be struck by the importance placed on Marilyn's status as the illegitimate child of an insane mother. What this does is present her as a victim of society's prejudices: she is both Society's Child and the Eternal Outsider in one. The issue of her illegitimacy is established early on and affects everything else in the narrative. Similarly, the absence of the father becomes so powerful a presence that it affects everything in her life. This is particularly true in the choices she makes in terms of men, with each man becoming a replacement for the absent father. In a similar vein, her romantic quest to achieve some form of identity defines another important thematic concern of the text. But it is principally in the tracing of the absence of the father that the vivid artificiality and fantasy of Hollywood inscribes its own powerful presence in the miniseries as a kind of substitute for the father. This is explicitly articulated in the action when the young Norma Jean is seen going off to the movies to which she is inclined to escape from the unsavory reality of her existence. As she gazes on the contrived Hollywood-derived imagery, a look of ecstasy overtakes her face, transporting her to a place of rapturous artifice and fantasy.

The scene of the young heroine at the movies signifies her complete susceptibility and surrender to Hollywood's power as total spectacle. Even at her young age, the spectacle of Hollywood becomes welded to her rich fantasy life until the two are indistinguishable from one another for her. Another means of escape for Norma Jeane is the creation of the imaginary friend she believes resides in her mirror. But this "Magic Friend" is not some mere narcissistic conceit. Instead, her mirror becomes a privileged trope of tremendous wonderment and, ultimately, empowerment for her. It is the combination of the idealized father with the fantasy world of her mirror and the contrived Hollywood fantasies that form the phantasmagorical backdrop against which the heroine seeks both a substitute for the father and, finally, her own identity. Accordingly, at its deepest level, *Blonde* asks to be viewed as a great myth. And in many ways, it is a highly wrought and richly detailed myth in which Marilyn's progress in the narrative follows the classic stages of the progress of the mythical heroine: from adventure to departure, initiation, a mysterious journey to the life force, transformation, and, finally, apotheosis. Yet, aside from these mythic elements just being reflected in the figure of Marilyn, there is also a further conceptualization of the mythical in the depiction of the various men she encounters along the stages of her great journey. These men become for her a series of powerful and often manipulative father figures, creating in the narrative a complex network of masculine imperative over every move she ever makes in her life.

The first such man she encounters is the overbearing photographer Otto Ose. He represents the initial adventure stage of Marilyn's mythic journey. It is his photographing of her that helps her realize her true potential. He is also the one responsible for the start of the planetary orbit, marking off the interstellar distance that eventually leads to her going from Norma Jeane to Hollywood starlet Marilyn Monroe. Further, Otto introduces her to the next important father figure of the text—legendary Hollywood superagent I. E. Shinn (*Blonde*'s obvious Johnny Hyde figure). He moves her from the departure to the initiation stage of her great journey when he introduces her to mogul Mr. R. (Daryl Zanuck), who, along with Shinn, is responsible for the heroine's initiation into the mysteries of Hollywood, transforming her from a mere starlet into the glorious Hollywood star—Marilyn Monroe. Now, she is woman as total Hollywood spectacle. As such, all the visual emphasis gets placed on the representational surface of her inviting and exciting sexuality. With this transformation, Marilyn has ironically achieved her apotheosis.

This apotheosis turns out to have both positive and negative implications. On the negative side, there is a deeper objectification of her than ever before.

On the positive side, her new stardom affords her greater access to a higher level of father figures, such as the Athlete and the Playwright. One of the flaws of this depiction is the fact that the development of her relationships with her two most famous husbands is only sketchy at best. Joe DiMaggio (signified as "the Athlete") suffers the most from this approach since he is depicted as an oafish man consumed with macho rage and jealousy over Marilyn's frequently promiscuous behavior. To a certain extent, Arthur Miller is better served. Even the feelings Marilyn expresses toward him seem more genuine and intense, as she hopes for a better life through him. Still, even her marriage to Miller is shown rapidly deteriorating in only a few brief scenes. This begins with her accusing him of not sufficiently supporting her in her battle with Olivier during the making of *The Prince and the Showgirl* and culminates with her losing her baby after reading the hurtful words he has written about her in his journal. Almost as a reaction to all her problems with Hollywood and the powerful father figures in her life, Marilyn sometimes rebels against the constraints their authority places on her. For example, while in the midst of filming one of her archetypal sexy blonde movie roles, she angers her director when she dares to question his authority with her own vision of the character she is playing. Further, her hedonistic affair with Cass and Eddie G. can also be viewed as another form of her rebelliousness.

Most strikingly, this text succeeds at depicting Marilyn Monroe by combining elements from the past (a concentration on biographical and psychological detail and some novelistic depth) with elements of the new millennium (the placement of less importance on narrative coherency and more on the use of artifice and elaborate visual patterning, color coding, and surface subjectivity). Although these new-millennial elements do sometimes overwhelm the narrative with all its many mythical allusions and the choppy structuring of the movie's final hour, what *Blonde* lacks in narrative coherency and a certain psychological depth it makes up for with the bold use of color. Only now, the color scheme is boiled down to just two colors—red and white. For example, the action begins with a spectacular example of the way red is employed. Marilyn, wearing a beautiful red dress, is sprawled out in an unconscious state on a deserted beach populated only by white seagulls swiftly darting in and out of the frame. Red continues to be foregrounded, emphasizing its association with possible harm and danger for the heroine, until it becomes a central part of the action, such as when, after her Grandmother Della dies, little Norma Jean is sent off to live with her unstable mother, who always wears red clothes. Later, when her stepmother, Elsie, forces her to marry Bucky, she appears on screen, her lips painted a glaring blood red (making her mouth look like a bloodied slash), defending her action against the girl.

In several other instances, red is once again associated with pain and blood (as it was in *Strawhead*), beginning with the mention of Marilyn's painful monthly periods and in the humiliating scene when Hollywood mogul Mr. R. forces himself on her in his private office, causing her to bleed over his white carpeting. Similarly, red will be linked to sexuality and pregnancy when the Playwright finds Marilyn in a pool of blood after she miscarries her baby. The symbolism of blood is consistently linked to the association of Marilyn's blood with her excruciating menstrual flow, her sexual initiation in Hollywood, her reproductive failure, and, finally, her suffering of several miscarriages.

White is also evident as an important symbolic color linking Marilyn to joy and hopefulness. At little Norma Jean's birthday party, she wears a pretty white dress, and Gladys presents her with a birthday cake with pure white icing. Soon after, Gladys purchases the white lacquered baby grand piano (that once belonged to Frederic March) for her as well. Then, at the start of her new life with Bucky, Norma Jean wears a flowing gown of white satin with white blossoms pinned in her hair. Yet another level of symbolism in the miniseries is explicitly more sexual. This is linked to the depiction of Marilyn as a woman objectified by men. As her wardrobe becomes progressively tighter and more revealing, her body gets presented to us as almost a series of eroticized body parts. And even after she becomes a star, Marilyn is not so much loved as she is doubly objectified. Not only is she the desired sex goddess of Hollywood movies, she is also a sexual object for the Hollywood studio executives to do as they will with. Thus, the linkage is repeatedly made of her stardom to her total sexual exploitation. Although we cannot credit director Joyce Chopra alone with these thematic implications (since all these themes are present in the novel), they are still fully realized by Chopra in an imaginative display of cinematic style. The director also deserves credit for the performance of Poppy Montgomery. The actress brings a warm naturalness to her portrayal of the role of Marilyn Monroe.

An even finer artistic achievement than *Blonde*—indeed, the most satisfying of all the new-millennial depictions of Marilyn Monroe thus far—is Donald Freed's 2001 play *American Iliad*. This American epic features Presidents John F. Kennedy and Richard M. Nixon and Marilyn as its central characters. On July 4, 2000, Nixon appears as a ninety-year-old senile wreck, babbling away to himself. The thirty-seventh president walks the New Jersey shoreline expounding on the book he is writing, *Going Home*, which he hopes will be a vindication of himself and of his role in American history. Suddenly, there is a shift in time, and Nixon is back in Chautauqua, New York, on July 4, 1900. He has been changed into a Bible-thumping assembly leader preaching before the faithful. Then, just as suddenly, he is back in 2000 again, informing his assistant Roberto of his intention to visit the eighty-year-old JFK, who is also still alive and living in complete seclusion on a mythical Greek island. The two presidents engage in some lively conversation touching on all the major events of their time. When Nixon tells JFK about his book, he beseeches him to tell the truth about himself and the rest of the Kennedy family. This makes Nixon angry, and he demands that JFK first tell him of his relationship with Marilyn Monroe. The action next unfurls into a bizarre scene of J. Edgar Hoover and his longtime lover and fellow G-man Clyde Tolson having a romantic candlelit dinner. Then, all of a sudden, Marilyn Monroe is conjured up, reclining on a golden couch being psychoanalyzed by her doctor (Nixon). After she talks of her unhappy childhood, she next appears standing before a microphone in Madison Square Garden singing "Happy Birthday, Mr. President." Then she fades away and exists only in the form of a tape recording, talking to First Lady Jacqueline Kennedy about how much she loves her husband. In her final appearance, Marilyn is a druggy femme fatale standing alone on the Santa Monica Pier. Nixon assumes the role of Secret Agent Conrad. He flirts with and comforts her before she vanishes into the starry night.

Nixon revisits JFK and demands to know who was responsible for Marilyn's death. Finally, JFK tells Nixon that the only way to get to the truth is to journey to Hell (which is represented here as Harlem). And Nixon's odyssey becomes that of anyone who wants to hold on to the American Dream despite everything to the contrary. Nixon goes to Harlem, where he encounters several strange individuals. These encounters serve to increase his paranoia until he pleads to be shown the way home. Nixon comes to realize that Marilyn Monroe was killed by powerful, evil political men and that the white race is doomed, until he is again back at Chautauqua preaching of America's great destiny to come in the new millennium.

In creating *American Iliad*, Donald Freed draws on Homer's great epic poem *The Iliad*. And while in the process of reinterpreting an ancient myth, he creates a new one. Freed fills the play with stylized, poetic dialogue and scenes of theatrical spectacle. Stretches of lyricism are followed by several wonderfully staged set pieces. And in the playwright's twenty-first-century reworking of Homer's epic poem, it is Marilyn Monroe who assumes the role of Helen of Troy. Her presence gets articulated in the play in three ways: 1) she is the elusive vision conjured by Nixon, the same way Dr. Faustus conjures Helen in Christopher Marlowe's theatrical masterpiece; 2) she is endlessly referred to by the other characters; and 3) the sound of her speaking through tape recordings is often heard in an eerie, disembodied voice. By being juxtaposed in these three ways, Marilyn's presence becomes so charged up with deep emotional meaning that she ends up dissolving the traditional boundaries of dream, history, and myth into a rich, theatricalized landscape. Much of the reason this occurs in *American Iliad* is because Freed explores the interface between dreams and myth and American history through the figure of Marilyn. This makes the play both ancient and modern at once. While the action looks to the ancient past for its inspiration, Freed's real aim is directed at creating a sense of the dramatic immediacy of today and beyond.

The playwright's sense of this immediacy comes with the play's very first reference to Marilyn. When Nixon, as the brooding Odysseus figure, travels to visit the wheelchair-bound JFK on his mythical Greek island, the two former presidents get into a nasty altercation regarding nature and morality in which an angry Nixon denounces JFK because of the affair he had with Marilyn Monroe. But what doubtlessly infuriates Nixon most about their affair is that he has to face the fact that it was JFK who knew Marilyn so intimately and not him. (As the action continues, we learn that Nixon also, understandably, holds a torch for her.) His mad rant against JFK continues unabated with his making several accusations about JFK having turned all of America into a big welfare queen looking for a lifelong government handout. Significantly, this eternal feud between the Democratic JFK and the Republican Nixon, between conservatives and liberals, between the right and the left, gets embodied in the figure of Nixon. But from out of this eternal conflict, an even greater distinction is made between the two presidents. This is the distinction of class difference in America and occurs when JFK condescends to Nixon for not having come from a privileged, elite class like himself.

This point of Nixon's inferior, poor beginnings will be further elaborated on when JFK goes on to describe most of the presidents who followed him as having been nothing more than this pack of drunks, psychopaths, and child molesters of the post-Camelot Cold War American Iliad. With this direct reference to mythology and legend, Kennedy's Camelot of the 1960s and the Golden Age are fused together into one great epic narrative. From then on, the play admits an avowedly nonnaturalistic, intensely stylized, mythologized dimension that projects the action into the more elemental and emotionally charged concerns of myth and legend. With this projection, Marilyn fully emerges as the play's Helen of Troy figure. In synthesizing aspects of Helen of Troy onto Marilyn, she becomes both divine and human—and, therefore, an anomaly. This makes her edges fuzzy and unclear and difficult to identify or classify. In linking Marilyn to the ancient and the classical, the play additionally employs the modern new-millennial use of color coding to enhance all her scenes.

In the first scene in which Marilyn appears, she reclines on a golden couch while being psychoanalyzed by Nixon. Her character is ageless and eternally beautiful; she has been emancipated from time and space, whereas the aged Nixon and JFK are prisoners of both. She wears a glowing white raincoat and dark glasses in an attempt to make her identity a mystery. For her second appearance, she wears the transparent Jean Louis gown she wore to JFK's birthday party at Madison Square Garden. She stands in a spotlight of golden light before a microphone while singing to the president. When she is finished, she dissolves into the surrounding darkness. And in both these scenes, Marilyn is depicted in a visual style inspired by classical mythology. She has a mysterious, dreamlike quality. In her final appearance, this aesthetic quality achieves its most complex pictorial expression when she appears on the Santa Monica Pier at nighttime. Her beauty takes on a remote quality as she is illuminated by only the glow of the star-filled black night sky. The glory of the heavens provide her with her key light, making her seem to be dematerializing into a completely visionary new spacing. She is alone on the pier, deeply lost within memories of the past. After a while, Nixon joins her, they talk, and it becomes clear from what she says that Marilyn is woozy from taking too many sleeping pills that have not helped her rest. Totally captivated, Nixon confesses that he also cannot sleep at night. In true dreamlike fashion, they melodramatically act out a love scene from Shakespeare, followed by her seductively singing a torch ballad to the enchanted Nixon. When finished, she simply dissolves into the star-filled night sky.

Following that metaphoric image, Nixon becomes even more obsessed with solving the mystery of Marilyn's death. With his newfound passion for her, it becomes his role to discover the truth. In his mythical movement toward exteriorization, Nixon revisits JFK and even threatens physical violence against him in his obsessive search for the truth. It is in this quest for Marilyn's murderers that Nixon comes to realize that she and the mystery of America's true greatness have become one and the same. In the very embodiment of Freudian condensation, while becoming one with America and her people, Marilyn also becomes one with the play's classically derived narrative schematic. In other words, both the whole of America and the whole of the *American Iliad* are signified by Marilyn Monroe. So, although she may have been tortured, raped, and driven insane while alive, as Nixon claims, Marilyn is finally also human and divine and undistinguishable from America, the truth and the classical art of epic narrative. And it is for this that the future of both her memory and America must be kept alive as Nixon is transported back to Chautauqua once again. And as he prepares to address the faithful, it is evident that Nixon's new passion for Marilyn has worked as an evolutionary force on him. Being the most noble form of indiscretion, his intense passion for her is a guarantee for true progress; it even gives the previously reactionary, negative Nixon the positive, progressive strength and power to rebuild first America and then perhaps the world.

Traces of Marilyn Monroe's association to legend and myth linger on in the remaining depictions of this chapter: *Killing Castro* (2002), *Just a Dream*

(2002), *LA Confidential* (2003), *Timequest* (2003), and *The Mystery of Natalie Wood* (2004). The first of these, the science-fictional *Killing Castro*, is also the first depiction to project Marilyn into the technological innovation of Cyberspace. The action takes place in an unspecified time in the future. America is on the brink of a full-scale nuclear war that eerily mirrors the Cuban missile crisis of the early 1960s. With Cuba merely ninety miles away, America is frantic to find a solution. It comes in the form of stem cell research that provides the ability to time travel via the stored DNA of an ancestor. Agent O'Donnell is recruited to go back in time. His mission calls for him to be the one responsible for "killing Castro."

This Internet thriller lasts only three minutes, but every second of it packs a wallop. This force comes from its mysterious depiction of Agent O'Donnell being tied down to a chair and savagely beaten the whole time by a shadowy group of sinister-looking men. Their physical assault on him causes his blood to splatter all across the screen in a visceral explosion of what seems like endless violence and red-hot gore. Since all this is captured in a swirling, gliding visual style, a feeling of nonstop movement is created. Yet, beyond the pyrotechnics of such stylized visuals, there is nevertheless a brutalized quality to the action. Along with the prevailing sense of mystery and mayhem, there is also an atmosphere of total political paranoia conveyed. Director Clark Westerman layers the action with a continuous stream of superimposed imagery that forms a delirious sense of visual free association. Fleeting images of President John F. Kennedy, Robert Kennedy, and even Fidel Castro go by on an almost subliminal level of consciousness. It is within this visual context that Marilyn Monroe appears as an enigmatic figure drifting in and out of all the free-flowing mise-en-scène. With this, Westerman projects her into the attention-getting artifice of twenty-first-century cyberspace—an apparently timeless, intensely stylized, high-tech space above and beyond the realities of the physical world. But because the physical reality of this text consists of a man being savagely beaten, Marilyn's presence comes as a much welcomed relief. She offers a palette of dramatic contrast, a promise of redemption, even a hope of love. Clad in her *Seven Year Itch* dress (in terms of color coding, the whiteness of her dress and the redness of O'Donnell's blood dominate the movie's color scheme), Marilyn carries the same mythical charge she possessed in *American Iliad*. Like the beauteous Helen of Troy of Freed's play, just the mere conjuration of her opens up the space of fantasy and desire in place of the hero's suffering.

From the future time of *Killing Castro*, the next depiction of Marilyn Monroe occurs in the 1960 setting of the movie *Just a Dream*. Twelve-year-old Henry Starbuck gets a summer job at the bar of the no-nonsense Cindy. While working there, he befriends Native American bartender Cecil Running Bear, saucy barmaid Lynette, and JM, a dignified black man who runs an auto-mechanic garage and idolizes Marilyn Monroe. During the course of the summer, JM teaches Henry how to drive and introduces him to the infinite wonders of Marilyn. In return, Henry takes him to meet his lonely, unhappy mother, Maureen, who suffers the indignities of Henry's constantly womanizing father, Dr. Hank Starbuck. When Henry learns that Marilyn will be coming to town to film *The Misfits*, he is beside himself with excitement and attempts to get JM to come and meet her with him. But JM refuses his offer, insisting it is for the best that Marilyn remain forever a fantasy to him. Further disappointment follows for Henry when Cecil Running Bear is stabbed to death and Henry discovers that his father is having an affair with Lynette. With this final indignity, his mother makes plans to leave his father and move away with Henry. But before that happens, he and JM encounter a physically ill Marilyn on the road one night. They drive her back to her hotel, and before going inside, she kisses JM. Thus, what JM believed could be only a dream becomes a reality.

The narrative of *Just a Dream* focuses on the coming of age of the twelve-year-old hero during the particularly memorable summer of 1960. In the evoking of this period, the movie operates on a nostalgic mode. Nostalgia for the 1960s can, then, be seen in the fashions, music, and vintage automobiles. But, mostly, nostalgia is there in the form of Marilyn Monroe. In the first scene in which she appears, she is glimpsed from a distance. In terms of color coding, she is associated with white and the three primary colors. She wears a white dress enlivened by an eye-popping design of red cherries. While in the process of having her golden blonde hair combed and makeup touched up, she projects the archetypal beauty of the distant Hollywood movie star. Her perfectly painted face projects a forbidden, distant beauty unrealistically without fault or flaw. Understandably, JM is anxious about meeting this flawless, forbidden goddess. When Henry asks him if he would like to meet Marilyn, JM refuses, stating he would rather she remain a beautiful and impossible dream forever out of his reach. As it turns out, however, they do get to meet Marilyn. But she is no longer the glamorized, immortal Hollywood goddess she initially appeared to be. Now, she is all too mortal, dressed in faded blue jeans, without makeup to cinematically stylize or idealize her perfect beauty. And yet, even without her makeup and glamorous clothing, she is, paradoxically, more perfectly beautiful than ever. So as JM drives Marilyn Monroe back to her hotel, she sits in the passenger seat next to him. Henry, seated in the back of the tow truck, watches in amazement as they converse effortlessly up front. After a while, Marilyn rests her head on JM's broad shoulder while the voice of Henry as a grown man is heard ruminating, in nostalgic voiceover, how he has learned that the best dreams to have in life are the ones you think will never come true but somehow do.

LA Confidential was the pilot episode for a proposed TV series based on the 1990 novel by James Elroy and the 1997 movie directed by Curtis Hanson. Set during the 1950s, the Los Angeles depicted is a seething morass of sin, seduction, scandal, and shame. Three different policemen are forced to respond to all this whether they want to or not. The overly ambitious Police Academy graduate Ed Exley takes to spying on his fellow officers. Rough-and-ready beat cop Bud White uses brutal force on suspects, yet he cannot tolerate violence against women. Weary and cynical Jack Vincennes takes to using his police work to further his own selfish ends. And, amazingly, none of this ever seems to escape the seemingly inexhaustible eye of Sid Hudgeons, sleazy reporter on the trashy gossip magazine Hush-Hush. During the course of the pilot episode, a guilt-ridden Jack sends money to a grieving widow for his role in her husband's death. Bud finds himself attracted to a beautiful aspiring movie starlet, Lynn Bracken, who is simultaneously being recruited by notorious Hollywood pimp and drug lord Pierce Patchett to join his stable of high-class Hollywood call girls. And Ed begins to investigate a blackmailing case involving Marilyn Monroe by a thug who's obtained an obscure pornographic movie in which she once appeared. The episode ends with one of Patchett's "girls" being brutally beaten to death in a field by an assailant. A close-up of her terrified face freezes on the screen. The words "To Be Continued" appear.

But, as it so turned out, this proposed TV series was never "to be continued" beyond this pilot episode. Therefore, at the end, we are left hanging in a state of perpetual suspense as to the fate of all the characters. Although Marilyn Monroe is only in one sequence, her appearance resonates with a visual power. After Ed is summoned by her, she appears elegantly attired in a crisply tailored, black-and-white suit, complete with a strand of ladylike pearls. Rather than mythical Hollywood sex goddess, her image is more that of a clear-eyed, well-bred Beverly Hills matron. As she tells Ed of her blackmailer, her demeanor cracks a bit. A flashback features a distraught Marilyn, with hair disheveled and makeup smudged, sobbing uncontrollably as her blackmailer forces her to watch explicit images of herself in the pornographic movie. In this grainy black-and-white pornographic footage, she is a very young Norma Jean—a fairy-tale waif who unexpectedly finds herself thrust into a forbidden, carnal world.

What is most striking about this sequence is the way it presents us with three different versions of Marilyn (as well-bred young matron, as hysterical woman, as eroticized porno goddess). The now obligatory use of new-millennial stylization and color coding coordinates her completely into the surface design of her surroundings. In brief, the crisp black-and-whiteness of her tailored costume dissolves into the unease of the out-of-focus, black-and-white pornographic imagery, which is juxtaposed against the disturbing vision of the dishabille Marilyn in her blue robe. The blondeness of her hair and the blueness of her robe are, ironically, the exact colors traditionally used in devotional images of the Virgin Mary. Reducing Marilyn to such a minimalistic and expressionistic color scheme codes her as a woman of sorrow: she's a lady in blue singing the blues in Los Angeles.

Marilyn Monroe makes her third appearance within a science-fictional context in the 2003 movie *Timequest*. The action begins in 1979. A group of male convicts is transported on a bus. The bus is stopped, and two government operatives take one of the men, petty thief Raymond Mead, off. The narrative jumps back in time to the morning of November 22, 1963. President John F. Kennedy and the First Lady prepare to leave their Dallas hotel room to take part in the presidential motorcade. Directly after having a frightening vision of her husband's impending doom, Jackie persuades him against going. Then, another shift in time occurs. It is now 2003. James—the third child of JFK and Jackie—makes the announcement that his elderly father has just died of natural causes. Returning back to 1963, the mysterious time traveler appears in Dallas to warn JFK and RFK of their assassinations. In private, he warns JFK against continuing with his dangerous connections to the Mob and his incessant womanizing. To prove his point, he shows the president holographic images of his passionate affair with Marilyn Monroe. Convinced of his claims, JFK and Jackie immediately fly back to Washington while RFK apprehends his brother's would-be assassins. JFK next disbands the CIA and forces the ever-malicious J. Edgar Hoover to resign as head of the FBI. He rejuvenates his marriage, cuts all his connections to the Mob, and puts an end to America's disastrous involvement in Vietnam. An alliance is formed with former enemy Russia, leading to an unprecedented era of world peace and prosperity. Meanwhile, Jackie begins a search for the man who saved her husband's life. He is Raymond Mead, who was taken off the bus in the opening scene. In gratitude, the Kennedys provide him with the resources to become an artist. The movie concludes with an evocative image from 1964 of Raymond as a small boy reaching his hand out to touch a grainy black-and-white image of Jackie Kennedy appearing on TV.

The hero of *Timequest* (like Agent O'Donnell of *Killing Castro*) is recruited by government operatives to travel back in time. Only now, rather than kill a dictator, the hero's mission is to save a president. Forgiveness and redemption take precedence over political paranoia and revenge, moving the action from a dystopian to a utopian spacing. Such a narrative movement affects the delineation of character, which causes a noticeable shift in the way JFK, Jackie, and RFK are depicted. All three are portrayed most sympathetically. Lending such affinity toward the meaning of the Kennedys causes Jackie especially to emerge as most sympathetic. Put simply, she is now wife and mother par excellence. Yet, whereas Jackie is rendered with more sympathy, Marilyn Monroe is once again the new-millennial site of total stylization and myth. Sensual artifice, spectacular color coding, and stereotypical prototype constitute the details of this depiction of her. From smooth glossy surfaces revealing her white-on-white decor, from soft lines and undulating curves collapsing into mounds of ornamental patterns and sumptuous fabrics, all this reflects the meaning of Marilyn vis-à-vis the movie. This begins before she even appears when a close-up of a bright red silk banner unfurls across the screen, covering over a field of white satin. From there, Marilyn is crystallized and brought into an alluring spell of the beautiful and seductive (especially when she re-creates for the president's private edification her famous nude calendar pose). Although this display of the beautiful and the seductive—Marilyn's desirable body, the bold juxtaposition of color, the suggestive words she and the president speak to one another—draws us into JFK's circle of deceit and infidelity, something morally justified still comes of it. Seemingly employed to veil reality, for a moment, the beautiful and the seductive become transformed, attaining the purpose of a higher, final truth. In JFK's new commitment to his wife and family, meaning shifts away from one image (JFK and the nude Marilyn frolicking on a sea of red silk) to another (JFK making love to Jackie to conceive another child). This process confirms his redemption as husband, father, and president. As for his love affair with Marilyn, that slips off into a category of a beautiful love affair that, though ended, remains a gorgeous memory forever.

A prevailing sense of ambiguity and a troubling lack of narrative closure echo through the 2004 TV movie *The Mystery of Natalie Wood*. Opening on the night of her death in 1982, the narrative flashes back to 1943. The young heroine is a six-year-old-girl named Natasha Grudin. Her mother and father, Maria and Nick, have come from Russia to America in search of the American Dream. Maria is the prototypical, overbearing stage mother. She focuses all her attention on Natasha. She fills the child's head with all sorts of dire warnings that she will die young while giving birth to a baby, or else drown at an early age. But Maria is also driven to make her daughter a star. In Hollywood, the child is transformed into Natalie Wood and cast in several movies. She meets Marilyn Monroe when they are making a movie together. They take an immediate liking toward one another. Natalie becomes a teenager and gets romantically involved with various actors and directors twenty years her senior. Eventually, she makes the transition into adult roles on the screen and at nineteen marries actor Robert Wagner (RJ). Despite her love for her new husband, Natalie is frequently plagued by countless fears and insecurities and abuses pills and alcohol. RJ's jealousy of Natalie leads to the couple's divorcing. She next begins a tempestuous affair with Warren Beatty. She also meets a totally distraught Marilyn Monroe at a party in Hollywood. When she confesses to Natalie that she feels all used up in Hollywood, Natalie fears the worst. All her fears are confirmed when Marilyn is found dead in 1962. So devastated is she over this that Natalie even overdoses herself not long after. During the 1960s, Natalie fires all her Hollywood agents, quits acting, marries English producer Richard Gregson, and gives birth to a daughter, Natasha. When she learns that Richard is having an affair, Natalie promptly divorces him and remarries RJ, with whom she has a second daughter, Courtney. The marriage runs relatively smoothly with the exception of RJ's periodic bouts of jealousy. This is seen at its worst when he and Natalie take actor Christopher Walken out for the weekend in 1982 aboard their yacht *The Splendor*. After much jealousy, arguing, and excessive drinking, Natalie falls into the sea and drowns at age forty-three.

In the constructing of this televisual version of Natalie Wood's life, the moviemakers have shaped the content so that it has the characteristics of a modern-day myth or fairy tale. Naturally, it is, of course, Natalie who is cast in the role of Beautiful Princess, while it is left to her mother, Maria, to assume the less flattering role of Evil Queen. With Natalie at the center of this primordial struggle of Beautiful Princess versus Evil Queen, the movie's director, Peter Bogdanovich, directs the action with confidence and style. And even despite the occasional contrivances and unevenness of the narrative flow, Bogdanovich mounts a physically impressive evocation of Wood's life and times. Naturally, with Natalie having spent so much of her life on the silver screen, many of the movie's best moments deal with the process of making movies. But this making of movies often serves as a painful ordeal sprinkled with all sorts of sadomasochistic flourishes all directed toward the understandably beleaguered heroine.

After witnessing Natalie being subjected to much cruel treatment by Hollywood, it only makes sense that she should feel such a close personal connection to Marilyn Monroe. From this initial meeting on, Natalie (like the young Susan Strasberg in *Nobody Dies on Friday*) profoundly identifies with Marilyn. In essence, Marilyn becomes a road map for her to emulate. This identification is only further complicated as a result of Natalie's own fears and insecurities. In her attempt to escape her inner pain, Natalie, like Marilyn, turns to pills, alcohol, casual affairs with powerful men, and even attempts of suicide. Despite the fact that she does achieve a relatively happy second marriage to RJ and becomes a mother, Natalie is so devastated by Marilyn's death that she instantly perceives it, as did Dorothy Dandridge, as a haunting premonition of her own. She tells her mother that Marilyn always felt as if she never really existed, and Natalie also feels the same way about her own life. It is in the wake of this distressing scene that the complete dissemination of the heroine begins. Despair and desolation creep in with such an all-encompassing finality that all traces of Natalie ever regaining any sense of rational order in her life disappear from view. Her mother's words of warning that she will die young just as Marilyn did fuse together in her mind until she feels herself hanging over the edge of the same dark abyss that claimed Marilyn Monroe.

Peter Bogdanovich makes good use of the new-millennial color coding as Marilyn is associated with whiteness once again in both of the scenes in which she appears. In the first, she wears a white bathing suit when she and the young Natalie first meet filming the movie *Scudda Hoo! Scudda Hay!* together. And in the second, in which she tells Natalie that at thirty-six she is now all used up in Hollywood, Marilyn wears an elegant, white, diaphanous gown, the coloration of which gives her an ethereal, Athena-like quality. Hence, on the last night of her life, Natalie also wears a similar luminously white, diaphanous nightgown. And because she has let her long, dark hair grow out and stopped straightening it, she's lyrically beautiful in a classical and most natural way. And still looking eternally youthful (as did Marilyn when she died), with her long, curly hair and pre-Raphaelite, flowing gown, Natalie recalls Shakespeare's heroine Ophelia hauntingly drowning to death.

NOTES

1. John Guare, *Cop-Out* (New York: Samuel French, 1969), 26. Used by permission.

2. George F. Custen, *BIO/PICS: How Hollywood Constructed Public History* (New Brunswick, N.J.: Rutgers University Press, 1982), 223.

3. Terry Johnson, *Insignificance* (London: Methuen), 8. Used by permission.

4. Debra Silverman, *Selling Culture* (New York: Pantheon Books, 1986), 11.

5. Barbara Klinger, *Melodrama and Meaning: History, Culture, and the Films of Douglas Sirk* (Bloomington: Indiana University Press, 1994), 123.

6. Cited in Mark Bego, *Madonna: Blonde Ambition* (New York: Cooper Square Press, 2000), 113.

7. Joseph C. Koenenn, "Marilyn: Alive and Kicking," *New York Post*, October 26, 1988, 7, 11.

8. Simone Signoret, *Nostalgia Isn't What It Used to Be* (New York: Harper & Row, 1978), 302.

9. Sue Glover, *Madame Montand and Mrs. Miller* (copyright Sue Glover, 1992). Used by permission of PFD.

10. Catherine David, *Simone Signoret* (Woodstock, N.Y.: Overlook Press, 1990), 122.

11. David J. Mauriello, *Body* (an unpublished play). Used by permission of David Mauriello.

12. Quotes from Mark Swed, "With Its World-Premiere Festival, New York City Opera Found That the Public and Press Have an Appetite for New Work," *Opera News*, December 25, 1993, 34–35.

13. Sigmund Freud, "The Uncanny," in *On Creativity and the Unconscious: Papers on the Psychology of Art, Literature, Love, Religion*, ed. Benjamin Nelson (New York: Harper Torchbooks, 1951), 148.

14. Gip Hoppe, *Jackie: An American Life* (New York: Samuel French, 1998). Used by permission of Gip Hoppe and Bret Adams, Ltd.

15. Robert Brustein, *Nobody Dies on Friday* (an unpublished play). Used by permission of Robert Brustein.

16. Jim Tommaney, *The Final Hours of Norma Jeane* (an unpublished play). Used by permission of Jim Tommaney.

17. Actually, beginning in the latter 1980s and continuing on into the new millennium, a by no means exhaustive list of just some who have participated in this unique pictorial system include actresses (Drew Barrymore, Julia Louis-Dreyfus, Daryl Hannah, Heather Locklear, Ashley Judd, Liza Minnelli, Jessica Alba, Scarlett Johansson), performers (Madonna, Deborah Harry, Courtney Love, Lisa Marie Presley, Gwen Stefani, Christina Aguilera), supermodels (Cindy Crawford, Linda Evangelista, Elizabeth Hurly, Naomi Campbell), *Playboy* pinups (Jenny McCarthy, Anna Nicole Smith), and, not to be undone, even members of the opposite sex (Jimmy James and Japanese artist Yasumasa Morimura).

18. Randy Taraborrelli, *Jackie, Ethel and Joan: Women of Camelot* (New York: Rose Books, 2000), 128.

· 2 ·

Marilyn Monroe as Roman à Clef

(Marilyn Monroe as a Thinly Concealed Character)

In the 1950s, there were four roman à clef depictions of Marilyn Monroe. The first two of these were the 1955 play and the 1957 movie versions of *Will Success Spoil Rock Hunter?* Written by George Axelrod, the 1955 play opened on Broadway with Orson Bean as George MacCauley and Jayne Mansfield as beautiful, blonde Hollywood sex goddess Rita Marlowe (the Marilyn Monroe character). George is employed as a lowly writer for *Movie World*. His only claim to fame is that he once wrote an article about movie star Rock Hunter, "Will Success Spoil Rock Hunter?" He is assigned to interview Rita Marlowe at her luxurious New York hotel suite. While there, he meets an assortment of Hollywood types: writer Mike Freeman, agent Irving La Salle, and producer Harry Kaye, who runs Rita's studio. Agent Irving La Salle turns out to be the devil in disguise. For a mere 10 percent of George's soul, he makes him a millionaire. For another 10 percent, he even casts a spell on Rita to make her fall madly in love with George forever.

Back in Hollywood, George assumes his place in Rita's bed and as vice president of her production company, Rita Marlowe Productions. He has been assigned to write the screenplay of Mike's controversial Broadway hit *No Hiding Place Down Here* as a starring vehicle for Rita. After many failed attempts, he ends up selling Irving even more of his soul in return for a successful screenplay.

George's screenplay wins him an Oscar. On the night of the Academy Awards, George and Rita return back to the offices of Rita Marlowe Productions to celebrate. There, they confront Rita's estranged husband, football star Bronk Brannigan. Bronk is determined to have Rita back even if it means killing George. Once again, Irving intervenes, and George ends up beating Bronk to a pulp.

After selling Irving 90 percent of his soul, George finally decides to abandon Rita and Hollywood and go back home to New York. Before leaving, George tells Mike all about Irving. Mike ends up outsmarting Irving by selling him 90 percent of his own soul in place of George's soul. Mike and George then head back to New York, leaving Irving, Rita (the spell to make her love George has been removed), and Hollywood all up to their own devices.

Essentially, what playwright George Axelrod has fashioned with *Will Success Spoil Rock Hunter?* is a kind of comic morality play that owes much to the Faustian myth. George, the poor, hapless hero, is willing to go to any lengths whatsoever (including even selling his immortal soul) to make it big in Hollywood. Even with Axelrod's satirical approach to the material, the scary image Hollywood projects is of this great, glittery facade, behind which lies a vast cultural and intellectual void.

The principal signifier of Axelrod's conception of Hollywood is personified in the character of studio head Harry Kaye. The first time Harry meets George, he tells the *Movie World* columnist to write that Rita's never wearing underwear is what actually made her such a big star. Yet despite Harry's rather low opinion of her, Rita shows she has a much higher opinion of herself when she expresses her deep longing to one day be looked on as less of a dumb Hollywood sex symbol and more of a serious dramatic actress. Although Marilyn often did express similar sentiments about Hollywood and the public's perception of her, those sentiments, coming from Rita Marlowe, as embodied in the outrageously voluptuous figure of Jayne Mansfield, cannot help but sound absurdly satirical. With all her physical excessiveness, her over-the-top sexy seductiveness, and her wild offscreen publicity stunts to get attention (whenever she was anywhere near a camera, she could always be counted on to let her swelling breasts come spilling out of her dress), Mansfield truly was Marilyn Monroe carried to the point of absurd satire.[1]

For all that ridiculous satire, however, there is something decidedly good-natured about this play written by the man responsible for creating one of Marilyn's biggest hit movies, *The Seven Year Itch*, as there also is about the endearing character of Rita Marlowe. Consequently, even if *Rock Hunter* is essentially a spoof on the vulgarity of the movie industry and the giggly, dizzy, dumb blonde take it had on Marilyn, it ultimately serves as a kind of fitting tribute to both the industry and the great star. Undoubtedly, the play's success was helped immensely by the remarkable presence of its leading lady—Jayne Mansfield. With her much publicized 42DD bosom, she was like the ultimate 1950s' overripened sexual fantasy sprung to life.

In adapting George Axelrod's play for the screen, writer/director Frank Tashlin transformed it into a brand-new work. Tashlin changed the focus of the piece from a wild satire on movies to an even wilder satire about the movies' chief rival, television. He also got rid of the whole metaphysical morality play angle. Instead, Tashlin's hero is now Rock Hunter, a lowly TV commercial writer at an ad agency. Despite his sorry status, Rock has the grand ambition of one day becoming a spectacular success by landing a major account. When beautiful, blonde Hollywood sex goddess Rita Marlowe comes to New York, Rock hears opportunity knocking. All he has to do is somehow convince Rita to appear in a TV commercial for his agency's biggest client, Stay-Put Lipstick, and he will have it made.

After much persuasion, Rita finally agrees to Rock's plan, but only on one condition. He must first transform himself into "Lover Boy" to make Rita's bodybuilder boyfriend Bobo Branigansky jealous. Frantic to land Rita for his commercial, Rock goes along with her crazy idea. The publicity that ensues when the media discovers he is Rita's latest "Lover Boy" changes Rock's entire life.

Rock's superiors at the agency begin to look at him with a newfound respect over the fact that he is now the virile lover of the sexy Rita Marlowe. To reward him, they promote Rock to vice president. However, his lovely but more modestly built girlfriend Jenny begins to feel inferior to Rock's "new girlfriend" and wears huge falsies to make her look more like her movie-star rival. When all else fails, she breaks off her relationship with Rock, leaving him free to carry on with Rita for real. Rock is finally made president of the agency, and his affair with Rita eventually runs its course. He finally comes to his senses and returns to Jenny, leaving Rita free to reunite with her long-lost lover, Georgie Schmidlapp.

Although it is true that Tashlin did alter most of George Axelrod's original play, he was smart enough to leave two things intact: the play's wonderful title and the actress playing Rita Marlowe—Jayne Mansfield. Most amazingly, in the movie Mansfield even goes beyond merely parodying Marilyn to become this two-dimensional cartoon version of her. Tashlin then takes what was already wittily eroticized to begin with and reinforces this with a powerful dose of the Freudian paradigm of extreme fetishism. With this, he makes Mansfield this new cartoonlike version of Marilyn, projects her into a cartoonlike space, and gives her cartoon language to speak. Still, clearly, much of what Rita says (and also what is said about her) owes a good deal to Marilyn's life. Yet there is such comic outrageousness about it that the movie often comes across as a Tex Avery cartoon come to life.

Of course, this cartoonlike quality of both Rita and the movie does make perfect sense if we consider that Tashlin began as a talented cartoonist before becoming a movie director. And in Mansfield he seems to have found his ideal cartoon movie star. This allows us to laugh at her various cartoonish foibles without seeming to laugh at a real human being. Virtually spilling out of her form-fitting gowns, with a squeaky Betty Boop–like voice—constantly erupting into high-pitched squalls—everything that comes out of her mouth has a comically absurd quality to it, particularly when she's spoofing Marilyn. An example of this occurs when Rita tells Rock that the latest picture she has completed in Hollywood is a Russian drama about two brothers in love with the same beautiful woman. Not coincidentally, one of Marilyn's own great artistic ambitions was to get to play one day the stunning role of Grushcenka, the beautiful, young Russian woman of questionable character loved by the father and eldest son in Dostoyevsky's great oedipal novel *The Brothers Karamazov*. Now Marilyn as Grushcenka is one thing, but with Rita Marlowe in the role, the movie would have been a true camp classic.

If Marilyn Monroe is only mildly eroticized in the play and movie versions of *Will Success Spoil Rock Hunter?*, she is totally eroticized in director Roger Vadim's 1957 movie *And God Created Woman*. Vadim's wife, Brigitte Bardot, stars as Juliette Hardy, a young orphaned woman who has been placed in a foster home with a childless couple, the Morins. Essentially, Juliette has three great loves in life: animals, children, and sunbathing in the nude. Not surprisingly, her last love does not go unnoticed, particularly by members of the opposite sex. This includes even her withered, old, wheelchair-bound, peeping-tom foster father, who gets off watching her. Her foster mother, however, is not the least bit amused by Juliette's antics. She calls her foster daughter a "slut" and threatens to send her back to the dreaded orphanage.

To keep herself amused, Juliette dallies about with various men. First, she gets involved with the good-looking Antoine Tardieu, who is battling to keep his small family shipyard afloat. At the same time, she also becomes the heated obsession of wealthy shipping magnate Eric Carradine, who happens to be the very person that Antoine is battling with. Then, in an effort to keep from being sent back to the orphanage, she ends up marrying a nice, upstanding young man, Michel, who happens to be Antoine's younger brother. The marriage is a disaster with Juliet sleeping with Antoine and continuing on with Eric. But by the movie's end, she realizes the error of her ways, and she and Michel go walking off together into the shimmery Riviera night.

In making *And God Created Woman*, Vadim and Brigitte Bardot saw their movie as a cinematic homage to Marilyn's early years, with many obvious similarities between her and Juliette. Both are unhappily placed in orphanages, both young women are taken advantage of in foster homes, both have a profound love for animals and children, both get involved with a number of men, and Juliette, like Marilyn, agrees to an arranged marriage at a young age to a nice, upstanding young man to prevent her from being sent back to the orphanage.

In 1957, *And God Created Woman* was considered hot stuff. And it did firmly establish leading lady Brigitte Bardot as Marilyn's rightful European counterpart. On the strength of this one movie, the French "sex kitten" became an international superstar. But with the many scenes of her romping around in various states of dress and undress in the movie, the nation's censors and moralists were fit to be tied. Bardot biographer Jeffrey Robinson describes how the Catholic Church in America immediately denounced the movie, declaring it "an assault on each and every woman of our community and nation, living or dead, our mothers, sisters, wives and daughters."[2]

When all is said and done, it still should be acknowledged, even with all its many censorship problems, that the depiction of Monroe in the person of Bardot is essentially a positive one. Blonde and beautiful, with a refreshingly uninhibited attitude toward her body, Bardot proves as irresistible as the golden sun and silvery sands of the movie's Riviera setting. Yet, despite the striking similarities between them, it would be unfair to look on her as nothing more than a Parisian carbon copy. Although it is true that she, like Marilyn, does exhibit similar qualities of extreme innocence and extreme eroticism, she also signifies an aspect of the infantile eroticized to the point where she is the naughty, little schoolgirl as bitch-goddess. This gives her star image a certain sexual perversity, which was very new to movies in the repressive 1950s. Because of this, an odd, infantile eroticism is the main mystique spread across her often pouty baby-doll face and lush woman's body.

A certain debunking of Marilyn Monroe's iconic status takes place in writer Paddy Chayefsky's 1958 *The Goddess*. Divided into three distinct parts—Portrait of a Girl, Portrait of a Young Woman, Portrait of a Goddess—Chayefsky's movie tells the moving story of Emily Ann Faulkner, an unloved child born without a father and unwanted by her mother. She dreams of going to Hollywood to become a rich and famous movie star. As she grows into her teenage years, she acquires a well-developed figure, which attracts the attention of the local boys. Although she does become something of a plaything for these boys, she eventually meets and marries John Tower, the intelligent but alcoholic son of a movie actor. The couple have a daughter, but their marriage is short lived. Emily Ann leaves her husband and child to seek her fame and fortune in Hollywood. She next becomes Rita Shawn, peroxided movie starlet; marries a second time, to ex-boxer Dutch Seymour; and drives him to drunken despair with her posing for nude photographs and her assorted sexual trysts with Hollywood big shots. Her marriage to Dutch crashes and burns just as her movie career finally takes off.

Rita Shawn does become a bona fide superstar, but she is also a complete mess. At only twenty-six, she is a profoundly unhappy, emotionally empty woman. Clearly, the Faustian-like bargain she has made with Hollywood has extracted from her more than its pound of flesh for whatever wealth or fame it might have bestowed on her. At one point, she turns to her self-righteous, Bible-thumping mother for help. Sadly, nothing comes of it. Later she goes back home, and when her mother dies, she breaks down at the funeral. Despite all her wealth and fame, the Goddess is essentially a lonely, unhappy woman just barely held together by pills, alcohol, and the manipulations of her domineering lesbian secretary.

Although Paddy Chayefsky always denied the charge, it is almost impossible not to reach the conclusion that *The Goddess* owes a tremendous debt to Marilyn. Here are just some of the similarities between his heroine and her:

- Both are born illegitimate and never know the true identity of their fathers.
- Their mothers try first to abandon them and later become religious fanatics.
- As young girls, each fantasizes about one day becoming a glamorous and famous movie star.
- Both pose for sexy photographs and end up using their bodies to get ahead in Hollywood.
- Each of them marries a moody athlete and a brooding intellectual type.
- Both of them suffer from profound loneliness and insecurity and end up addicted to pills and alcohol.

Even with all these striking similarities, *The Goddess* is hardly a rip-off of Marilyn's life. On the contrary, Chayefsky has taken all these biographical details and shaped them into a powerful viewing experience. Clearly, Chayefsky went to great lengths to create a heroine with psychological nuance and detail who is presented to us in all her novelistic complexity as the always probing narrative carries her from her sad and lonely childhood to the fantastic heights of Hollywood stardom. And, in all of this, Chayefsky takes a definite point of view. Like novelists such as Dickens, the Brontës, and Thomas Hardy, he openly challenges and is critical of the ways in which society (signified by Hollywood) contributes to her tragic circumstances. He makes all his points by showing us the profoundly damaging effects that it has on her psyche in the end.

There are also operatic aspects of the heroine that make her reminiscent of some great tragic opera diva of the nineteenth century. Like Puccini's *Madame Butterfly*, Bizet's *Carmen*, or Verdi's Violetta from *La Traviata*, Rita Shawn is depicted as a neurotic and sultry prima donna who, although she has the power to taunt and entrap men, must, in the end, be punished. Her transgressive sexuality must be brought back under masculinist control and dominance. But, as is also befitting a true opera prima donna, Chayefsky has also provided her with extended passages of dialogue and long soliloquies that are always rich in imagery, highly stylized, and poetically lyrical. Chayefsky's language has the same effect as a showcase aria in an opera.

To play his highly dramatic and operatic Goddess, Chayefsky chose Kim Stanley. One of the leading stars of Lee Strasberg's Actors Studio (Strasberg would later most famously become Marilyn's teacher as well), Stanley had caused a sensation in 1955 when she originated the role of Cherie in William Inge's *Bus Stop.* (Of course, this same role would also be a great triumph for Marilyn in Joshua Logan's 1956 movie.)

Having found his diva, Chayefsky next turned to old Hollywood pro John Cromwell to direct her. Using Chayefsky's masterful words, Cromwell directed Stanley into giving a deeply intense, interior performance. For her part, the actress pulled out all the stops, perfectly hitting every single note of Chayefsky's complex, lyrical arias. In Part One: Portrait of a Girl, she becomes lost in her Hollywood fantasy. Then in Part Two: Portrait of a Young Woman, she is seen embracing this Hollywood fantasy with all her body and soul. She has completely transformed herself into a new being—sexy, peroxided movie starlet Rita Shawn. Along the way, she has ditched her first husband, abandoned her daughter (the same as her mother had abandoned her), and made a second marriage to a celebrity—ex-boxer Dutch Seymour. But inside she still basically remains the same lonely and insecure little girl she has always been. When Dutch tells Rita of his plan to leave Hollywood and go back to St. Louis, she frantically pleads with him to let her first become a star so that people will love her.

In the concluding act, Part Three: Portrait of a Goddess, Rita has attained her Hollywood fantasy. She truly is the Goddess, living in an exclusive Bel-Air neighborhood inside a luxurious mansion. Now she signifies a totally stellar dialectic. Sadly, her private life is no longer her own: it is for public consumption. She belongs to Hollywood and the public. In fact, she belongs more to Hollywood and to her admirers than she does to herself anymore. And she understands this, for she has even transformed her private home, as she has her private self, into a celebration of the public figure she has become—Rita Shawn. Paradoxically, she now has everything but feels nothing. The movie was considered strong stuff back in 1958, and it still packs quite an emotional punch today. In terms of artistic depictions of Marilyn, it is undeniably a seminal work. For Chayefsky presents his heroine to us, warts and all. Yet, for all that, she is more victim than victor. Her story is not so much a star born in Hollywood as it is a star destroyed by Hollywood. Lurking beneath Hollywood's glittery surface, there is much that is dark and ugly. True, Hollywood may grant her all her dreams of wealth and celebrity, but what does any of it matter in the end? For after Emily Ann Faulkner has been transformed into seductive superstar Rita Shawn and Hollywood has taken from her all that it possibly could, nothing is left in Rita for herself.

Playwright Arthur Miller originally conceived of *The Misfits* (1961) as a cinematic valentine to his then wife Marilyn Monroe. He based so much of his heroine Roslyn Taber on her that in many ways this depiction could even be viewed as Marilyn playing Marilyn. In the movie, Roslyn is an incredibly beautiful—but also incredibly unhappy—blonde dancer temporarily living in the Reno rooming house of spirited divorcee Isabelle Steers. After obtaining her divorce, Roslyn and Isabelle meet Gay Langland, an aging, rough-and-ready, divorced cowboy and his mechanic buddy Guido, a widower. They invite the two women to visit Guido's partially completed ranch house. Because of his wife's sudden death, Guido has never been able to finish constructing his home. After a day of partying, Roslyn and Gay discover they are strongly attracted to one another. The couple soon move into Guido's place.

One afternoon, the foursome go to the rodeo. On the way, they meet up with battered and disillusioned rodeo performer Perce Howland. After almost getting killed at the rodeo, Perce is comforted by kindred spirit and fellow "misfit" Roslyn. Later that night, Roslyn exhibits strong maternal instincts when she comforts all three men, each of whom has had way too much to drink for his own good.

The next morning, the men take Roslyn with them when they go to round up wild mustangs in the high hills and mountains of Nevada. But this is no simple roundup. The reason the mustangs are being hunted is to sell them to a dog-food manufacturer. As the three men try to tie down the lead stallion— that is also, like themselves, something of a "misfit"—Roslyn is no longer able to remain silent. She offers $200 for the mustang's freedom. Insulted by her offer, Gay becomes even more relentless in his fierce resolve to capture the mustangs. Roslyn finally reaches her breaking point when the men try to tie down a mare and her colt. She wildly shrieks at them for their cruelty, becoming, at once, a signifier of the calming, more feminine force of civilization against the brutes.

Continuing in her totally desperate state, Roslyn later appeals to the more sensitive of the men, Perce, who frees the horses for her. But Gay, furious over what Perce has done, goes to single-handedly recapture the lead stallion. After a particularly torturous and prolonged battle, the mustang relents to Gay's will. Then, Gay does just as Roslyn has wanted all along: he sets the animal free. More understanding and respectful of one another after the harrowing experience, Gay and Roslyn make their way back home together.

There would be no such happy ending for Arthur Miller and Marilyn Monroe in real life because, in truth, *The Misfits* proved to be anything but a

Valentine's Day story for either of them. Their marriage was already in pretty rough shape even before they arrived in Nevada to begin the movie. And further complicating things, Marilyn's pill and alcohol consumption was at an all-time high. Yet even with all this, whenever the camera started to roll, she could somehow always pull it together. Marilyn not only looks luminously beautiful in *The Misfits* but also gives one of her most beautiful screen performances.

In *Hollywood: 1920–1970,* John Baxter considers the way in which Miller created a role for Marilyn that fully allowed her to "express a naturalness and vitality her admirers, desert drop outs and small-time adventurers, recognize as the spirit of a West none has seen, but with which they are totally entranced."[3] Consequently, the very presence of Roslyn is a constant reminder to the men of just how very far they have all fallen from the noble idea of the true West. And her presence in the movie transforms her into a figure of the imagination. Like a great, floating dream, she is a beautiful impossibility whose approval each of the wounded, aging, grief-stricken men must somehow gain in order to go on functioning as men. This idea is even borne out in the movie's imagery. Russell Metty's black-and-white photography presents Roslyn's golden blonde hair as pure white, making her a symbol of purity and hope among the dark-haired men, all so rough, cynical, and world-weary. Perhaps the greatest expression of Miller's intention happens when the men take Roslyn with them to round up the wild horses to be used for dog food. When she becomes aware of their heartless intent, she simply cannot contain her revulsion. When Gay finally frees the horses and allows them to live, he gives his relationship with Roslyn a second chance as well. His generosity leads directly into the movie's magisterial final scene. Driving back home through the starry night, the couple talk of "the passage of time, and we see the closing of an era of great stars and the passage of Hollywood itself."[4]

As Neil Carson points out, what Gay learns from Roslyn "is an openness to life and hope for the future."[5] After having taught her lesson so well, Roslyn safely rests her weary head on her man's shoulder as they both fix their eyes on that big, bright star that will lead them back home. And the glow from that bright star charges her face with a radiant beauty. Her physical beauty in the scene comes to take on a pure, interiorized richness, and Roslyn comes to represent here the feminine force of civilization winning out in the end. Then, again, civilization must always win out, and the "misfits" all must ultimately fit into the great jigsaw puzzle of existence or else perish completely from the earth. So, despite the odds against her, Roslyn is a very hopeful woman in possession of a true redemptive love. Fittingly, she is responsible for bringing about the movie's highly hopeful conclusion in which she and Gay recapture for themselves a kind of sweet innocence. This essentially upbeat conclusion reflects the general atmosphere of hopeful optimism that is associated with the early Kennedyesque 1960s.

This same 1960s hopeful optimism is also expressed in a big, comical way in the screen comedy *The Ladies Man* (1961) as it is in two theatrical romantic comedies that opened on Broadway in 1962, *Venus at Large* by Henry Denker and *Come on Strong* by Garson Kanin. The first of these, *The Ladies Man*, is a fantastically stylish-looking cinematic confection produced and written by its multitalented leading man Jerry Lewis. The comedian plays Herbert H. Herbert, a hapless, small-town hick who has the misfortune of catching his terribly shapely—but also terribly unfaithful—fiancée making passionate love to the hunky captain of the college football team. So traumatized is the downtrodden Herbert over her betrayal that he vows to swear off all women forever and leaves home for Hollywood (of all places) for good. After several humiliating failed attempts, he lands a job as a handyman in what has got to be one of the most elaborate boardinghouses in the history of the movies. Unbeknownst to Herbert, however, is the crucial fact that the house is also occupied by room upon room of gorgeous, young women.

Less of a coherent movie and more of an episodic series of humorous vignettes and one eye-appealing set piece after another (held together by the flimsiest of narratives), *The Ladies Man* chronicles Herbert's zany antics as he wreaks havoc of many different varieties on the utilitarian orderliness of the feminocentric theoretical space he has intruded on. The phallocentricity of his role makes him the hero of a Freudian sex fantasy, and each of the women he encounters comes to represent assorted feminine archetypes of the male sexual imagination (the lethal vamp, the luscious girl next door, the free-loving hedonist, the bitchy man hater). Although the women do tend to exploit Herbert's generosity, by the end both they and he find newfound respect for one another.

Two of the more memorable aspects of *The Ladies Man* are, first, the vivid use it makes of Hollywood artifice in its palatial, four-story, cutaway Victorian dollhouse set (which cinematographer W. Wallace Kelley photographs in beautiful, bright, candy-coated Technicolor) and, second, the use that Lewis makes of Marilyn Monroe. As a great admirer of hers, he pays her a special cinematic homage. While Herbert is busy delivering the mail to the women, he is dumbfounded when he runs into Marilyn. To his utter amazement, she reacts to him with such an unbridled eroticism that he instantly becomes the very embodiment of male sexual frustration run amok.

If *The Ladies Man* reminds us of Frank Tashlin's *Will Success Spoil Rock Hunter?*, this is not coincidental. After all, Tashlin was for Lewis a great mentor, and the two of them made eight films together. As was previously mentioned, Tashlin's expertise as a professional cartoonist afforded him a rare ability to combine his training with all sorts of sophisticated cinematic flourishes, to transform the real world into a more exciting, hyperkinetic space where anything at all could happen. And this is the same space where *The Ladies Man* takes place and where a yutz like Herbert H. Herbert can exist in a fantastic cinematic dreamscape full of beautiful women, including even a perfect replica of Marilyn Monroe.

In Henry Denker's *Venus at Large*, the Marilyn Monroe–inspired character is named Olive Ogilvie. She is a beautiful, blonde Hollywood sex goddess fed up with the way her studio, Classic Studios, absolutely refuses to take her seriously. She flees to the much more cultured environs of New York, where she hopes to become a "real" actress on the Broadway stage. She is encouraged in all this by her ambitious agent, Sonny Stone. But, unbeknownst to Olive, Sonny is actually planning to start Olive Ogilvie Productions with himself as the newly formed company's president. His lovely and sophisticated wife, Betty, attempts to talk him out of his crazy scheme to no avail.

Sonny arranges for famous, in-your-face, Broadway playwright Nick Mandelbaum to write a play for Olive. When this doesn't pan out, he next arranges for Hollywood scriptwriter Alec Grimes to pretend he is writing a play to placate Olive. Meanwhile, Olive enrolls in the Actors Studio to study method acting. While Olive is working on a scene, the head of Classic Studios, J. B. Bannister, shows up and demands to know why she isn't in Hollywood filming the movie she was assigned. Olive promptly informs him that she has absolutely no intentions whatsoever of ever returning to Hollywood again.

In the hope of impressing the head of the Actors Studio, Mr. Kronheim, Olive enacts the last scene from Ibsen's *A Doll's House* for him. Kronheim's verdict: Olive is a great star, but she will never be a "real" actress. Initially crushed by Mr. Kronheim's low opinion of her talent, Olive rebounds in the end. When Alec comes clean and confesses that he deceived her about writing a play for her, she not only forgives him but also confesses her love for him, at which point Alec promises to write her a great movie role. Sonny patches up his differences with Betty and successfully negotiates a lucrative deal with J. B. Bannister, making himself president of Olive Ogilvie Productions.

Clearly, *Venus at Large* is a knowing satire about Marilyn Monroe's famous involvement with Lee Strasberg and the celebrated Actors Studio. Like Marilyn, the play's heroine, Olive Ogilvie, desperately longs to find her place among the New York theater's elite. And all this does make for an entertaining enough theatrical excursion. Admittedly, there are times when the play's plot grows predictable, but Denker always seems to maneuver his characters in and out of their outlandish predicaments with ease and style. Just when things get too bogged down, he comes up with a particularly witty situation or a stretch of dialogue that puts things back on track again. Time and time again, there is then the surety of Denker's delightful comic touch, which is at its very best in his conception of luscious heroine Olive Ogilvie.

On one level, there is definitely something Rita Marlowe–like about Olive (the plot of the play also owes something to *Rock Hunter*). Still, on another level, Denker gives her a more realistic quality than Rita ever exhibited. He also makes certain to add in generous amounts of poignancy and intelligence with her lush sexiness. Therefore, when she declares her desire to be taken more seriously as an actress, we tend to believe in what she says because she says it so as to make it sound both funny and wise at the same time. There's a sense here that in learning to act, Olive will gain a new depth and stature. And as her physical desirability vanishes, she will still be able to radiate something beautiful from the screen: her great talent. This will not only give her a chance at longevity but also afford her an excellent chance to go beyond herself to create a totally different reality from the increasingly unsatisfactory one of her everyday existence. *Venus at Large* opened on Broadway to only mixed reviews. Joyce Jameson as Olive Ogilvie, however, did receive her fair share of decent notices.

The other romantic comedy that opened on Broadway in 1962, *Come on Strong*, was written and directed by Garson Kanin. The play looked at the trials and tribulations of sexy, blonde actress Ginny Karger and her on-again, off-again relationship with her hunky photographer boyfriend, Herb. Ginny and Herb live together in New York, where Ginny is also involved with the mega-rich but also mega-ancient, widower Arthur Murchison. When Herb refuses to make an honest woman of Ginny, she accepts a proposal of marriage from Arthur. On the night of their honeymoon, Ginny's elderly bridegroom drops dead while having sex with her. This then leaves Ginny a very rich widow.

Two years later, at the luxurious home of vulgar Hollywood producer Mike Anadem, Ginny and Herb meet again. Both have reinvented themselves. Herb is a successful documentary filmmaker, and Ginny is now beautiful, blonde movie starlet "Vanessa Karr." She is also, however, Mike's girlfriend of the moment. Mike wants Herb to direct Ginny in a movie loosely based on one of his documentaries. Ginny is amenable to Mike's idea; Herb is not. Herb leaves Hollywood; Ginny remains.

Two more years later, Ginny is well situated at the Plaza Hotel in New York. She is now glamorous Hollywood sex goddess "Ginia Kerr," and Herb arrives to photograph her for *Life*. While in the middle of taking pictures of Ginny, Herb stops to make love to her. Then he proposes to her, and she more than gladly accepts.

The actress Garson Kanin chose to play Ginny, Carroll Baker, first became famous for starring in a movie role that Marilyn Monroe had wanted to

A Gallery of Marilyns

1. Lucille Ball as Marilyn in *I Love Lucy*, 1954. Courtesy Photofest.

2. Lloyd Bridges and Kim Stanley in *The Goddess*, 1958. Courtesy Photofest.

3. Marilyn Monroe in
The Misfits, 1961.
Courtesy Photofest.

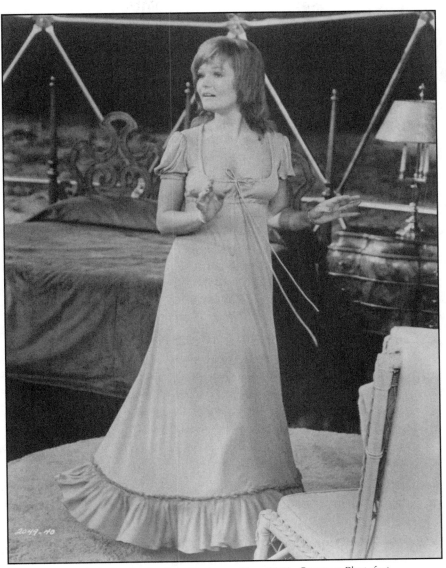

4. Valerie Perrine in *Slaughterhouse-Five*, 1972. Courtesy Photofest.

5. Christopher Plummer and Faye Dunaway in *After the Fall*, 1974. Courtesy Photofest.

6. Catherine Hicks in *Marilyn, The Untold Story*, 1980. Courtesy Photofest.

7. Karen MacDonald in *Strawhead*, 1983. Courtesy Daniel Vachon and Karen MacDonald.

8. Jimmy James as
Marilyn Monroe,
c.1985–1995. Courtesy
Richard Armas.

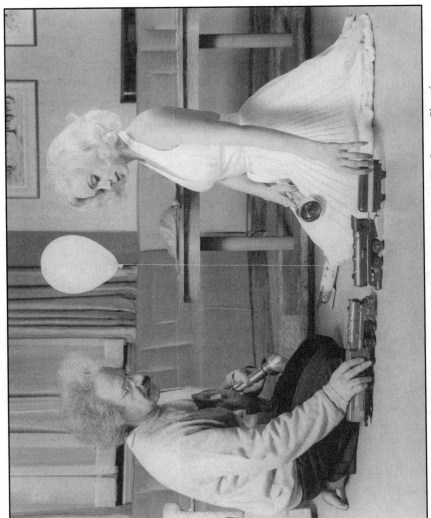

9. Michael Emil and Theresa Russell in *Insignificance*, 1985. Courtesy Photofest.

10. Heather Thomas in *Hoover vs. the Kennedys: The Second Civil War*, 1987. Courtesy Sunrise Films Limited.

11. Larry Pennell and Susan Griffiths in *Quantum Leap,* 1993. Courtesy Photofest.

12. Kathryn Gamberoni in the opera *Marilyn*, 1993. Courtesy Carol Rosegg.

13. Jessica Lange in *Blue Sky*, 1994. Courtesy Photofest.

14. Mira Sorvino in *Norma Jean and Marilyn*, 1996. Courtesy Photofest.

15. Naia Kelly in the play by Jim Tommaney, *The Final Hours of Norma Jean*, 1999. Courtesy Toni Parras.

16. Garry Shandling, Jenna Elfman, and Warren Beatty (in polar bear costume) in *Town & Country*, 2001. Courtesy Photofest.

17. Nana Kazari as Marilyn Monroe for Stylezone TV in *Zink,* September 2004. Courtesy Miguel Starcevich.

18. The immortal Marilyn singing "Happy Birthday, Mr. President," 1962. Courtesy Photofest.

play herself: the fantasy child-bride in director Elia Kazan's screen adaptation of Tennessee Williams's infamous *Baby Doll* (1956). Baker also shared many other connections with Marilyn: she studied acting with Lee Strasberg, was one of Paddy Chayefsky's first choices for *The Goddess*, and ended up playing Jean Harlow, a role originally slated for Marilyn.

Although not in the same exact league as Kanin's 1946 play and 1950 movie *Born Yesterday*, *Come on Strong* still has its strong points. The dialogue has a lively sparkle and snap, especially when the heroine Ginny is spoken of or speaks for herself. Kanin has a good deal of fun turning the stereotypical Hollywood perception of Marilyn as a dumb blonde airhead upside down. Ginny may be blonde, but a dumb airhead she most certainly is not. Like Olive in *Venus at Large*, she knows the score—only more so. She tells Herb that she likes to think of herself as something new in the world—the Smart Blonde. All this is the main reason that the best thing by far about *Come on Strong* is heroine Ginny Karger. True, Ginny is one hot Hollywood babe, but the real knockout is her sharp wit and keen intelligence. She is neither a "dumb blonde" nor a tragic victim. She's a realist, with both feet planted firmly on the ground and a good head on her shoulders. Not only does she make it in Hollywood, but she also gets her man in the end—which all adds up to a representation of the sex goddess surprisingly refined and redefined as the new empowered woman of the twentieth century. There's even an attempt being made here to work toward a new model of male/female relations. For in the last act, there's no question that Ginny is Herb's equal. True, he might still appear to embody the idea of male authority, but Ginny has discovered all kinds of clever new ways to shift the balance of power, ever so slightly, so that it doesn't always seem so one-sided anymore. She's introduced a brand new possibility of tit for tat in the modern terrain of 1960s relationships. The play ends with the couple having resolved their differences, keeping their relationship intact. And it is this happy ending, which we also saw reflected in *Venus at Large*, that places Kanin's play firmly within the codified tradition of countless Broadway and Hollywood romantic comedies. Additionally, such an ending perfectly reflects all the optimism of the early 1960s.

Now, an infinitely more cynical take on Marilyn Monroe is presented by her third husband, playwright Arthur Miller, in *After the Fall* (1964). Directed by Elia Kazan, *After the Fall* tells the story of Quentin, a twice-divorced lawyer in his forties. Quentin is hugely successful but also hugely unhappy and guilt ridden. At the start of the play, he is poised between relationships with two women: Maggie, the beautiful blonde pop singer, and Holga, a young Nazi concentration camp survivor. About to marry Holga, Quentin remembers many disturbing scenes from his life, beginning with his mother's death, his unhappy marriage to his first wife Louise, and his betrayal of his good friend

Lou, which causes the man to commit suicide. His marriage to Louise ends when she learns of his affair with Maggie. After Louise divorces him, Quentin embarks on a new life with Maggie. Initially, Quentin is drawn to her astonishing golden beauty and childlike innocence. He sees her as his gateway to some lost Eden.

In time, Maggie becomes famous for her sensual looks and seductive singing style. But she also harbors many inner demons. Neglected by her mentally disturbed mother, exploited by an endless line of cruel men, Maggie turns to Quentin to provide her with nothing short of her salvation. For a while, he does all that he can for her. But her growing dependency on pills and alcohol and her unbearable neurotic energy increase to the point where she makes life all but impossible for him.

Quentin grows increasingly disgusted and resentful of Maggie's viciousness and abuse. His disgust and resentment culminate in his attempt to strangle the dissolute, drug-sodden Maggie. Eventually, he leaves Maggie, and she kills herself. In the wake of her death, Quentin aligns himself with Holga as his new post-Fall companion.

After the Fall is a dark, brooding, multilayered text that operates on many different levels. There's the drama of the surface—the faces the characters show to each other, the words they speak, and the almost mechanical actions they go through as their lives unfold. Then there's the subterranean realm of the conscious and subconscious. This is the real realm of Miller's work. In the telling of Quentin's story, Miller projects a metaphorical interior journey rather than a straightforward narrative. But this journey has no beginning, middle, or end in the traditional sense. Much of the narrative is mixed up, fragmented, and splintered into an elaborate series of kaleidoscopic scenes that tell the story of Quentin's life. Past, present, and future converge on one another, often making it difficult to distinguish one from the other. In this constant movement, backward and forward and forward and backward, Quentin sifts through his memories, illusions, dreams, and deceptions, trying desperately to make sense out of his life and his relationship to others.

In the creation of the play's characters, Miller turned to the people from his own life for artistic inspiration. The character of Quentin is based on Miller himself, while Quentin's three wives are based on Miller's: Louise is his first wife Mary, Holga is his third wife Inga, and the character of Maggie is the play's Marilyn-inspired character. The similarities between Marilyn and Maggie are striking and inescapable:

- Both are the illegitimate daughters of disturbed mothers.
- Both are beautiful and blonde and idolized and desired by millions.

- Each has an affair with a senior professional associate (for Marilyn this man was Hollywood superagent Johnny Hyde, for Maggie, Judge Cruse) and are forbidden by his family to visit his deathbed.
- Both suffer from self-destructive addictions to pills and alcohol.
- Both undergo psychoanalysis.
- Each stands by her husband when he has problems with the House Un-American Activities Committee.
- Each works on her chosen craft with a legendary teacher (Marilyn, of course, studied the method with Lee Strasberg; Maggie goes to vocal coach Ludwig to make a great artist of herself).
- Both die, at a young age, from a drug overdose.

Even with all these obvious similarities, Miller always denied that Maggie is based on Marilyn. Still, in his harsh 1964 review, Robert Brustein wrote that Maggie reminded him of the "image created by Marilyn Monroe's press agents, and by Arthur Miller himself."[6]

It was mainly because of this highly negative portrait of Marilyn that many American critics tended to dismiss the play out of hand. But in Europe, the critics were far more receptive, and with time many American critics have followed suit. Clinton W. Trowbridge calls *After the Fall* "one of the few genuinely tragic plays of our time."[7] And nowhere in the play is the powerful sense of the tragic greater than in the depiction of the sad fate of Maggie. Before getting into the depths to which Maggie falls, it is important to understand the fantastic heights to which she first rises. Our very first glimpse of her is provocative and enticing: Maggie rises up from the total darkness, like some mythical goddess clad in a sensational-looking, skintight gold lamé gown. She is seen in the center of a crowd of men. She laughs teasingly, calls out Quentin's name, and then, just as quickly as she appears, she disappears, completely engulfed by the surrounding darkness. Besides paying homage to Marilyn's great "Diamonds Are a Girl's Best Friend" number from *Gentlemen Prefer Blondes*, this image operates as a signifier showing us just why it is that the crowd of men, as well as Quentin himself, all so desire Maggie.

It is precisely this desirability, along with her perfect, golden blonde beauty and seductive singing, that catapults Maggie to the highest heights of pop music stardom. In his transference of the Marilyn-inspired Maggie from movie star to pop star, Miller is doing something interesting in this play. Maggie goes from being associated with the alluring image that is seen (the movies) to the seductive sound that is heard (record albums). It is then the ear rather than the eye that becomes the means by which her full powers of seduction get played out. Now, in *After the Fall*, it is music itself that becomes the possessor of the allure. And because music can easily carry the listener to places where the image can unexpectedly drop off completely, music becomes the site of overindulgence and excessive effect. And this is precisely the space that Maggie occupies. Her seductive singing style and golden blonde beauty combine to make her a double threat. And, as such, she becomes not only the object of desire but also the object to be worshipped, adored, and even feared.

When Quentin first encounters Maggie, he cannot resist her. In fact, he becomes so enthralled with her that he selfishly abandons his wife and small daughter to devote himself exclusively to her. In effect, he becomes her ultimate fawning worshipper. But with time, he notices that his golden girl is more than a little tarnished. When Maggie tells him of her numerous erotic encounters with men, he seriously begins to question if he can possibly go on loving her. His disgust leads to his harsh mistreatment of Maggie. Miller actually uses an incident that occurred between himself and Marilyn to show the extent of this cruelty. Toward the end of the play, Maggie tells Quentin of how she has read some hurtful things he wrote of her in his journal that caused her to want to kill herself. This leads to his trying to strangle her. It is, finally, this disturbing depiction that Miller gives us of Marilyn Monroe that makes the play one of the most tragic and problematical of all the depictions in this book. Miller gives us a version of Marilyn as this devouring endless pit demanding of a totally unrealistic, limitless, unconditional love. At the same time, she is also depicted as being too far gone, too self-destructive, too psychoneurotic ever to give love back to anyone, least of all Quentin. When, toward the end of the play, Maggie attempts suicide, Quentin goes from her avenger—calling her doctor to save her from herself—to her destroyer, grabbing her by the throat to strangle her to death. And no matter how many times we are exposed to this shattering scene, we cannot but be riveted by it.

Long gone is the idyllic, romantic, and redemptive view of love, capable of surmounting all the obstacles, as was seen in *The Misfits, Venus at Large,* and *Come on Strong.* In its place, there is this supremely negative view of love being pushed so far to its breaking point that it must shatter apart. Coming at a time when the initial hope and promise of the 1960s was beginning to wane, *After the Fall* taps into the encroaching darker aspects of the political cultural Zeitgeist, presenting a view of Marilyn etched in a lingering despair.

Yet another variation of the same sort of late 1960s despair—albeit here that despair is served up in a decidedly melodramatic, satirical, and campy mode—comes with the 1966 appearance on Broadway of the musical *The Apple Tree.* With music by Sheldon Harnick and book and lyrics by Jerry Bock, *The Apple Tree* was based on three famous stories by Mark Twain ("The Apple Tree"), Frank R. Stockton ("The Lady or the Tiger?"), and Jules Feiffer ("Passionella"). For our purposes, however, we will focus on Feiffer's allegorical, parable-like contribution to the show only.

"Passionella" begins with the smudgy little chimney sweep, Ella, living alone in New York lamenting the cruel misfortune of her lowly status in life and fantasizing of becoming a glamorous and famous movie star. One night, while watching *The Late, Late Show*, Ella's Fairy Godmother (in the improbable form of a TV announcer) grants her wish. The ordinary Ella is miraculously transformed into the extraordinarily exotic/erotic Passionella, but only for the nighttime hours. Despite these limitations, she is immediately launched on a brilliant career in Hollywood as the world's most alluring sex goddess. Soon, she is wealthy, famous, and endlessly worshipped and adored beyond even her own wildest fantasies.

For all this wealth, fame, and constant adoration, Passionella is lonely and miserable inside. She longs to be taken seriously; she longs to be truly loved. Then she meets Flip Charming—a nonconforming, Marlon Brandoesque, black-leather-clad motorcyclist. More into "digging" Allen Ginsberg and Timothy Leary, Flip declares Passionella not "real." His total rejection of Passionella and all she represents sets in motion her final rejection of the "unreal" Hollywood. Leaving fame, fortune, and glamour far behind her, Ella settles down with Flip to a life of "real" blissfulness.

Pitched at the level of a maniacally imaginative melodramatic satire on the way Hollywood exploits the Marilyn Monroe–like heroine, "Passionella" picks up on some of the same darker themes explored in *The Goddess* and *After the Fall*. Only now, there is a noted movement toward toning down, softening up, and satirizing all those negative aspects. Yet this does not cause the text to deconstruct itself, as we might at first expect. Instead, it works to demystify the heroine, as it also paradoxically remystifies her for us as well. In this way, the writers pay tribute to both Hollywood and Marilyn. Two key factors that contribute much to this procedure are the characterization of the heroine played by Barbara Harris (who, with her "sexy, sweetly shell-shocked look,"[8] brings much innocence and tenderness to the role of Ella/Passionella) and the witty songs Harnick and Bock provide her with which to tell this incredible tale.

From her very first song, "Oh, To Be a Movie Star," to the highly parodic "Gorgeous" (in which Passionella celebrates the voluptuous Hollywood construct she has been transformed into), the songs quote the conventions of the classical Broadway musical as they send up those same codified traditions. In essence, the songs criticize Hollywood and its cruel treatment of the Marilyn-like heroine. But, despite the use of this critique, the irrational power that music possessed in *After the Fall* vanishes. Here, music ends up taking on a gentle, more comical tone that serves to temper the more bitter twists and turns of the narrative, ultimately softening the harsher impact of the story. In turn, Passionella becomes less like Rita Shawn and Maggie and much more like Rita Marlowe and Olive Ogilvie.

In this regard, when we first witness Ella being transformed into Passionella—in a bravura display of theatrical pyrotechnics, featuring exploding bright lights and puffs of 1960s psychedelic-colored smoke—she emerges (much as Maggie did) a glittery goddess of campy excess in a skintight gold lamé gown, Marilyn Monroe platinum blonde wig, and a set of breasts the size of Hollywood. Still, even with all this outrageous excess, the beleaguered Passionella may become resplendent, but she also perpetuates an aura of such childlike poignancy through it all that she is never less than completely endearing.

Similarly, aspects of the same sort of late 1960s despair (also mixed with traces of melodramatic camp) get carried over into the 1967 movie version of Jacqueline Susann's best-selling novel *Valley of the Dolls*. The movie begins with the classy Anne Welles leaving her tony New England home for New York. She lands a job at a prestigious theatrical law firm and soon gets involved with aging, hard-boiled Broadway diva Helen Lawson; talented singer Neely O'Hara; and beautiful, buxom, blonde showgirl Jennifer North. Anne also finds herself romantically involved with her handsome boss Lyon Burke, while Neely marries her boyfriend Mel and Jennifer marries nightclub singer Tony Polar.

Neely's career takes off; she also becomes addicted to pills and alcohol and divorces Mel. Anne and Lyon also break up. She goes on to win wealth and fame when she stars in a series of TV commercials as "The Gillian Girl." Eventually, they reconcile and convince Neely to enter a sanitarium. While recovering there, Neely meets Tony, who is dying of an incurable degenerative disease. To pay for Tony's exorbitant medical bills, his domineering sister Miriam forces Jennifer to go to France to make smutty adult movies. When Jennifer returns home, she discovers she has breast cancer and takes a fatal overdose of sleeping pills. Meanwhile, the recovered Neely makes a comeback on Broadway and sets her sights on Lyon. His involvement with Neely causes Anne to turn to pills to deal with the betrayal. Neely, now totally incapable of facing an audience, ends up drunk and stoned out of her mind in her Broadway theater's back ally. But Anne wins her battle of pills and returns back home.

Unlike Arthur Miller, Jacqueline Susann never made a secret of the fact that the characters in *Valley of the Dolls* were modeled on famous show business personalities. Her heroine Anne Welles is based on the beautiful and talented Oscar-winning and later Princess of Monaco, Grace Kelly. The inspiration for the troubled Neely O'Hara is the equally troubled but also quite legendary Judy Garland. The fire-breathing, aging Broadway diva is modeled on Broadway legend Ethel Merman. And although the tragic figure of Jennifer North is based principally on Marilyn Monroe, there are also some elements from the lives of Jayne Mansfield and Carol Landis. Of course, the sweet vulnerability and trust; the improvised childhood; the distant, cold mother; and the sensational looks all recall Marilyn.

On casting the movie, director Mark Robson initially tried to sign Candice Bergen to play Anne, Ann-Margaret to play Neely, and Raquel Welch to play Jennifer, but none of these actresses expressed much interest. He did succeed in hiring Judy Garland for the role of Helen Lawson. Unfortunately, only three days into the shooting, she was fired for her secret drinking and drugging. Her replacement was the Oscar-winning Susan Hayward.

Eventually, Robson was successful in casting his movie with three distinctly different actresses in the leading roles. Barbara Parkins, who played Betty Anderson on the long-running TV soap opera *Peyton Place*, was cast as Anne. Fresh from her stint as the star of *The Patty Duke Show*, Oscar-winner (*The Miracle Worker*, 1962) Patty Duke was cast as Neely, and Sharon Tate was cast to play Jennifer. Tate manages to give Jennifer a deeply touching quality that is most affecting. As a desirable woman whose desirability is completely associated with her lush sexuality and excessive voluptuousness, Jennifer, much more than either Anne or Neely, also provides the story line with its most tragic element. This is especially true when she is forced to face the fact that what has so rigidly defined her—her remarkable cleavage—is now being cruelly taken from her. Because she has been so rigidly defined as a sexualized woman within the patriarchal construct of desirable femininity, Jennifer is now without a meaning after her double mastectomy. As a sex goddess without her excessive voluptuousness, she is a signifier without signification, a reference without a referential. Without her defining attributes, her tragic death becomes a sad inevitability.

There were six roman à clef depictions of Marilyn Monroe in the 1970s: two were theatrical productions (*The White Whore and the Bit Player* [1973], *Fame* [1974]), two appeared on television (*The Sex Symbol* [1974], *After the Fall* [1974]), and two were theatrical releases (*Slaughterhouse-Five* [1972], *Winter Kills* [1978]).

Based on Kurt Vonnegut's brilliant novel *Slaughterhouse-Five or the Children's Crusade: A Duty Dance with Death* (1969), the 1972 movie version of the celebrated book is the first instance of a Marilyn Monroe–based character (Montana Wildhack) being depicted in a science-fictional context. The story follows Billy Pilgrim, a man who lives two different lives. In one life, Billy is an ordinary if even unremarkable man who serves in World War II. At the Battle of the Bulge, he is captured and brought to Dresden as the Allied forces devastate the legendary city with firebombs. After the war, Billy becomes a successful optometrist, gets married to a rich man's overweight daughter, has a couple of kids, loses his wife in a bizarre auto accident, becomes the prophet of stoicism, and is assassinated in 1976 while speaking of flying saucers and the mystery of time.

In Billy Pilgrim's second life, he is unstuck in time. This means he can move from one moment in his life to another. One moment he might find himself still a prisoner of the Nazis, and in the next he might be in bed making passionate love to the gorgeous, Marilyn Monroesque Hollywood sex goddess Montana Wildhack on the futuristic planet Tralfamadore. In his being taken to the planet, Billy comes to understand that all time is coexistent, and therefore man's past, present, and future, even his birth and death, are merely random acts on a longer time continuum. The key to happiness is in forgetting the bad moments and concentrating on only the good. The movie concludes on a great moment. After Montana has given birth to a baby, she and Billy are blissfully happy on Tralfamadore.

Director George Roy Hill, aided by the genius of his editor Dede Allen, does an admirable job at bringing Kurt Vonnegut's phenomenally successful cult novel to the screen, leaving much of its complex, literary richness intact. The movie's unlikely hero, Billy Pilgrim, has the ability to move back and forth within all the periods of his life much as we saw Quentin do in *After the Fall*. But whereas Quentin often struck us as an extraordinary man whose behavior could be quite ordinary, if not downright petty at times, Billy is an ordinary man whose life becomes most extraordinary. It is precisely for this quality that he is chosen by the Tralfamadorians in the first place to be taught the wisdom of their knowledge of time. Billy also exhibits a more chivalric attitude (than Quentin ever showed toward Maggie) when he is granted his wish of possessing the golden girl of his fantasies, Montana Wildhack, for all eternity. Throughout the course of the narrative, the moviemakers almost subliminally incorporate various images of Montana Wildhack in nude pinup photos and explicit scenes from her movies as a way to cue us into this aspect of Billy's rich, secret fantasy life.

But then again, there is much more to the character of Montana than her awesome Marilyn Monroesque physical splendor alone as depicted in the movie. Once Billy gets to know her, he is rather pleasantly surprised to discover she also possesses a lovely and touching innocence that makes her a naive in a hostile world much as Billy is himself. Even more, by the end of the movie, both we as well as Billy come to realize that Montana is not meant to signify a dumb, Hollywood sex goddess at all, as she is instead a woman-as-Earth-mother symbol when she positively glows with an otherworldly luminosity after giving birth to a beautiful baby boy. In celebration of her feat, the Tralfamadorians light up the whole of the stratosphere in a wild explosion of dazzling fireworks as Montana and Billy display their newborn son. In fact, such a joyous conclusion looks like an erotic dream come true combined with ideal matrimonial blissfulness, the sweet innocence of Adam and Eve before the Fall re-created on a futuristic Eden forever. This optimistic ending then gives *Slaughterhouse-Five* more the feel of an early 1960s depiction of Marilyn Monroe as Billy becomes a modern-day Candide, believing that he is now in the best of all possible worlds.

A more comically pessimistic roman à clef depiction of Marilyn Monroe comes in 1973, with playwright Tom Eyen's off-off-Broadway play *The White Whore and the Bit Player*. This dark comedy is freely inspired by the life and death of Marilyn Monroe. Set in an insane asylum, the play features the split personality of a great Hollywood sex goddess. The setting has a metaphoric dimension in that it presents the asylum as the repressive, soul-crushing world the Star has been forced to inhabit. One side of the tormented Star is the White Whore. The other side of her is the Nun, or Bit Player. As the play progresses, it becomes apparent that both sides actually represent the split halves of Marilyn's divided psyche. The Whore is Marilyn as she appears to the world, and the Nun is Marilyn's own sad image of herself. In the ten seconds it takes for the Star to kill herself, her two, dualistic sides remember scenes from her tumultuous life.

The Nun sits rigidly on a regal papal chair, while the Whore poses most seductively, in her fancy white apparel, on a white-on-white-silk–covered chaise lounge. (White was Marilyn's favorite color.) And with the celestial sounds of Gregorian chants, African Mass music, and the ever-present smell of burning incense, the Nun and the Whore get into an extremely intense battle of wits in which they constantly attack and counterattack one another. These confrontations take on a mythic intensity, involving everything from the Star's questionable parentage, improvised childhood, troubled love life, rise and fall in Hollywood, and the various sadistic ways each side of the Star wishes to see the other side killed off. This struggle for power continues on unabated until the Whore eventually strangles the Nun with her rosary beads, after which she, like Jesus Christ, is crucified on a giant cross.

If the Nun and the Whore represent the two split halves of Marilyn's divided psyche, there is a rather perverse little twist going on: the Whore is often angelic and virtuous, and the Nun is cheap, negative, and joylessly domineering. Hence, in Eyen's vision, the Whore represents Marilyn's glamorous surface side, her beauty, her famous sensuality, which, like one part of Eyen's heroine, were her ticket out of her abject beginnings and into the world of Hollywood fame. The Nun side of the Marilyn schism is the internal voice of her own nagging conscience, which never stops rebuking her for her many indiscretions and addictions. It is then within the context of this strictly bipolar notion of Marilyn's psyche that the Nun speaks almost entirely from the more willful, authoritarian side of the dichotomy, and her judgments are almost always emphatically harsh and condemning. Her ultimate plan would seem to be to limit the Whore part of herself, completely restricting her from ever getting away with anything or from making any sort of judgments. If it were left up to her, the Nun would effectively problematize the Whore's very existence into mere nothingness. And if victorious, the Nun would constitute a total menace. Her final victory over the Whore would then not only enslave her power to perpetuate this part of her own identity but also imbue the Whore with a Christ-like martyrdom. And, tragically, all this oddly does reflect the sad reality of Marilyn's own life. For no matter what heights she attained, Marilyn was unsuccessful at preventing the dark side of her inner self from plaguing and tormenting her. For this reason, she remained a personality hopelessly divided against itself.

If the insane asylum setting of the play becomes a powerful metaphor for the destructive world at large, the power of Hollywood that is projected is of an ominous and ever-threatening space that dominates the imagination completely. Hollywood, initially, lures the heroine in with all its seductive allure and its promises of endless love and glamour and fame and glory. But once Hollywood gets its hooks into her, it destroys her, becoming the giant cross she must first bear. And when it is all finished with her, Hollywood becomes the cross on which she is finally crucified. Almost in spite of its bold anti-Hollywood stance and its boldfaced use of Christian symbolism, *The White Whore and the Bit Player* is a harrowing theatrical parable of the life of Marilyn Monroe filtered through Eyen's dark comic vision.

The year 1974 saw three distinct roman à clef depictions of Marilyn Monroe. The first of these was in the form of the TV movie *The Sex Symbol*, a fictionalized version of Marilyn's life based on the 1966 novel by Alvah Bessie. Actually, so similar is Bessie's heroine, Kelly Williams, to Marilyn that the book even had to come with a disclaimer:

> This story is fiction. Neither its characters nor the situation in which they are involved are intended to represent any persons now living or dead (or both), although the milieu in which they exist has produced many like them.[9]

The television version of Bessie's novel begins with beautiful, blonde Hollywood sex goddess Kelly Williams getting fired from her latest movie because of her addictions to pills and alcohol. In a fit of desperation, she calls her psychiatrist on the telephone and tells him the story of her life. Kelly remembers her sad childhood as the lonely, unwanted little girl Emmeline, who always dreamed of becoming a glamorous movie star. Her reminiscence goes on to include her rise to the top in Hollywood by sleeping her way straight up the ladder, her failed marriages to rugged ex-football player Buck Wischnewski and famous painter Calvin Bernard, her pill and alcohol abuse, her scandalous affair with handsome Senator Grant O'Neal, and her feud with the powerful and vindictive gossip columnist Agnes "Aggie" Murphy. The action concludes on the last night of Kelly's life with her totally wiped out on pills and alcohol while making desperate telephone calls to some of the men she had once loved. Immediately before dying, she pleads for a strong, handsome man to come and rescue her.

Bessie's disclaimer notwithstanding, the many similarities between the life of Kelly Williams and Marilyn's own life are both obvious and too numerous to mention in detail. As to the quality of what Bessie has achieved in adapting his book *The Symbol* into the TV movie *The Sex Symbol*, the best that can be said is that the final results are uneven. Unquestionably, the biggest problem of all he faced was how to find a way to compress his three-hundred-page chronologically told novel into a ninety-minute movie. To accomplish this, he strips away much of the book's more fascinating detail. Then he attempts to cover up the many huge gaps left in the narrative's cohesion (to say nothing of the occasional gap in logic) by telling his story in that old Hollywood standby the extended flashback. Although Bessie's creative solution to the problem moves the action along at breakneck speed, in the end it proves to be wanting at best. There is just no possible way that the dramatic and complex tale of Marilyn's life (even as presented in Bessie's roman à clef version) can be done proper justice when transformed into a TV melodrama lasting only ninety minutes.

Also, not surprisingly, within such a truncated narrative structure, the figure of the Marilyn-inspired Kelly Williams cannot help but suffer as well. Stripped of all the thoughtful, literary context and depth that fleshed her out in the novel, now she is made to seem the very embodiment of a certain neurotic, excessive female sexuality. With only her mere presence, she frequently seems capable of inciting catastrophes for anyone or anything that gets too close to her. These catastrophic tendencies not only affect the men in her private life but are equally destructive to the people in her professional life as well. Her behavior toward everyone in the movie becomes so cruel and abusive that Kelly even slips into a sadomasochistic space. This narrative movement posits the question of whether she is victim or victimizer. But because she is depicted as being alternately both passive and aggressive, both loving and hateful, both sadistic and masochistic, she ultimately collapses all such oppositions into an entirely new dynamic. Unfortunately, the ending of the movie never does fully resolve these dynamic conflicts. Despite everything, however, Connie Stevens as Kelly Williams manages to deliver a credible enough performance. She is especially good in the last twenty minutes of the movie. Here, Stevens's accomplished playing ennobles the final scenes with a bittersweet eroticism that was very rare for American television of the time.

The 1974 Broadway play *Fame*, by playwright Anthony J. Ingrassia, was so cruelly castigated by the New York critics when it opened that the show's producers closed it down directly after opening night. For all that, however, the play was handsomely mounted in a monochromatic white-and-yellow set on which a series of briskly moving scenes unfolded depicting the rise and fall of the Marilyn Monroe–based Hollywood sex goddess Diane Cook. The action began with the nude corpse of Diane spread across her bed, hordes of photographers and reporters crowding all around her (just as they had throughout her life). From that essentially realistic scene, there was a shift into a more surrealistic space wherein the dead Diane miraculously lifted herself off the bed, put on an extravagant gold lamé gown, applied her makeup, brushed her blonde hair, and finally told the audience the story of her life.

Ingrassia supplied his sexy heroine with a generous amount of clever dialogue as she then enacted scenes from her life, which began with her illegitimate birth to an insane, unwed mother, through her disastrous marriages to her three husbands (including a great athlete and a famous writer), her rise to Hollywood stardom, her self-destructive addiction to pills and alcohol, and her untimely death at thirty-six.

If *Fame* is all but totally forgotten about today, it deserves to be mentioned for both the sleekness of its ingenious design and the performance of Ellen Barber as Diane Cook. So good was she in the role that Martin Gottfried of the *New York Post* wrote that "playing an insecure, ambitious actress who has learned to use her body and her beauty to get what she wants, Ellen Barber is excellent and she has the looks to carry it off." [November 19, 1974]

A better-critically-received roman à clef depiction of Marilyn came with the 1974 television adaptation of Arthur Miller's *After the Fall*. Following the play's debut on Broadway in 1964, MGM purchased the rights to the property to become a lavish movie produced by Carlo Ponti. Sophia Loren was set to star as Maggie, and Paul Newman was to play Quentin. Miller himself was able to persuade revered Oscar winner Fred Zinnemann to direct the movie. After MGM's big plans fell through, Paramount Pictures next took up the option on the project in 1967 to no avail. *After the Fall* finally did see the light of day in 1974, not as a theatrical movie but as a TV special for NBC. In this television production, Christopher Plummer was cast as Quentin, and Faye Dunaway played Maggie to much critical acclaim.

An entirely different but highly influential approach toward the depiction of a character based on Marilyn Monroe is found in the 1978 movie *Winter Kills*. Adapted from the best-selling 1974 novel by Richard Condon, *Winter Kills* is the first work to project Marilyn's death into the cinematic context of the shadowy realm of political paranoia and conspiracy. In the movie, the charismatic JFK-like President Tom Kegan is gunned down by lone assassin Willie Arnold on February 22, 1960. But nineteen years later, the president's younger brother, Nick, is brought new information that Arnold was merely a fall guy for the real assassination conspiracy that occurred. Aided by his ruthless and powerful billionaire father, Pa Kegan, Nick begins his search for his brother's real killers, exposing himself to a multiplicity of conspiratorial scenarios, false identities, and conflicting motives. Among those he encounters along the way are sleazy nightclub owners, strippers, call girls, corrupt police and politicians, glamorous ex-mistresses of his brother, and, most important, the mysterious beauty Yvette Malone (*Winter Kills*' Marilyn Monroe–inspired character). After Yvette is brutally murdered, Nick comes to the painful realization that it was his own father, Pa Kegan, who had her killed as well as his own son, the president, assassinated. A violent shootout concludes with Pa throwing himself out of his skyscraper penthouse office, falling to his death below. With this, the great patriarch is exposed as homicidal, and Marilyn Monroe's death (in the form of Yvette's murder) constitutes the scene of a crime.

Like Alvah Bessie, writer-director William Richert had the same problem of doing justice to a fairly complex novel in the narrative space of a ninety-minute movie. To do so, Richert speeds up the plot's action so that it is often too difficult to follow completely. The worst part of this is that, buried within the narrative of *Winter Kills*, there is an amazing collection of the complicated conspiracy theories concerning the 1963 assassination of JFK. It seems that with each new character whom the sleuthlike hero Nick Kegan (well played by Jeff Bridges) encounters, both he and we learn of yet another conspiracy theory. These include the president having been killed by the FBI, the CIA, the Mafia, corrupt big business, and anti-Castro Cubans, among others. (Interestingly, many of these alleged assassins will later figure in conspiracy theories of Marilyn's death as well.) Thus, as all the twists and turns of the narrative overwhelm Nick, so too are we equally overwhelmed. Also, as each new conspiracy theory displaces the one before, a texture of total political paranoia is built up so that nothing in the movie is ever as it first appeared to be. Contributing to this overall sense of political paranoia is the movie's shadow-soaked imagery, dark-toned mise-en-scène, and the tragic use made of its Marilyn Monroe–based character—Yvette Malone. What is most striking about this cinematic incarnation of Marilyn is the way it taps into the heretofore unseen aspect of her image: her sultry, mysterious side. Yvette Malone is Marilyn Monroe as femme fatale. Therefore, Yvette is also very much a difficult-to-figure-out enigmatic figure.

Consequently, along with everything else going on in the movie to confuse him, Nick is constantly baffled by Yvette's erratic behavior toward him. Just when he thinks he's finally gotten a handle on her—who she really is—the rug is pulled out from under him again. Over the course of the movie, he finds out that Yvette is not really a journalist, that she doesn't live where he believed she lived, that she's really the spoiled daughter of a superrich, right-wing fanatic, that she was one of his brother's many mistresses, that she had him assassinated after he dumped her, and that she is an out-of-work actress, hired by Pa Kegan, only to pretend to be all the above. The movie's deployment of her false identities thus joins up with its narrative complexity to suggest how the discourse of Marilyn's death will become enfolded within the tropes of deception and unsolvable mystery in the future.

Finally, *Winter Kills* becomes, as stated, the first cinematic depiction to place a Marilyn Monroe–based character within the frightening context of a larger political conspiracy. And it is this specific use of Marilyn that will be further developed and explored in exhaustive detail in many later depictions. S. Paige Baty addresses the exact meaning of this representational development:

> Whether or not one chooses to accept that a battle has been staged on Marilyn's living body, mass-mediated versions of it have certainly been mapped onto her remembered figure. These cartographic rememberings assert that she was not a suicide but a homicide. They argue that Marilyn's body figured in a plot to defame and contaminate the sanctified and moral persons of both President John Fitzgerald Kennedy and Attorney General Robert Kennedy. Other characters in the plot include underworld mobsters related to Sam Giancana and Jimmy Hoffa, intelligence agencies such as the FBI and CIA, and a host of individuals ranging from Fidel Castro to actor Peter Lawford to Nikita Khrushchev to Marilyn's maid Eunice Murray.[10]

For all intents and purposes, *Winter Kills* marks one of the last of the truly original roman à clef depictions of Marilyn Monroe. In future decades, this form of depiction would seem to have pretty much served its purpose and fallen out of artistic favor. In fact, two of the remaining roman à clef depictions are Roger Vadim's remake of *And God Created Woman* (1988) (which had nothing like the impact or success of the original) and the movie *Everybody Wins* (1990) by Arthur Miller (whose female lead, Angela Crispini, can be viewed as Miller's extension and elaboration on his earlier characters of Roslyn and Maggie). More creatively daring is the approach taken by David Lynch and Mark Frost with their cult TV soap opera *Twin Peaks* (1990).

Roger Vadim's *And God Created Woman* starred Rebecca De Mornay in the role that made an international star of Brigitte Bardot in the 1957 original. In this 1980s update of the tale, De Mornay plays Robin Shay, a poor girl who finds herself in prison. Although she does succeed in escaping, she is surprised when ambitious gubernatorial candidate James Tiernan promptly deposits her back there. Once returned, she succeeds at seducing handsome young carpenter Billy Moran, who ends up marrying her and wins her parole.

Despite all Billy does for her, Robin refuses to have sexual relations with him. Instead, she pours all her considerable energy into becoming a rock-and-roll singer with the band of lusty men she puts together. Also, she finds the time to carry on an illicit affair with the married Tiernan. To retaliate, Billy picks up a woman. But soon, he and Robin come to realize how much they mean to one another. However, Billy blows up when he sees Robin performing her raunchy rock-and-roll act. When all her uninhibited behavior gets her in trouble with her parole board, Robin turns to the powerful Tiernan for his help. Jealous over her love for Billy, he refuses, but the repentant Billy helps Robin win her freedom.

Over thirty years after Vadim had made Brigitte Bardot an international star in *And God Created Woman*, he attempted to do the same with Rebecca De Mornay. But, unfortunately, lightning did not strike twice for either Vadim or De Mornay. And in some ways, this is too bad because De Mornay gives a solid performance. She's most persuasive as a beaten-down young woman who has been so used up by life that she is now hell-bent on using life to get her what she wants out of it for a change. Instead of Marilyn Monroe struggling to be a movie star in the Hollywood of the 1940s and 1950s, Vadim's Marilyn Monroe–inspired heroine struggles to make it as a rock star in the Santa Fe music scene of the late 1980s. And, sadly, things don't appear to have changed all that much in all that time. All throughout the narrative, De Mornay's Robin has her talent and ambition denigrated by powerful men who constantly exploit her.

What is markedly different between the real Marilyn and Vadim's 1980s version of her is that both he and De Mornay work hard to give the heroine such a tough, hard edge that she ends up having much more in common with Madonna's 1980s reinterpretation of Marilyn than she does with Marilyn herself. At the end of the movie, Robin becomes a successful rock star, and she also gets her man. But this doesn't happen to her by chance alone. No, it happens because once she wills it to happen, nothing can stand in her way.

The protagonist of Arthur Miller's *Everybody Wins* is private eye Tom O'Toole. He lives in a small, decaying industrial town in New England with his sarcastic, spinster schoolteacher sister Connie. One day Tom is summoned by mysterious blonde beauty Angela Crispini, a woman of less-than-spotless reputation. Angela convinces him to investigate the case of Felix Daniels, a young man wrongly convicted of brutally murdering his wealthy old uncle. After Tom agrees to help Felix, Angela rewards Tom by seducing him. Lured into the mystery by Angela, Tom learns many unsettling things from her: Angela is a mentally unbalanced woman who believes she is several different women in one, she is a sometimes prostitute who was brutally raped by her father as a child, she is part of a huge drug ring involving the police and many local officials, and she is a lapsed Catholic who has told her priest, Father Mancini, that Tom is her lifeline.

Connie, growing increasingly distrustful of Angela, gets upset when Tom goes to her aid after she is savagely beaten by one of her many ex-lovers. But in this, Tom learns that although Angela was implicated in the crime, she is also his only real hope of ever clearing the innocent Felix. On Tom's advice, Angela goes to see powerful Judge Murdoch to confess her guilt and tell him everything she knows of the town's corruption. Although Judge Murdoch does free the innocent Felix, he does nothing about the town's corruption. When Tom expresses his disappointment at the Judge's decision to Angela, she informs him that she and Judge Murdoch are now lovers. Angela then goes to a lavish party at the Judge's palatial mansion, while the defeated Tom heads off into the engulfing blackness and uncertainty of the dark night.

In creating the character of Angela, Arthur Miller turns to Marilyn Monroe once again for his creative inspiration for the third time. And the cinematic vehicle he has constructed around her character is a complex puzzle of a movie filled with all sorts of metaphysical, theological, and psychological overtones. Ostensibly, the plot of the movie takes the form of a traditional murder mystery. However, what ends up lifting it high above the formulaic narrative pattern of its genre is the way Miller chooses to place the Marilyn-inspired character of Angela at the pulsating heart of both the densely plotted action and the final mystery.

In *Everybody Wins*, what is at stake is the innocence of a young man, Felix, wrongly convicted of murder. Because he so strongly believes that Angela holds the key to setting Felix free, Tom finds himself becoming deeply involved with her to solve the mystery. But each time, Angela only ends up frustrating his efforts, thrusting him deeper and deeper into a state of uncertainty. The truth for Tom must, then, always remain frustratingly elusive and forever out of his reach. In this way, the truth is much like Angela herself with all the multiple personalities that inhabit her troubled soul. Much like an actress who does not know when to stop her acting, Angela is an enigma. She is a tempting child-woman. She is an archetype. There is no way that Tom (or any other man) can ever understand why Angela is the way she is or why she does the things she does.

Even with all her different personalities, there is something of both Roslyn from *The Misfits* and Maggie from *After the Fall* (and therefore also much of Marilyn) in the character of Angela. She is most like Roslyn whenever her warm, loving, seductive side emerges, as when she makes love to Tom, defends the innocent Felix, and turns to Father Mancini to save her soul. Yet whenever Tom believes that he might be falling in love with Angela and has a handle on her behavior, he is soon confounded on both accounts when the disturbing Maggie-like side of her personality suddenly surfaces. This happens when Tom goes to the mill to question a suspect and instead finds Angela there. Only now she is no longer the Angela he thinks he knows. She has become the exceedingly haughty and derisive figure of Renata, behaving as if she doesn't even know who Tom is.

In one scene, Angela pleases; in the other, she provokes. In both modes, her behavior opens up a narrative space in which mystery and madness are crystallized. But in this crystallization there is never much clarification. Still, if Angela's behavior ends up distancing Tom from her, their relationship never descends to the level of psychological despair reached by Quentin and Maggie in *After the Fall*. And *Everybody Wins* does not conclude as pessimistically as *After the Fall* did with Maggie made into a dead body. No, in this depiction, Angela is still very much alive and in control, as was Roslyn at the end of *The Misfits*, as she assumes her final role, that of the traditional Hollywood femme fatale. Like the character of Angela that Marilyn played in *The Asphalt Jungle*, this Angela also aligns herself to security and wealth as the mistress of the rich, old, and powerful Judge Murdoch. And when she tells Tom at the end of the movie that everybody wins, it is with only the bitterest irony that he must accept her interpretation of the surprising turn of events.

A similar ironic tone also runs through the TV soap opera *Twin Peaks* (and especially in the way that it can be viewed as a roman à clef depiction of Marilyn Monroe). It seems that after the critical and commercial success of his cult movie *Blue Velvet* (1985), director David Lynch, along with his writing partner Mark Frost, was hired to develop Anthony Summers's *Goddess* (which served as the basis for the documentary *The Last Days of Marilyn Monroe*) into a roman à clef movie about the death of Marilyn. With the new title of *Venus Descending*, the team created a narrative that begins in 1962 with the mysterious death of famous Hollywood sex goddess Rosilyn Ramsay (the obvious Marilyn Monroe figure). Before her demise, Rosilyn descends into a state of depression and drug addiction after her last lover, Attorney General Phillip Malloy (who is also the brother of the president), abruptly ends his affair with her. Lynch and Frost actually go much further than even Summer did in *Goddess*. For they make Attorney General Malloy the heroine's murderer. When the financing for *Venus Descending* dried up, Lynch and Frost basically reworked the better part of their characterization of Rosilyn Ramsay into the doomed figure of Laura Palmer in their TV series *Twin Peaks*.

Bringing an unprecedented artistic sensibility to American television, Lynch and Frost placed a great emphasis on sophisticated visual imagery, lighting, music, and evocative sound effects as they told their darkly brilliant tale of the small American town Twin Peaks being totally torn apart when it learns of the brutal murder of the sweet and innocent Homecoming Queen—the blonde and beautiful Laura Palmer. Not long after her battered, nude, plastic-wrapped corpse is washed ashore, all sorts of deep, dark secrets about Laura's hidden private life are revealed. It is in the revelation of the dualistic nature of Laura's troubled psyche that Lynch and Frost extensively draw on the characterization of Rosilyn Ramsay (as they derived her from the portrayal of Marilyn Monroe in the pages of *Goddess*). As it happens, the similarities between Laura Palmer and Summers's conception of Marilyn are too numerous to list in full. So we shall just point out some of these. Both are the daughters of mentally unstable mothers, both pose nude for sexy photographs on red velvet drapery, and both keep secret red diaries in which they record the intimate details of their love affairs with powerful, exploitive men. Finally, the fact that both Rosilyn Ramsay and Laura Palmer are brutally murdered by their last lovers speaks volumes about the harsh psychosexual realities of the sinister worlds they inhabit (that is, Hollywood and *Twin Peaks*).

NOTES

1. We are most particularly influenced in our discussion of Jayne Mansfield and her "star" image by the powerful biography by Martha Sexton, *Jayne Mansfield and the American Fifties* (Boston: Houghton Mifflin, 1975).

2. Jeffrey Robinson, *Bardot: An Intimate Portrait* (New York: Donald I. Fine, 1996), 73.

3. John Baxter, "The Sixties," in *Hollywood: 1920–1970*, ed. Peter Cowie (New York: A. S. Barnes, 1977), 255.

4. Charles Higham, *The Art of the American Film 1900–1971* (New York: Doubleday, 1973), 272.

5. Neil Carson, *Arthur Miller* (New York: Grove Press, 1982), 107.

6. Robert Brustein, *Seasons of Discontent* (New York: Simon and Schuster, 1965), 246.

7. Clifton W. Trowbridge, "Arthur Miller: Between Pathos and Tragedy," in *Arthur Miller*, ed. Harold Bloom (New York: Chelsea House, 1987), 47.

8. Pauline Kael, *Reeling* (Boston: Little, Brown, 1976), 451.

9. Alvah Bessie, *The Symbol* (New York: Random House, 1966).

10. S. Paige Baty, *American Monroe: The Making of a Body Politic* (Berkeley: University of California Press, 1995), 116.

• 3 •

Marilyn Monroe as a (Documentary) Subject

The 1960s saw four different documentaries about Marilyn Monroe's life and death. She hadn't even been dead a week when CBS threw together the half-hour documentary *Marilyn Monroe, Why?* (1962) as part of its *Eyewitness* program. The overall tone of the piece is respectful enough, even if there is something of a slapdash quality to it all. Featured are clips from *The Misfits* (1961) and some footage from one of her very rare television appearances (in 1955) on Edward R. Murrow's famous interview program *Person to Person*.

Marilyn Monroe, Why? also features brief interviews with some of the more important people from her life: Emmeline Snivley, head of the Blue Book Modeling Agency, who signed the young Norma Jean Baker to a contract in 1945; Lee Strasberg, artistic director of the Actors Studio, who became Marilyn's teacher and mentor; George Cukor, legendary Hollywood director of such classic movies as *Dinner at Eight* (1933), *Camille* (1936), *The Philadelphia Story* (1940), and *A Star Is Born* (1954) as well as Marilyn's *Let's Make Love* (1960) and her unfinished last movie, the 1962 *Something's Got to Give*; Jean Negulesco, who directed her in her early movie hit *How to Marry a Millionaire* (1953); and Clifford Odets, renowned playwright of such acclaimed stage dramas as *Awake and Sing* (1935) and *Golden Boy* (1937). An Odets play was also the basis for one of Marilyn's better early movies, *Clash by Night* (1952).

Although *Marilyn Monroe, Why?* has this rather thrown-together feel, it does serve its ultimate purpose because it activates and actualizes many of the more important themes of future Marilyn Monroe depictions. Such themes include her questionable childhood and early environment of emotional deprivation, her own psychological instability, and her often-cruel exploitation by the men in her life and by the powerful men of Hollywood.

The 1963 documentary *Marilyn Monroe* seems to have relied on whatever available film footage that the producers could get their hands on. There is then that same rather slapdash feel that we experienced with the 1962 *Marilyn Monroe, Why?* Fortunately, however, there is Mike Wallace to help hold everything together with his concise and informative narration. Additionally, Andre de Dienes (Marilyn paramour and photographer who took some of the most beautiful photographs ever taken of her when she was very young) designed the superb photo sequences, which, along with Wallace, are the best things about the documentary.

A second, more costly documentary produced in 1963 took a much different approach to Marilyn's life. For instance, sweeping, romantic movie music is first heard, and the name "Marilyn"—in glowing white letters!—appears against the luxurious, silky blue backdrop. Thus begins this fittingly loving cinematic tribute to the late Marilyn Monroe by her own home studio, 20th Century-Fox. Essentially, what we are presented with is a veritable cinematic feast of many of her most memorable Fox movies (*All About Eve, Niagara, Gentlemen Prefer Blondes, The Seven Year Itch, Bus Stop*) accompanied by the snappy narration of Rock Hudson.

It is unfortunate that *Marilyn* uses only the movies that she made for Fox. Not only does this tend to limit the ultimate scope of the documentary, it also means that some of her best movie roles are absent, most notably, her sultry gangster's moll in *The Asphalt Jungle* (1950), her luscious Sugar Kane in *Some Like It Hot* (1959), or her immensely moving portrayal of Roslyn in *The Misfits* (1961).

These problems aside, the one place where *Marilyn* does get it right is in its generous sampling of clips from Marilyn's movies. *Variety* acknowledged the cinematic magic of these clips that show Marilyn "at the absolute apex of her beauty yet so near the end." [June 14, 1963]

In 1966, David L. Wolper (of TV's *Roots* and *The Thorn Birds* fame) produced *The Legend of Marilyn Monroe*. Director John Huston's sonorous narration guides us through the highlights of Marilyn's life. Starting off with her early modeling days at Emmeline Snively's Blue Book Modeling Agency, the film moves on to her eventual rise in Hollywood. Initially, she is locked into the image of the eternal dumb blonde; only later does she successfully fight the studio bosses to prove herself a fine screen actress in such films as *Bus Stop* (1956) and *Some Like It Hot* (1959). Huston describes how in her hands the worn-out cliché of the dumb Hollywood blonde became elevated to the level of true cinematic art. And it is during the making of Huston's *The Misfits* (1961) that Marilyn's dependence on pills and alcohol is at an all time high, causing him to remark,

> Roslyn, Miller's heroine, of course, closely resembled Marilyn. Sometimes
> I had the sense that we were in another dimension, that we were hearing
> Marilyn's own cry against the many brutal violations of her life.

Huston goes on to tell of how after *The Misfits* was completed, Marilyn's marriage to Arthur Miller fell totally apart, which sent her into an emotional tailspin. From this point on, the pace of the documentary tends to grow a little too abrupt for its own good, as it more or less rushes through the last year of Marilyn's life. We are either told or else briefly shown images of her looking increasingly depressed and confused. Although she is fired from her last movie, *Something's Got to Give*, she buys her first home in Brentwood: a Spanish Colonial hacienda, with the Latin inscription *Curium Perficio* on the doorstep, translating to "I have completed my journey." Marilyn found great comfort in that message, which oddly seems to have foreshadowed her imminent death.

Finally, it is through his connection to the Democratic Party that Wolper was able to get use of the only known footage of Marilyn's singing of "Happy Birthday" to President Kennedy at his birthday party in Madison Square Garden. This extended sequence is one of the documentary's true high points. If the last part of *The Legend of Marilyn Monroe* leaves us feeling somewhat unsatisfied, then it is to Wolper and his associates that credit must go for coming up with a documentary about Marilyn that is honest, fair, and, for the most part, insightful.

The only documentary of any real note about Marilyn Monroe produced in the 1970s was *Marilyn Remembered* (1974). But it was really nothing more than a revised version of the documentary *The Legend of Marilyn Monroe*. Along with some new footage, additional commentary was added from two people who knew Marilyn very well, Peter Lawford and Shelley Winters. It should be pointed out, however, that the production of documentaries about Marilyn in the future would become a considerable cinematic oeuvre worthy of a whole separate study of their own.

After the paucity of documentary depictions of the 1970s, the 1980s seem a more fertile period. For there were three documentaries produced about the life and times of Marilyn Monroe: the 1985 *The Last Days of Marilyn Monroe* (a.k.a. *Marilyn, Say Goodbye to the President*), the 1987 *Marilyn Monroe: Beyond the Legend*, and the 1988 *Remembering Marilyn*. The first of these, *The Last Days of Marilyn Monroe*, is a BBC-produced documentary that puts forth the question, Did Marilyn Monroe actually commit suicide on the night of August 5, 1962, or was she instead the victim of foul play? Certainly, the question was not exactly new in 1985. For there had been considerable speculation as to the exact cause of Marilyn's premature end all throughout the latter part of the 1960s.

And as the 1970s progressed, these speculations found their most complete expression when Norman Mailer, with the publication of his 1973 biography *Marilyn*, became the first mainstream writer to print the names of JFK and RFK in connection to Marilyn's decline in the last year of her life and also in connection with her death. It was finally with the publication of investigative British journalist Anthony Summers's book *Goddess: The Secret Lives of Marilyn Monroe*, as well as the major role he plays in the making of this 1985 documentary, that one of the more detailed filmic cases is made supporting the allegations that Marilyn's death was actually more along the lines of a homicide rather than a suicide.

The Last Days of Marilyn Monroe begins by establishing the fact that Marilyn was indeed intimately involved with both John and Robert Kennedy. A battery of surveillance experts attest to the fact that many of her romantic trysts with the Kennedys took place at the beachfront home of their brother-in-law Peter Lawford. Unbeknownst to all of them was the fact that Lawford's home was thoroughly wired for sound. This meant that Marilyn's intimate interludes with the Kennedy brothers were captured on tape for all of posterity. Not too surprisingly, many people were interested in these sexy tapes for one reason or another. This cast of curious characters included many. Joe DiMaggio—who detested the Kennedys and was distrustful of their motives regarding Marilyn—was one. Another was Teamster boss and another profound Kennedy hater, Jimmy Hoffa. The documentary makes the claim that Hoffa, in fact, got hold of copies of the tapes and that he was ready to use them, if need be, to destroy the political careers of his two hated archenemies. But the question of whatever became of this important evidence is left unanswered and unsolved.

Along with DiMaggio and Hoffa, some of the other characters in the cast are unsavory agents from the FBI, CIA, and KGB and even the infamous Mafia kingpin Sam Giancana and company. Complicating things even further is the fact that so many of the important file documents and the results of medical tests performed on Marilyn during the coroner's autopsy have gone missing. And several individuals, including the first police officer to arrive at her home, positively insist that her death was definitely a homicide.

One of the most intriguing aspects of *The Last Days of Marilyn Monroe* is the crucial role that Robert Kennedy played. After JFK had more or less passed Marilyn onto his younger brother, matters became much more complicated because of Bobby's more genuine affection for her, which was diametrically opposite to the love-em-and-leave-em attitude JFK always took toward his various glamorous mistresses. Perhaps it is the complex feelings Robert had for Marilyn that account for much of what this documentary claims to have happened. Since this was no small affair for him, he found it extremely difficult to end the relationship. And, according to many of those interviewed, Marilyn's own mental and emotional states were such at the time that RFK's rejection of her proved to be a most devastating blow. Thrust into the role of a woman scorned, she is said to have made plans to call a press conference to reveal to the world the full truth about the Kennedys. At this press conference, she purportedly planned to reveal all sorts of secret information he confided to her about the Mafia–CIA plot to kill Castro and the various schemes to bring down Jimmy Hoffa.

Although RFK always claimed he was in San Francisco during the final weekend of Marilyn's life, many refute this account. Instead, we repeatedly hear that he was at her Brentwood home on the day of her death and that he fled the scene of the crime in a helicopter so as not to implicate himself. As RFK made his escape from the death scene, the ambulance driver who found the unconscious Marilyn claims that she was still alive and did not die until much later at the hospital. This is all said to have occurred three hours before she was "officially" found dead in her bed.

The depiction of Marilyn's death here is a troubling one. In her precarious mental state, she proves a tremendous danger to all these powerful men involved with her. If even the least bit of knowledge were to get out of her intimate connection to Camelot, it could mean the destruction of all those involved. We have seen Marilyn depicted in a comparable way in the movie *Winter Kills*, within a totally fictionalized context, and in the role of a supporting player. Here, however, she is the leading lady, and the context is intended to signify the "real, unvarnished truth." Still, we cannot help but be struck by just how equally fantastic and fictional seeming are the Byzantine twists and turns of the conspiracy as well as the general unsavoriness of the cast of characters.

The other two documentaries of the decade celebrate Marilyn Monroe in different ways. *Marilyn Monroe: Beyond the Legend* is a tribute that focuses almost exclusively on her achievement as a movie actress. It is made up of a compendium of movie clips (thankfully, now even her non–20th Century-Fox great roles are included), along with newsreel footage, still photographs, and interviews with those who either knew her or worked with her.

Among those interviewed for this production are Celeste Holm, Joshua Logan, Robert Mitchum, Don Murray, and Shelley Winters. All these interviewees offer up some interesting observations about a fact that is all too often glossed over or simply ignored: Marilyn's intense devotion to her chosen art—screen acting. Celeste Holm makes several astute observations about her unique approach to acting. Many of her remarks touch on that side of Marilyn's talent that flourished during the 1950s at the Actors Studio in New York, where Marilyn went to experience a higher level of artistic expression and a heightened dramatic reality over what Hollywood offered her. While enrolled as a student there, she is said to have enacted dramatic scenes from *Golden Boy*, *A Streetcar Named Desire*, and *Anna Christie*. She would then apply all that she had learned at the Actors Studio to arguably her best movie performance in *Bus Stop*. The movie's director, Joshua Logan, appears to attest to the meticulous preparation and care that went into her magnificent performance of Cherie:

> Marilyn got all the ideas. She had the accent down perfect. It was sort of a hillbilly, Southern accent. She knew how to speak it so easily. She had re-hearsed it perfectly. And when they sent drawings to us of show costumes, she said, "I'd like that if only we can just make it look more real." I sud-denly realized that she was a wonderful girl with great, imaginative, funny ideas. She was a wonderful comedian and she was any kind of a serious ac-tress you wanted her to be. She was brilliant. And she was Cherie. That's all. She was just so wonderful in the role. I'd suddenly realized, I had a chance of working with the greatest artist I had ever worked with in my life. And it was—Marilyn Monroe.

Remembering Marilyn is similar to *Marilyn Monroe: Beyond the Legend* in that the approach taken toward Marilyn is a very positive one. But rather than con-centrating exclusively on her achievement as an actress, the film's main em-phasis is an assessment of her overall mystique. The film is narrated by Lee Remick, the actress that 20th Century-Fox lined up to replace Marilyn in the movie *Something's Got to Give* until the film's leading man, Dean Martin, re-fused to act opposite any other leading lady except Marilyn. Later, Remick ad-mitted that she never truly believed the studio would replace Marilyn with her. Instead, she felt they were just using her, as they had always used Marilyn, as leverage to force her to return to work.

If a large part of what we see and hear in this documentary is by now fa-miliar, it nevertheless holds our interest. And the most fascinating aspect of *Re-membering Marilyn* comes in the form of the observations about her made by Su-san Strasberg, Gloria Steinem, Robert Mitchum, and Robert Wagner, among others.

Steinem, who also wrote the excellent revisionist biography *Marilyn/Norma Jean* (1986), brings a sharp, perceptive feminist interpretation to her re-marks. She mentions the fact that although Marilyn did indeed use her body to get ahead in Hollywood, she did so only as a means to get work and not to not have to work. Steinem even attempts to explain what might have become of Marilyn had she not died so young. She imagines all sorts of extraordinary possible Marilyns of the future had she lived.

Actors Robert Mitchum and Robert Wagner reminisce a bit about their working with Marilyn, but Susan Strasberg offers insightful observations that are more along the lines of Steinem's. In a sense, this documentary might be described as "Marilyn seen through women's eyes." In keeping with this over-all feminine impression of things, there is also the voice of Marilyn speaking for herself. In one scene toward the end, she is shown horrendously besieged by hordes of photographers and reporters. In a poignant voiceover, she remarks, "I mean they kind of like taking pieces out of you. And I don't think they realize it. You know, they're kind of like grabbing pieces out of you. And, yes, you do want to stay intact."

In the 1990s, there were seven documentaries devoted to Marilyn Monroe. The first three of these, *Marilyn: Something's Got to Give* (1990), *The Discovery of Marilyn Monroe* (1991), and *Marilyn: The Last Interview* (1992), offer reassessments of her life and career but from three completely different angles. The next two documentaries of the 1990s, *The Marilyn Files* (1992) and *Marilyn: The Last Word* (1993), focus on the seemingly inexhaustible topic of her death. These two documentaries take up where the 1985 documentary *The Last Days of Marilyn Monroe* left off. The final two documentaries, *Marilyn Monroe, Life after Death* (1995) and *Marilyn, The Mortal Goddess* (1996), essentially harken back to the more celebratory tone of Marilyn's life and achievements—albeit now with more of an unflinching honesty—that was first established in 1963 with the documentary *Marilyn*.

The 1963 *Marilyn* was made by her home studio, 20th Century-Fox, which was the same studio that fired her from her last movie, the incomplete *Something's Got to Give*. For years, there has been great intrigue surrounding the quality of Marilyn's appearance and acting ability in the movie. Rumors were circulated by Fox that her physical and mental states were so bad that all the footage she shot for the movie was virtually unusable. Fortunately, writer-director Henry Schipper was able to put together the 1990 documentary *Marilyn: Something's Got to Give*, which allows us to judge for ourselves the veracity of those claims. Schipper assembled twenty minutes of extraordinary scenes from Marilyn's ill-fated last movie that show us a beautiful and most elegant-looking Marilyn being directed by George Cukor and acting most charmingly. As Schipper states, "To the very end, Marilyn Monroe had a beauty and sexual glory that no other actress could touch. And that came across in all her films even the one that never got made."

Something's Got to Give was a remake of the sparkling 1940 screwball comedy *My Favorite Wife*, starring Cary Grant and Irene Dunne. In the 1940 movie, Dunne plays a woman who has returned from a desert island after seven years. Grant has had her declared legally dead, and just as he is preparing to embark on a honeymoon with his new stuck-up wife (Gail Patrick), Dunne reappears to complicate his intentions.

The role that Dunne played in the 1940 movie would seem to be a perfect one for Marilyn in the 1962 remake. With Dean Martin as her leading man and George Cukor as her director, *Something's Got to Give* had all the earmarks of being a sparkling 1960s sophisticated comedy. The movie was even to have included a groundbreaking scene of Marilyn swimming in the nude to entice Martin.

Like many of the heroines in Cukor's movies, the character of Ellen displays many of the same remarkable qualities. As Allen Estrin points out in his study of the director,

> The Cukor heroine may generally be described as intelligent and clever; she is also high-spirited, usually more than a little neurotic, and most importantly, fiercely independent. Although the manner in which these characteristics are expressed differs from heroine to heroine, the impulse behind them is similar. . . . Cukor's heroines are always involved in a personal struggle to prove to themselves and the world their worth as human beings.[1]

This same struggle Estrin describes was not only a part of the character Marilyn played in the movie but also her own personal struggle. Sadly, she would lose this struggle while making Cukor's movie. Traditionally, the blame for the film's failure has been placed solely on Marilyn. In the "official" version of the story, it is because of her chronic illnesses and her alcohol and chemical dependencies that the studio heads at 20th Century-Fox fired her. At the time, a highly placed studio source declared, "Something has to be done with these unprofessional stars—Marilyn Monroe included. We have to sit on them or else forget about the industry!"

In this 1990 revisionist documentary, however, we are given an entirely different version of the facts to consider through a series of interviews with the movie's sympathetic producer, Henry Weinstein, and several members of the cast and crew. According to them, it is not so much the making of Marilyn's sophisticated little romantic comedy that gave the studio brass so much grief as it was the hedonistic and exorbitant costly antics of Elizabeth Taylor on the set of the epic *Cleopatra* in Rome. Between Taylor's adulterous couplings with costar Richard Burton and her own illnesses, *Cleopatra* was well on its way to becoming the most expensive Hollywood movie ever made. In firing Marilyn, the studio was, in effect, both attempting to placate nervous stockholders and using her as their scapegoat. Rather than pull the reins in on Liz Taylor (who was being paid a cool million for *Cleopatra* as opposed to the bargain-basement $100,000 Marilyn was getting for *Something's Got to Give*), the corporate decision was made: Marilyn was expendable.

Without question, the spectacular centerpiece of this documentary is the twenty minutes of footage of Marilyn Monroe starring in *Something's Got to Give*. In *The 50 Greatest Movies Never Made*, Chris Gore sadly laments that her last movie was never finished. He also provides an excellent description of the star as we see her in the scenes from the movie:

> This is not just any Marilyn Monroe. This is a Marilyn Monroe who had come through the experience of making John Huston's *The Misfits*. This is a Marilyn Monroe well on her way into maturing into a great actress. This is a Sixties Marilyn. . . . This Marilyn has a natural, flowing sensuality, with long loose hair and an air of sublime reality.[2]

If the 1990 documentary gave us Marilyn Monroe at the end of her career, *The Discovery of Marilyn Monroe* shows us how the photographic potential of the young Norma Jean was first discovered by David Conover back in 1944. At the time, Norma Jean was only eighteen and doing her effort for World War II by working on the assembly line of the Radio Plane Factory. We are told the story of how Conover went to the factory in search of pretty girls to transform into pinup models to help boost the morale of the American boys fighting overseas. And in one particularly memorable case, his camera does indeed find its perfect subject in the form of the young Norma Jean. Conover is immediately struck by her fresh-scrubbed, apple-pie, all-American-girl charm and beauty. He senses at once the sort of beauty that is the source of the "star quality" that fuels the star system. The narration describes the young, beautiful Norma Jean captured in Conover's images:

> The girl is fresh. She's a youngster. She looks beautiful, healthy, vibrant, and very much the innocent. This is a complete paradox to the general preconceived notion of Marilyn Monroe as the Sex Symbol. And it is such a direct counterpoint, we are stung by it.

The carefree young woman depicted in Conover's photographs juxtaposed against the Hollywood star she will become is actually only one of the many paradoxes the text will open up for us. But in characterizing the young Norma Jean as being so different from the star to come, the moviemakers overlook the even more profound paradox of just how much of Norma Jean got carried over into—and always remained a significant part of—Marilyn Monroe. Almost as if in spite of itself, the documentary opens up several of such paradoxes but never attempts to solve or properly explain them. Perhaps the biggest paradox of all about this documentary is all that lies in between, as it were. It is this "in between" that becomes most fascinating: these unexpected spaces that the text keeps opening up, only to discard or dismiss as irrelevant, are precisely those that are most important.

For example, when the documentary expresses regret over how Norma Jean had to vanish in order to make way for Marilyn, it ignores one crucial fact: when Norma Jean first stepped in front of Conover's camera and came to realize just how much the camera loved her, her life was irrevocably changed forever. And as Conover also realized, there was no way that she could simply remain some anonymous pinup girl after that. Although it is true that in her pinup poses there is the emphasis on her body, there is something more going on in these images as well. For even in these standard pinup poses, her charismatic personality shines through. And it is this charismatic personality that leads directly into Norma Jean the pinup girl becoming first a Hollywood starlet and then finally a genuine star. And with her attaining full-fledged Hollywood stardom, another paradox develops: as a pinup girl and then as a lowly starlet, Marilyn Monroe tirelessly sought out the camera's gaze, but once she became a star, the reverse would occur, and she would flee from the oppressive force of the camera's often much too penetrative gaze.

In 1992, HBO presented the documentary *Marilyn: The Last Interview*. It contains excerpts of an eight-hour audiotaped interview that journalist Richard Meryman conducted with Marilyn Monroe for his August 3, 1962, article in *Life*. The Marilyn interviewed by Meryman comes across as a witty, thoughtful, deeply subjective woman who is at times justifiably angry at the way she has been used and exploited during her life. She begins by expressing her feelings on fame, and much of what she says has a lively, epigrammatic wit and polish to it:

> Fame. It's like caviar. It's good to have caviar, but if you had it every damned day, it's too much caviar. And yet, fame can stir up envy, fame. Who does she think she is, Marilyn Monroe?

As the documentary's narrator, Meryman describes Marilyn experiencing "roller-coaster moods" during the interview, her moods do, however, seem appropriate. When she describes her childhood, a pronounced sadness comes into her voice. This is especially so when she wistfully remarks, "Happiness wasn't something I ever took for granted." And later, while the film shows a wedding photograph of Marilyn and her first husband, Jim Dougherty, whom she married when she was sixteen, Meryman informs us that she emphatically told him in advance that she would not discuss her three husbands. All she says about her marriage to Dougherty is that she wasn't all that much of a housewife because she had "too many fantasies" she wanted to make a reality as a way to make herself happy and find fulfillment.

Marilyn's sense of happiness disappears when she describes how she began to feel at odds with the prescribed role that Hollywood insisted she always play: the dumb, blonde sex goddess, which was something she no longer wanted for herself. Instead, she prefers to be thought of as a serious actress, an artist of the cinema. Although she understands that her physicality will always

be a considerable part of her appeal, she struggles to be recognized for her acting ability. The combination of her physical beauty confining her to roles she
has long outgrown, with her obsessive drive to act against the grain of Hollywood and its conventions, cannot help but make her feel angry and discon-
tented. In fact, it is in her quarrels with the studio bosses and all the dumb,
blonde sexpot roles they forced her to play, to their constant ringing up of
more profits from her movies, right up to their firing her off of *Something's Got
to Give*, that makes them the bane of her existence.

Perhaps the most astonishing thing revealed in this documentary is that
despite everything that Marilyn was subjected to during her life, the woman
who ultimately emerges is a defiant survivor with a wonderfully ironic sense
of humor about it all. Meryman himself tells of how he has gone back to listen to the tapes he made many times to see if there was perhaps something he
could have missed in all the time he spent with Marilyn shortly before her
death. Although he does acknowledge that at various points she would be angry or sad, Meryman claims he never once saw anything of the completely
broken woman who would soon take her own life. What he witnessed instead
was a vital woman, full of all sorts of imaginative plans for the future. So struck
is Meryman over this that, even thirty years afterward, he still finds it difficult
to believe that she actually took her own life.

The next two documentaries of the 1990s, *The Marilyn Files* and *Marilyn:
The Last Word*, like the 1980s documentary *The Last Days of Marilyn Monroe*,
depict Marilyn Monroe as a figure caught up within the machinations of an
out-of-control political conspiracy and its subsequent cover-up. Based on the
book by Robert Slatzer, who claims to have once been secretly married to
Marilyn for a short time (see the 1991 TV movie *Marilyn and Me*), *The Marilyn Files* was a two-hour show broadcast live from Hollywood in 1992. Hosted
by Bill Bixby and Jane Wallace, the documentary is in the form of a mock
courtroom trial. Five former district attorneys and attorneys general listen to
all the evidence to determine if a grand jury should reopen the investigation
into Marilyn's mysterious death.

To keep things moving at a lively pace, the program's producers construct
the documentary as something of a three-ring circus. There's the main action
of the mock trial that takes place live. Then there are the various filmed interviews featuring several witnesses giving testimony that often contradicts the
"official" version of Monroe's death. Finally, there are other filmed sequences,
reenacting the last day of Marilyn's life. Besides Marilyn herself, Robert
Kennedy, Peter Lawford, her psychiatrist Dr. Ralph Greenson, and her house-
keeper Eunice Murray are portrayed by actors. Murray is most fascinating in
this context because her version of Marilyn's death seems to change every time
she tells it, making the "truth" seem ever more elusive and difficult to discover.

In one of the documentary's more harrowing reenactments, ambulance driver James Hill claims to have been present, along with Peter Lawford on behalf of the Kennedys, when Dr. Greenson supposedly injected a lethal dose of a drug directly into the heart of the semiconscious Marilyn, killing her instantly. It is in the depiction of such scenes as this that the documentary moves away from presenting a fact-based investigation and moves more into the realm of embellished, fictionalized speculation and conjecture. Consequently, it often becomes difficult to believe fully in everything that is being depicted.

Interestingly, the matter of Marilyn's "secret" red diary, which she is said to have kept (and which was only briefly mentioned in *The Last Days of Marilyn Monroe*), becomes a most crucial piece of evidence here. Actually, there is much evidence that Marilyn was known to have religiously kept such a daily diary as early as 1951. According to one of the documentary's witnesses, coroner's aide Lionel Grandison, the diary's pages held,

> A very interesting series of stories, or assessments, of evaluations about many things that were apparently going on in Marilyn's life—John F. Kennedy, Robert F. Kennedy, the Mafia—those kinds of catch phrases. . . . There was something to look at a little more thoroughly, to see what she was saying there.

Along with being the first depiction to place such prominent significance on the role of Marilyn's diary, this documentary posits a concise outline, consisting of the conglomeration of major questions all relating to the events of August 5, 1962, to form a supertheory of conspiracy:

- Although Marilyn is said to have taken forty sleeping pills to kill herself, why were there no traces of capsules found in her stomach? Also, with no water in the bedroom or even a glass found there, how was she able to swallow the pills?
- Why was she "officially" pronounced dead after 4:00 A.M. when the condition of her body suggests she died hours before?
- Although two of her doctors attest to giving her needles in the last three days of her life (and even billed her estate), why were no needle marks found on her body?
- What happened to all the official autopsy reports, body parts, and pieces of tissue conducted on Marilyn?
- Even though it was always claimed that RFK was in San Francisco on the night of August 4, 1962, why do at least half a dozen people swear to have seen him in Los Angeles on that night?
- Why did so many of Marilyn's neighbors claim to have spotted various ambulances outside her house on that night?

- What happened to her secret red diary?
- What did Dr. Greenson confide to the district attorney that convinced him Marilyn's death was not a suicide?
- Was Marilyn worth more to the studio dead? How much was 20th Century-Fox able to collect on the insurance policy it had on her?
- What role did the CIA play?
- What about the Mafia?
- What role did the Kennedys play in Marilyn's death? Did they later orchestrate a massive cover-up?

The Marilyn Files concludes with the five-member jury voting unanimously for the grand jury to reopen the Marilyn Files to learn what actually did happen to Marilyn Monroe on the last day of her life in order that justice might, finally, be served.

A call for justice is also at the heart of *Marilyn: The Last Word*. Hosted by Barry Nolan and Terry Murphy, this documentary takes up the rallying cry of *The Marilyn Files* one year later. Once again, a complex network of theories and hypotheses concerning the cause of Marilyn Monroe's death is presented. And once again the cast of characters includes the Kennedys, Dr. Greenson, Eunice Murray, Peter Lawford, J. Edgar Hoover, Jimmy Hoffa, Sam Giancana, and the Mafia, among others. The film also places a tremendous amount of significance on the importance of Marilyn's secret diary, even claiming that RFK had read the diary and was enraged over its explosive contents.

The diary incident and several other episodes from Marilyn's life are meticulously re-created in the form of these elaborate, vérité-style reenactments. The most amazing thing about these reenacted sequences is just how cinematically engaging they turn out to be. Conceived and directed as something of a suspenseful narrative, these sequences depict Marilyn as being full of hope and optimism, something that is borne out in the early mise-en-scène. The elaborate use of color coding is as involved and intricate as it was in Norman Mailer's *Strawhead*. The colors surrounding Marilyn are generally warm and gentle, signifying the order and consistency of her life. There is a preponderance of the colors white, pale yellow, and soft pastel tones in the organization of the contents of the frame. And Marilyn, with her pale gold hair and dressed in pink, lavender, and mint green, blends in altogether perfectly with her setting. The mise-en-scène suggests a perfect, feminine space where the heroine and her world are one and the same, together, in complete and perfect harmony.

In opposition to the symbolic unity of Marilyn's feminine world, the documentary depicts the other world of powerful men. It is in this shadowy world that the Kennedys reside, as do J. Edgar Hoover and the FBI, the CIA,

Jimmy Hoffa, Sam Giancana and the Mafia, Frank Sinatra, Peter Lawford, the Hollywood studio bosses, and so on. In this frightening nighttime realm, everything is dark, ominous, and dangerous. Everything is so harsh in this world, and when there is color, it is torrid and garish, and it appears in occasional, disturbing flickers, like the jarring flash of deep red scattered all throughout the masculinized mise-en-scène.

It is in this dangerous world of powerful men that Marilyn is most cruelly mistreated, manipulated, and sexually debased and abused. Her abusers include not only the Kennedys but also Frank Sinatra and Sam Giancana and an operative for the CIA who attempts to set her up in a sexual tryst with President Sukarno of Indonesia as a means of blackmailing him. It is also in this masculine world that one of the more disturbing reenactments occurs. In this sequence, Sinatra lures Marilyn to his Cal-Neva Casino at Lake Tahoe. After plying her with drink and drugs, both he and Giancana take turns brutally raping her until she loses consciousness.

Yet, as bad as the scene with Sinatra and Giancana undeniably is, even it pales in comparison to what occurs to both Marilyn and her harmonious, feminine world when the chaotic masculine world forcefully intrudes on it. When this happens, we become acutely aware of the incompatibility of these two separate spaces. And, regrettably, it is the keeping of Marilyn's own "blood-red" secret diary that causes the world of powerful men to come crashing so forcibly into her own. This occurs when RFK finds out about the secret diary and, accompanied by the sycophantic Lawford, goes to Marilyn's home on the night of August 4 to confront her and retrieve the diary from her. With their harsh treatment, Marilyn becomes hysterical, causing the two men to heavily drug her and put her to bed. They leave without finding her diary. Later in the evening, two of Giancana's henchmen next go to Marilyn's home and kill her by administering a lethal suppository. When Eunice Murray later discovers the unconscious Marilyn, she phones Dr. Greenson, who arranges for an ambulance to take her to the hospital. After she dies in the ambulance, her body is then returned back to her bed. RFK is notified, and it is under his orders that government agents (possibly the CIA or FBI) are brought in, first to sweep her home of all possible traces of her relationship with the Kennedys and then to set the stage so that it looks as if she took her own life. Empty pill bottles are scattered all about the bedroom, and a telephone is placed in her hand. And, in the end, it is the aggressively masculine that wins out over the doomed figure of woman in the form of Marilyn's dead body.

The 1994 documentary *Marilyn Monroe, Life after Death* is essentially a cinematic tribute to Marilyn Monroe's beauty, talent, and continuing popular appeal. One of the more notable elements about this documentary is that it was produced with the full cooperation of Anthony and Joshua Greene, sons of the late, great photographer Milton Greene, who was so instrumental in Marilyn's rebellion against Hollywood. It was this involvement with Greene and his wife Amy that served as the basis for the play *Strawhead*.

Not too surprisingly, the presentation of Greene's photographs of Marilyn proves to be one of the two main reasons why this documentary is so memorable. The other is the haunting musical score of composer Peter Carl Ganderup. The documentary opens with an evocative black-and-white sequence of endless rows of Marilyn masks being mass-produced on an assembly line. Ganderup's music is most compelling with its rippling yet still subdued lyricism. The music then quietly drops off as we are next shown black-and-white film footage of the night of Marilyn's death and the day of her funeral. These elegiac scenes are interspersed with color segments in which people who were acquainted with her discuss their responses to the sudden news of her death. Lee Strasberg is next heard delivering his eloquent eulogy for Marilyn:

> When she first came to me, I was amazed at the startling sensitivity, which she possessed. . . . Others were physically as beautiful as she was, but there was obviously something more in her, something people saw and recognized in her performances and with which they identified.

As Strasberg concludes by stating that Marilyn's talent was no mirage, a montage of Greene's images appear, while Ganderup's music perfectly captures the mood created in the eulogy for Marilyn juxtaposed against Greene's ravishing images of her in life. At the completion of Strasberg's eulogy, a close-up of a smiling Marilyn fills the screen. But then, the unexpected occurs. The "positive" of her face is suddenly transformed into a negative. The photograph of a glowing, happy Marilyn becomes a haunting, shadowy presence. This effect serves to remind us that no matter what we or even all the people in this documentary may think we know about her, there is still much that will remain forever unknown and mysterious.

Although the rest of the documentary is nowhere near as rich as this sequence, it does present an interesting assortment of individuals who all contribute their various perceptions on Marilyn's rise to stardom and her ultimate immortality. Donald Spoto, who wrote the 1993 biography *Marilyn Monroe, The Biography*, highlights her bravura performance in *Bus Stop*. And Amy Greene speaks of the Marilyn that she came to know so well in the 1950s. The last section of the documentary details the many ways that Marilyn continues to live on through her life and movies and as the divine muse who inspires so many. From Andy Warhol's pop-art images, to all the books that have been written about her, to all the thriving Marilyn merchandise—dolls, posters, calendars, telephones, mugs, even wine—she has become a significant part of the texture of our everyday lives.

If the six other documentaries of the 1990s have examined specific aspects of Marilyn Monroe's life from six different perspectives, the final documentary of the 1990s, *Marilyn: The Mortal Goddess*, takes a different approach. In this documentary, Marilyn's life is presented in full. The rich narrative begins with an account of her mother, Gladys, being confined to an asylum and the unwanted child Norma Jean being forced to live in a series of dehumanizing orphanages and foster homes. In keeping with the overall moral tone established from the outset, the documentary judges and condemns what Norma Jean is made to suffer as a child:

> It is while she is in the care of couples that took her in only to profit from government welfare assistance. And the little girl felt isolated and insecure and easy prey to the horrors of emotional and even sexual abuse.

Consonant with this is the fact that even in spite of her predicament, Norma Jean is a beautiful child who perfectly fits the model of the pretty little girl. And from pretty little girl, she soon grows into a beautiful young woman. But with the circumstances of her life such as they are, it becomes imperative for her to escape from the harsh reality of her daily existence. She accomplishes this by projecting herself into the more fantastic, imaginary realm of Hollywood and the movies:

> Hiding in the shadows of the silver screen, Norma Jean could escape into a world where men like Clark Gable and women like Jean Harlow used glamour and sex to obtain power. Emotionally alone, Norma Jean craved attention, especially the kind she saw lavished on her beloved screen idols.

But before that can happen, a shift occurs in Norma Jean's focus, and the beautiful, young woman first attempts to play the role of a housewife when she gets married to Jim Dougherty. Projecting a dignified presence, Marilyn's first husband even appears to attest to the happiness of their marriage. Despite Dougherty's obvious sincerity, we know that her real destiny lays in the fantasyland that helped shape her imagination: Hollywood. Thus, the fine line between fantasy and reality becomes inextricably blurred for her. Yet Marilyn always manages to keep her head about her whenever the need arises no matter what. When the press discovers she is the beautiful nude woman depicted in all the gas stations and locker rooms across Eisenhower's 1950s America, Marilyn honestly admits that she is indeed the popular calendar's shapely subject:

> By facing the scandal head on, Marilyn dealt a devastating blow to the conservative standards of 1950s America. She now represented a refreshing reinterpretation of the Modern Woman. One who was not willing to equate sex with sin.

The documentary depicts Joe DiMaggio as it does Johnny Hyde, as being one of the most heroic and decent of the men in Marilyn's life. The only problem, however, is that she once again rejects her Prince Charming. For all his wealth and fame, Joe is nothing more than a glorified version of her first husband. And if she didn't want to play the role of devoted wife when she was only the ordinary Norma Jean, why would she want to play it as the extraordinary Marilyn Monroe? Her problems with Joe are relatively minor ones compared to what she faces from 20th Century-Fox. Refusing to accept any more of the lightweight, forgettable roles offered her, Marilyn turns her back on Hollywood, goes to New York, and forms Marilyn Monroe Productions with Milton Greene.

It is while in New York that she begins her work with Lee Strasberg at the Actors Studio. If Marilyn triumphs as a dramatic actress under Strasberg's guidance, in many ways her victory is a Pyrrhic one at best. The intense style of acting Strasberg espoused required her to use much of her private inner life to create her art, forcing her to confront a tremendous amount of psychological pain and anguish for the first time in her life. In *The Actors Studio, A History*, Shelley Frame writes,

> The painful past Marilyn offered Strasberg . . . included a haunting moment when, as a very young child in her hometown of Los Angeles, she was told she was just going for a ride and then abandoned at the orphanage. She screamed and protested that it was all a mistake. She had no father. She was led to believe that she was illegitimate, the product of sin. She was worthless. And her mother could never come to her aid; she was a paranoid schizophrenic who had tried to smother Marilyn in her crib when she was an infant . . . and the list of painful memories only mounted.[3]

As a direct result of Strasberg's teachings, all of Marilyn's deep-rooted fears and insecurities surface and take a devastating toll on her. She grows anxious and develops problems sleeping, and her reliance on pills and alcohol intensifies. Yet she withstands the pain of her chaotic life in order to obtain recognition and acceptance as a serious dramatic actress. The documentary suggests that her eventual marriage to Arthur Miller is also a part of her constant longing for respectability. So in awe of the Pulitzer Prize–winning playwright is she that he quickly becomes a major component of her goal for her life as well.

The documentary depicts Arthur's having many reservations toward Strasberg, though he essentially stands back and allows Marilyn to get more deeply involved with Lee and Paula Strasberg, who soon becomes a proxy for her husband. It is Paula who becomes Marilyn's constant companion and personal acting coach, and it is her very presence on the sets of Marilyn's movies that creates numerous problems. Simultaneously, her marriage to Arthur goes through serious problems of its own. Her inability to carry a baby to term, her pill and alcohol abuse, and her affair with Yves Montand soon spell an end to the union. Although the tone of the narrative grows noticeably somber as Marilyn sinks deeper and deeper into a downward spiral of drug abuse and total despair, resulting in her death in 1962, the documentary's concluding images are of all the Marilyn Monroe books and merchandise that are now available for consumption on a worldwide scale. And, in the final analysis, the film reinforces the notion that today Marilyn has become "an ageless deity, her platinum hair has become a golden halo, her sensuous face a shining icon." But if Marilyn has become such a sterling goddess, the last words we hear are her own, confirming that she herself always knew she was all along simply just the Goddess of the People.

The four documentary depictions produced thus far in the new millennium give us examples of how the meaning of Marilyn Monroe can be replayed, reinterpreted, and even contradicted to fit the creative developments of the new century. The first documentary, *The Death of Marilyn Monroe* (2000), owes a certain debt to Norman Mailer's *Strawhead* (in its use of color coding) and to the three earlier documentaries: *The Last Days of Marilyn Monroe, The Marilyn Files,* and *Marilyn: The Last Word.* It cannot be said of this new documentary that it does much in the way of adding anything new or dramatically different from those others. It does, however, manage to come up with some perceptive observations from two writers who had recently written books about Marilyn—Joyce Carol Oates (*Blonde,* 1999) and Donald Wolfe (*The Last Days of Marilyn Monroe,* 1998). And, as has been stated, the influence of the technique of color coding also warrants attention.

With regard to this matter, Marilyn gets rendered in this depiction as a most seductive collision of color, design, and alluring texture. What this does is make us initially think that this text is going to be something of a celebration of her lush physical beauty (as was seen in the documentary *Marilyn Monroe, Life after Death*). But suddenly, that impression dissolves away as she is soon rendered as being something of a blonde beauty who is also a blonde dumb bunny, like a windup life-size doll with a sleepy-little-girl voice and glowing, come-hither eyes. But then, even that impression quickly changes when she is next rendered as a suicidal neurotic prepared to cut herself off from all traces of the signified in a moment. We are informed that she had attempted suicide several times in the past and often with barbiturates.

Marilyn as suicidal blonde then emerges as the condition for a new possibility for reflection, originally grounded and even sanctified in the so-called official version of her death as being classified a probable suicide. It takes the more reflective presence of Joyce Carol Oates to uncover the possibility of a truth disclosed between the alternatives of Marilyn as blonde dumb bunny and

Marilyn as suicidal blonde: "The Marilyn persona was constructed at the time of *Gentlemen Prefer Blondes*. Before that she played roles that were very different. Loreli Lee is a kind of hyper-feminized, slightly comic, slightly parodied female seductress." With her expert ability to construct the persona of this mythical female seductress "Marilyn Monroe," Marilyn shows she fully understands what Hollywood and the world want of her: to be this seductively alluring good-girl, bad-girl, blonde stereotype, endlessly cuddly and available and seemingly forever helpless. But behind this clever construct, Oates perceives that there was always a fully conscious young woman who had expertly constructed her persona and always displayed a lot of perseverance and a fierce determination to get what she wanted out of life. In Oates's view, Marilyn's cuddly, sexy, dumb blonde routine becomes nothing more than a means to an end, pure and simple. But what was this end? According to this text, that end was to find love and respect for herself.

The legendary facts of Marilyn's love life (her three husbands and affairs with JFK and RFK) and her attempts at winning the respect of Hollywood (studying at the Actors Studio and demanding better movie roles) are all briefly detailed. Interestingly, however, it is the detailing of her love affairs with the two Kennedys that is given the most attention here. To be sure, this does make dramatic sense, as the last half of the documentary focuses solely on the subject of her death and its aftermath. This narrative turn allows for the use of the same sort of dramatic reenactments and the *Strawhead*-influenced color coding and visual patterning also used in *Marilyn: The Last Word*. As in that earlier documentary, these reenacted sequences are meticulously conceived of and designed in very precise colors.

Initially, Marilyn is depicted as existing in a harmonious, female space of soft, dreamy earth tones—pale blues (which complement the color of her eyes and the sky), greens, soft browns, with an occasional touch of yellow (mostly in her pale golden hair). At first glance, the filmic image is one of nobility, and we as viewers are invited in a postclassical manner to partake in the imaginal dispersion of this generous nobility. But then, a closer look reveals the pointing to of an erosion of the noble harmony of the female ground. Enframed on the edges of the compositional perfection is the shadowy, black velvet world of powerful men (the Kennedys, Jimmy Hoffa, the Mafia, the CIA, and the FBI) preparing to encroach on and collide with the stately beauty of Marilyn's classical order. Once again, as in *Marilyn: The Last Word*, it is the color red that signifies the rise of aggressive, masculine power and the fall of her female, more passive, nobility. And while the power of this new ground rises and nobility dissolves, representation itself shatters as the color red suffuses the screen. Red is so intense here and fired up that it glows red hot like the sweeping emotionalism of a Hollywood melodrama or the coils of an electric heater.

Not only is there the blood-redness of Marilyn's secret diary (cryptically referred to as "The Book of Secrets"), but there's also the scarlet dress she wears shortly before her death, the glowing red lights of the police cars and ambulances that come to her home on the night of her death, and even the harsh redness of the enema bag allegedly used to administer the lethal dose of drugs that killed her.

Also, the so-called official version of her death is once again taken to task for all its glaring discrepancies (most of which were copiously detailed in *The Marilyn Files*). In keeping with this understandably skeptical tone, Donald Wolfe states that he believes the reason for our unending interest in the problematical matter of Marilyn's death is due principally to our not having been aware in 1962 of all the pertinent events connected to the death. So, as we have previously seen before, Marilyn is again depicted as an innocent and neurotic victim caught up within the evil machinations of a political conspiracy. What this ultimately does is evince this harboring sense of all the latent paranoia and cynicism that crept its way into the American psyche in the late 1960s and 1970s and that has consistently refused to drop out of view. Although it is true that the depiction of Marilyn in the 1980s and 1990s was not totally about such political paranoia and cynicism anymore, still the impact of those elements remains so strong and pervasive that they have now exceeded far beyond the boundaries of their epochal occurrence and continuously bleed into each succeeding decade. As a result of this negative presencing, Millennium Marilyn cannot help but convey feelings of a certain groundlessness and mysterious otherness. Within this context, Coroner Thomas Noguchi (who conducted the autopsy on Marilyn) describes the mystery of her death as being much like a jigsaw puzzle with some of the pieces missing. And it is in these missing pieces of the puzzle Noguchi mentions that the metaphorical possibility of enigma opens up into the new century.

Despite its misleading title, the 2000 documentary *E! True Hollywood Story: The Many Loves of Marilyn Monroe* covers much of the same contextual ground as *The Death of Marilyn Monroe*. This is not meant to imply that the details of Marilyn Monroe's love life are totally ignored (Arthur Miller, Joe DiMaggio, Frank Sinatra, and the Kennedys are among the cast of familiar male characters here). What it does imply, however, is that the text's title promises one thing, while its content delivers another. Because of this, a certain dramatic conflict is manifested. This tension soon takes the form of a narrative that introduces a discursive disposition in which form and content are often seemingly at odds with one another. For example, as images of a stunning Marilyn singing "Happy Birthday, Mr. President" to JFK are projected on screen, we are informed in a conflicting voiceover that at the time of the event, she was both irritatingly late and heavily intoxicated.

Throughout the course of the narrative, this same sort of conflict keeps occurring until we realize that both the narrative drive and the figure of Marilyn have become interchangeable. With this occurrence, Marilyn is then depicted as an exceptionally beautiful but deeply flawed woman. Every time something good happens to her, it seems just a matter of time before it wanes and fades. This begins with the breakup of her marriage to Arthur Miller, which plunges her into a depression so deep that she has to be institutionalized. Although her affairs with JFK and RFK do initially seem to offer some momentary hope, soon those relationships also end in dismal failure. Concurrently, after she is fired off of *Something's Got to Give*, her professional life lies in tatters before her. Surrounded by such abandonment and uncertainty of the future, she turns to the reliability of her pills and alcohol, which are, at least, always there when she needs them. Once again, it is then her own self-destructive tendencies that are inexorably linked to her inevitable destruction in this depiction. And with this sudden shift from an epistemic to more of an existentialist spacing, Marilyn is plunged into the dark abyss. The peculiarity of this new millennial change in narrative terrain causes the words of Marilyn in defeat to collide with the images of Marilyn triumphant. Beyond the inevitable antinomy created by the clash of negative and positive, this depiction reveals a surprising texture of transformative possibility. Accordingly, with this transformation, a new means of expression is needed to convey this more positive side.

This arrives in the theatricalized and highly aestheticized moment of pure visual pleasure that occurs at the narrative's end. A seductive finale of *Strawhead*-like color coding explodes on the screen in the form of a montage of Milton Greene's photographs of Marilyn. Gorgeously beautiful within their own right, these images have a special purposiveness here in relation to their being the first images of Marilyn to be presented in color. Before their appearance, all other images of her consisted of only black-and-white photographs and newsreel footage. So with the appearance of Greene's images, there is a stylized leap from the existential method of judgment to a more aesthetic manner of seeing. She is strikingly depicted in the three primary colors—red, yellow, and blue—against either a black or a white backdrop. Reflecting this new spacing, the final image is of Marilyn in her luminous Jean Harlowesque white ermine fur against an equally luminous white backdrop. With the projection of this concluding image, the final leap to a transcendental space has been completed. Simultaneously, along with the opening up of this imaginal site, the documentary moves her into an archetypal, mythical space that is further complemented by the delivering of the last words we hear spoken by Hugh Hefner. He describes Marilyn's life as being ultimately about the impossible magically made possible.

In the next two documentaries of the new millennium—*Marilyn Monroe: The Final Days* (2001) and *Marilyn Monroe: Medical Secrets* (2003)—the extreme fragility of Marilyn Monroe's physical, mental, and emotional states becomes a matter of the utmost narrative importance. Ostensibly, *Marilyn Monroe: The Final Days* means to replay much of what was previously so well documented about the making of her last uncompleted movie in the documentary *Marilyn: Something's Got to Give*. Although we do get a similarly detailed account of the making and the unmaking of the movie, there is now a major difference in the way in which these events are contextualized. This difference is firmly established at the start, with narrator James Coburn complaining of Marilyn's constant tardiness and her growing dependence on pills and alcohol:

> Marilyn Monroe's constant tardiness was now legendary in Hollywood. She had been blamed for creating costly delays on nearly every film in which she ever starred. To make matters even worse, her four year marriage to playwright Arthur Miller had just ended in divorce. And the actress was finding consolation from a growing dependence on pills and alcohol.

Following this strong lead, the trajectory of the narrative proceeds to go out of its way proving the truthfulness of Coburn's claims. Walter Bernstein, one of the writers of *Something's Got to Give*, speaks of his negative impression of Marilyn having many psychological problems. And all his harsh words are confirmed by one of her own costars from the movie, Cyd Charisse. Directly after the laity has had its say on the matter, various experts are brought in to further elaborate on the precariousness of Marilyn's condition. Among those interviewed are representatives for the late Dr. Ralph Greenson, Marilyn's Freudian psychoanalyst during the last years of her life; Dr. Hyman Engelberg, her personal physician; and Dr. Lee Siegel, the studio doctor employed by 20th Century-Fox. As these various experts present their interpretations of her, we suddenly come to realize that the figure of Marilyn depicted here becomes interesting to them only as she is systematically converted by them into a case history. And precisely because she is made just such a case history, she is no longer so easy for us to understand anymore. In the wake of this conversion, all these medical and psychological experts must be brought in to help make her comprehensible to us once again. The task that lies before them is to help us understand all that is inscrutable of Marilyn. As they put forward their various assorted analyses and interpretations, their words begin to exert an unexpected power over the proceedings. In a postmodern sense, their expertise assumes an authority that allows them to see what cannot be seen. Implicit in all their authority is the power to remake Marilyn Monroe into their own image of her. Thus, it becomes the main focus of this particular text to dig down through her inscrutable surface to reveal, as it were, all that lies beneath. The tools used to get the job accomplished are the wonders of modern medicine and psychology. One after another, all these experts put forward their learned hypotheses as to what is going on in her body and mind. Dr. Engelberg appears to confirm the validity of Marilyn's claims of truly being physically ill during much of the making of *Something's Got to Give*.

A great deal of this depiction is concerned with theorizing about the exact condition of Marilyn's mental status. She is by turn described as always being depressed; excessively needy; severely addicted to pills, alcohol, and sex; and a bipolar manic-depressive. And as each of the expert opinions of her vie for dominance, her desirable female body is suddenly transformed before our eyes from being the site of alluring Hollywood spectacle to an element in the discourse of modern science and psychology. In other words, an attempt is made to reduce her to a collection of medical problems and symptoms to be diagnosed, cured, and, ultimately, explained away. She may still be an inscrutable mystery, but now she is a mystery that can be solved and brought under controlling expert male containment. So once again, in a depiction of Marilyn, power shifts away from the weak and defenseless woman and into the hands of more powerful (due to their expert status), even much wiser, men than she. With this shift in power, she goes from being a subject to an object. Rather than being the great star, her status drops back to just some anonymous starlet to be ground down, chewed up, and spat out by those great, monolithic machines of first Hollywood and then modern science. And in the process, her unique movie star individuality is virtually obliterated, and she is thrust into an artistic limbo, as it were.

Yet, despite the constant efforts of these powerful men to control and contain Marilyn, in the end, they all fail. Why they fail in their reductivist tactics is fittingly contained within the body of the text itself. For as the running discourse erects a scientific and psychological superstructure, the text's visual component totally undermines its veracity. As we also saw happen in *The Many Loves of Marilyn Monroe*, the words these men speak of Marilyn are one thing, while the visual imagery tells a whole other story. Accordingly, what we see is a woman who is ravishingly beautiful and perhaps at the height of her talents. She is most definitely not the broken-down, paranoid, drug-addicted Hollywood has-been they make her out to be. In this way, the text contains its own deconstructive negation. With this breakdown, a schism opens up. And through this opening, Marilyn is able to break out of the process of the critique to which she has been so relentlessly subjected. As the verbal component of the text then is erased, a new dynamic of spectatorial power emerges that frees Marilyn from the impaling of the taint of the word and allows her to resurface once again.

The final proof of all this comes in the last half hour of the documentary, which consists of a superb reconstruction of *Something's Got to Give*. In this pristine restored footage, there is Marilyn in her groundbreaking nude swimming scene. And, despite all the words we had heard to the contrary, she looks extraordinarily lovely and delivers an elegant and refined performance of skill and charm. Interestingly, although these scenes were filmed over forty years ago, they adhere to the same bold use of color coding and design that have now become such a strong element in the depiction of Millennium Marilyn. Highly colored deployments of white, red, and blue appear to have supplied Cukor with the key motif for expressing his idea of her in the movie. There is extensive footage of her costume tests for the movie in which she appears in a white so pure and so luminous that it, poetically speaking, becomes supernatural. Red is sometimes used to accessorize white as a means of conveying a distinct sensuality. For Marilyn's nude scene in the swimming pool, Cukor insisted that the water be tinted a special sapphire blue and illuminated with only blue and amber spotlights. This gives the water an otherworldly, iridescent shimmer, in turn giving Marilyn's nude body an incandescent glow as she emerges from the sapphire-tinted water, strangely weightless and ethereal, like the apparition of divine beauty.

The 2003 documentary *Marilyn Monroe: Medical Secrets* also presents us with Marilyn Monroe as something of a case history that can be made comprehensible only through the explanations of various medical experts, although in this case an attempt is made to consider her life in full rather than in the context of simply the last year of her life. Also, the narrative takes on the mood of a murder mystery as the medical experts (referred to here as "medical detectives") attempt to unravel the mysteries of her medical secrets. This mood is established at the start when we are told of medical detectives who meticulously search through Marilyn's medical records, psychiatric history, and autopsy reports to solve the mystery of her life and death once and for all.

This quest to solve the riddle of her life and death begins with the medical detectives first putting forth the following key question: "Was Marilyn Monroe mentally ill?" The sad history of the insanity of her mother and grandmother is explored as a way of providing evidence that Marilyn herself was indeed highly susceptible to mental illness like them. It is in the telling of this possibility that narrative patterning is used most effectively in conjunction with visual patterning for a change. Rather than conflicting, narrative and visual components complement one another. This is achieved in the way the narrative is organized around three specific visual motifs: 1) filmed sequences of the various medical detectives offering their theories, 2) black-and-white newsreel footage of Marilyn's life, and 3) *Strawhead*-like color-coded, theatricalized reenactments from the last year of Marilyn's life. If there is a vague feeling at times that she is in danger of being reduced to pure speculation and figurative artifice, the overall intelligence of what many of these medical detectives have to say keeps this from ever happening entirely.

Dr. Louise Kaplan considers what Marilyn was subjected to in childhood in her illegitimate birth and in her being passed around to a series of orphanages and foster homes, which made her feel worthless and unloved. And, as Dr. Kaplan speaks, her words are interspersed with these stylized, black-and-white images of a blonde little girl, standing alone, her face obscured from the camera's gaze. Additional footage of the melancholic child appears whenever the topic of Marilyn's childhood is discussed. The portrait that begins to emerge is of a lonely, unwanted child who eventually grows into an intensely unhappy woman.

An unseen but crucial presence in all this is the pathetic figure of Marilyn's mad mother Gladys. The story of Gladys going incurably insane and getting locked away in an asylum for life entangles the daughter with fears of echoing a similar fate. In some ways, Marilyn is so crippled by Gladys's failure as a mother to her that she comes to view herself as duplicating her mother's tragic identity through her own personal history. Fiercely determined to avoid such a wretched fate, Marilyn turns to intensive Freudian psychoanalysis as a means of escape. However, Dr. Peter Swalen claims that such deep psychoanalysis ultimately did her far more harm than good. While embracing the tenets of her therapy, she would often find herself plunging into an ever darker, more frightening abyss of greater doubt and uncertainty. In this domain, she finds herself thrown into an alienated state of postanalytical madness.

As Marilyn becomes more and more an unwilling captive of all these frightening memories of her past, she turns to pills to obliterate her pain. We are informed that by 1956, she is a full-fledged drug addict. Images of pills even become something of a fourth visual motif at this point. In narration, we are told of how her growing dependency on all her pills—her Seconal, Nembutal, Demerol—are what "make Marilyn shine during the day and bring sleep to all her restless, fitless nights." Throughout the course of this narrative, a kaleidoscopic array of pills is depicted. Sometimes in bottles, sometimes free-falling surrealistically through space, or else being poured directly into Marilyn's trembling hands. These pills create a visual interplay that has the power to dominate the narrative. And in keeping with the new-millennial use of stylization and heightened color, the pills are color coded. At first, the pills are white and pale yellow. Then, as they become more of a problem for Marilyn, the pills become a shocking pink and electric red in color.

Further, this same sort of surface concentration on the visual emerges in the way color is associated with Marilyn herself. In most of the re-creations in which she appears, she is connected to a pure, luminous whiteness. But as her depression, mental illness, and various forms of addiction overtake her, the color red (and, later, black) predominates. This visual configuration reaches its disturbing conclusion when, at the end of the documentary, her nude body is viewed face down on her bed of luminous, white satin sheets. Although she does initially appear oddly at peace in her death, that feeling is soon disrupted by all the black-clad men who invade the frame. Insidiously, they violate the peacefulness of her death scene until they have swallowed up her physical and spiritual sanity. She becomes the very embodiment of her own tragically violated bedroom: a space without dignity or privacy. There is no longer then a separation between her and these black-clad, strange men as they engulf and absorb her totally.

For all that, once again *Marilyn Monroe: Medical Secrets* finishes on a note of elusive ambiguity. Although all the medical detectives have done their best to solve the enigma of Marilyn, when all is said and done, they are forced to admit what we already know: Marilyn will forever remain an enigma, "and yet, despite all of her many problems, Marilyn Monroe has no equal. She leaves behind for us the image of an unforgettable star forever."

NOTES

1. Allen Estrin, *The Hollywood Professionals: Frank Capra, George Cukor, Clarence Brown* (New York: A. S. Barnes, 1980), 106.

2. Chris Gore, *The 50 Greatest Movies Never Made* (New York: St. Martin's Griffin, 1999), 189.

3. Shelley Frame, *The Actor's Studio, A History* (Jefferson, N.C.: McFarland, 2001), 122.

Marilyn Monroe as a Referent

$\mathcal{A}$lthough Walt Disney had purchased the rights to James Barrie's classic play for children *Peter Pan* in 1939, he didn't actually get around to transforming it into an animated film until 1953. The story of the rebellious boy who refused to grow up was given the typical Disney treatment: the darker implications of Barrie's play were eliminated or played down, making the text that much more edifying for the America of Eisenhower. Other significant changes included the role of Peter Pan being enacted by a boy for the first time (perhaps to eliminate any possible traces of lesbian overtones). Traditionally, Peter had always been played by a woman (Maude Adams, Eve Le Gallienne, Mary Martin, Jean Arthur, and others). And traditionally, the role of Tinker Bell has usually been represented as only a beam of golden light.

For Disney, however, this timeworn theatrical rendition of Tinker Bell portrayed as only a beam of light, though simply achieved, was completely unacceptable. Instead, he instructed his illustrators to base their design of her on the current conception of female attractiveness. Since this process began in the late 1930s and continued throughout the 1940s, the look and spirit of the character went through various transmutations—all of them unacceptable to Disney. Then, finally, in the 1950s, Disney found his perfect role model for Tinker Bell—Marilyn Monroe. The traditional golden beam of light that had been used to represent Tinker Bell had been made alluring flesh and blood in the form of America's new golden girl. The imaginary had been made real, only to be made the imaginary once again.

In Disney's movie of *Peter Pan*, the character of Wendy incarnates the ideal of "Mother." And with her domestic aptitude and the way she cares for Peter and all the Lost Boys of Neverland, she is consistently associated with the maternal role. In opposition to Wendy, Tinker Bell becomes a signifier for

"Mistress." Her immense erotic energy (even in this toned-down animated context) spreads first to all parts of Disney's favorite little fairy and then to all parts of the narrative as well. By this same impulse, Peter's growing interest in the domesticated charms of Wendy does not go unnoticed by Tinker Bell, who grows more angry and jealous. With this emotional transition, she goes from signifying "Mistress" to "Jealous Wife." Henceforth, she does all that she can to dispose of her more maternalistic rival. Small but far from submissive, she summons a now destructive eroticism that reaches its peak when she betrays Peter's secret hideout to the evil Captain Hook as a means of getting rid of Wendy. With this knowledge, Hook plants a time bomb in Peter's hideout. But in the end, Tinker Bell does do the right thing. She saves Peter from the blast, then rescues the kidnapped Wendy from Hook. And with this movement, Tinker Bell grows, perhaps less sublime but still wonderfully magical and all the more lovable for it.

In the classic 1954 *I Love Lucy* episode "Ricky's Movie Offer," Lucille Ball paid tribute to Marilyn Monroe in her own inimitable way. Now, with her exaggeratedly wide blue eyes, shock of tangerine-colored curls, and rubbery, shape shifting tomato-colored mouth, Ball would at first seem to be an odd choice to be the first artist to pay tribute to Marilyn. But that's just what occurs in the episode. Ricky tells Lucy that he has an opportunity to land a contract to star in a Hollywood movie about legendary Latin lover Don Juan. But Lucy almost ruins everything when she mistakes Ricky's agent for a burglar and knocks him unconscious. On the night of Ricky's audition, Fred and Ethel show up in these moth-eaten Spanish dancer outfits, Mrs. Trumbull delivers a geriatric version of an antiquated love song, and even Pete, the grocery boy, gets into the act with his trumpet.

Of course, Lucy manages to top them all. Wearing a platinum blonde Marilyn Monroe wig, corseted up within an inch of her life, and clad in a skintight, strapless gown, similar to the shocking pink gown Marilyn wore in *Gentlemen Prefer Blondes*, Lucy makes her grand, hip-wiggling entrance to the utter amazement and astonishment of everyone. After Ethel asks Lucy who she's supposed to be, Fred says Lucy looks like Humphrey Bogart in drag. But Lucy pays them no mind at all and simply goes on paying tribute to Marilyn Monroe in her own inimitable way.

The next depiction in which Marilyn Monroe was used as a referent did not occur until twenty-one years later with the Broadway premiere in 1975 of playwright Robert Patrick's *Kennedy's Children*. In the play, five lonely people gather, on a cold, rainy February afternoon in a New York bar. They are Wanda, a dignified, middle-aged woman obsessed with JFK, Jackie, and the whole Camelot mythos; Sparger, a campy, articulate drunken off-off-Broadway actor; Mark, a pill-popping, beer-guzzling, burnt-out Vietnam vet; Rona, a wilted flower child of the 1960s who comes to the bar mostly to avoid her drugged-out, abusive husband, Robbie, and to reminisce about her days of former student glory; and the ultraglamorous Carla, a sexy, blonde go-go girl whose only ambition in life is to be Marilyn Monroe.

Although it is true that *Kennedy's Children* was produced on Broadway in the 1970s, it is first and foremost a play about the 1960s. It therefore reflects both the initial hope and all the later despair associated with the decade. Each of these five people live lives that intersect the 1960s at its great historical waves. And as the decade unfolded, it seems to have meant different things to each of them. For Rona, the 1960s were a time of political activism and consciousness raising. She and her husband, Robbie, have done everything from marching for civil rights to protesting the war in Vietnam. She also admits that they both got heavily involved in the drug scene.

To Sparger, the 1960s began on the night he was brutally raped and savagely beaten by three rough-and-ready, gay-bashing sailors. He is mercifully helped and cared for by Buffo, the gay owner of the underground theater "Opera Buffo." Buffo and his lover Corso invite Sparger to join their campy acting troupe.

Mark's experience of the 1960s is tied in with his increasingly bizarre and surrealistic time spent in Vietnam. The horror of the war and his drug abuse cause him to develop a messianic complex over his best friend Chick, a bright, talented writer who helps Mark not to let his head go to bad places. But for all Chick's hard work, Mark's head to a bad place always does seem to go. While Mark heads for his bad place, the indefatigable Wanda does all that she can to take all her negative feelings about JFK's tragic death and to transform those feelings into positive action. Motivated by the president's message of hope, she quits her job and goes back to school to become a teacher, while Carla's impossible quest to transform herself into the next Marilyn Monroe takes a rather twisted route of all the rampant promiscuity of the 1960s. And as the 1960s wind down, all but Wanda grow more and more disillusioned. In the end, only she is able to find a way to keep all the hope and beauty of the Kennedy mythos alive. She becomes a teacher to special needs children and remains steadfast in her admiration of JFK and Jackie and all they stood for.

Marilyn Monroe is used in *Kennedy's Children* not simply as a glamorous sex symbol alone, although there is that undeniable aspect to this depiction of her. Rather, she is used here in a way similar to her use in both *The White Whore and the Bit Player* and *Tommy*. In other words, she is depicted as a total goddess projecting a perfect but unattainable beauty. Despite that unattainability, Carla still attempts to transform herself into just such a sex goddess. For Carla, Marilyn is this bright, shining beacon to lead her out of the encroaching darkness of the late 1960s. Yet if Marilyn didn't want to be looked on as a mere sex goddess, Carla longs to be considered as such. Having chosen the course of her life, Carla bleaches her hair blonde; perfects her makeup; wears only fine, expensive lingerie; and dresses in skintight, clingy dresses that hug her curvaceous body.

If Carla does produce a reasonable facsimile of Marilyn's surface sexuality and eroticism, in the end that is all that she can ever produce. We then see Carla's manufactured construct of Marilyn-inspired sexuality eventually collapse into a kind of free-floating, chaotic disaster. She is never able to achieve the stardom she so desperately seeks, and using her considerable sexuality as capital to attain her goal takes a most profound toll on her. So while sex and drugs did work for Marilyn, at least for a while, anyway, Carla is not quite so fortunate. Her quest to be Marilyn leads her to a dead end. Early on in the play, Carla proclaims to have learned from all the mistakes Marilyn made. But not only does Carla *not* avoid making the same mistakes as Marilyn, she even ends up making several of her own. Carla finally copies Marilyn even in death when she confesses she has come to the bar only to wash down the sleeping pills she had taken earlier that day. With the depiction of Carla's tragic death here, while poignantly echoing that of Marilyn, it can also be seen as a final reminder that both Marilyn and JFK and the whole Camelot mythos remain the most powerful symbols of the fairy-tale glory of the early 1960s.

The 1980s provide us with three texts that use Marilyn Monroe as a referent from three completely different approaches. In the first, the movie *Fade to Black* (1980), Marilyn Monroe is the symbol of erotic desirability and exquisite feminine beauty for the hero Eric. This introverted and alienated young man lives with his nagging, wheelchair-bound Aunt Stella. He works at a film stock company where his abusive boss and bullying fellow employees also mistreat him. His only real pleasure in life comes from watching old Hollywood movies. One day, he is astonished when he meets a beautiful blonde young woman who looks exactly like his favorite movie goddess—Marilyn Monroe. Much to Eric's further astonishment, Marilyn (coincidentally her name is also Marilyn) agrees to go to the movies with him. Although he waits hours for her, she never shows up. Disappointed, Eric attempts to pick up a hooker who only scorns him. Returning home, he watches *Kiss of Death* (1947), in which Richard Widmark plays a giggling, psychotic killer who shoves a wheelchair-bound old lady down a flight of stairs. Later, Eric does the same to his nagging Aunt Stella.

Now, completely transported into his fantasy world of old movies, Eric dons various cinematic guises (such as the Mummy, Dracula, and Hopalong Cassidy) as he kills off all his enemies. Throughout it all, he eludes the police and continually obsesses over his beloved Marilyn. He next pretends to be a photographer and hires her to be his model. He dresses as Laurence Olivier in

The Prince and the Showgirl and makes her dress as Marilyn's showgirl in the movie. After he serves her drugged champagne, he escapes with the semiconscious Marilyn as the police close in on him. He carries her up to the top of Grauman's Chinese Theatre. Believing that he is now James Cagney in the 1949 *White Heat*, he lets Marilyn go as the police shoot him down.

In *Fade To Black*, the king of Eric's world is James Cagney, and his queen, of course, is Marilyn Monroe. Her photographs cover the walls of his bedroom. And thoughts of her fill his head by day, and highly eroticized visions of her are the stuff of all his dreams at night. Therefore, Eric is beside himself with excitement when he actually meets an exact replica of Marilyn Monroe. The meeting happens in a nondescript-looking diner where she is having lunch with her girlfriend Stacy. Eric actually gets up the nerve to speak and flirt with her and regale her with his encyclopedic knowledge of old movies. And much to his—and our—surprise, Marilyn agrees to go to the movies with him. This turn of events proves potent enough to make him feel his life does have some real meaning to it after all. In less than twenty-four hours, Eric goes from being a hapless toad of a boy to becoming the princely escort of Marilyn Monroe. But when she fails to show up for their date, Eric is transformed from a withdrawn teenage slug into an avenging angel with a fiery sword to strike down all who have wronged him. Since he is an avid movie buff, it's only fitting that he should go about his deadly deed of wiping out all his enemies while dressed in the guises of his various movie heroes.

Eric's last guise in the movie as Laurence Olivier is the most complex by far. For when he dons it, he does so to avenge himself on Marilyn for rejecting him. After he has lured her to his studio, he addresses her just as Olivier did in *The Prince and the Showgirl*, telling her that fate has taken a hand in their love for one another. But the real hand that fate takes is much different from what Eric had originally planned. There is no way that he can ever bring himself to destroy his Marilyn as he did all those others. In a way, his powerful love for her redeems him. In the climactic scene at the end of the movie, Eric may die re-creating the famous "Top of the World" finale from *White Heat*, but Marilyn must live on eternally.

In 1987, another layer of meaning was added to Marilyn Monroe's referential potential when Spalding Gray's 1984 one-man stage show *Swimming to Cambodia* was made into a movie by acclaimed director Jonathan Demme that was based on Gray's experiences when he played a small role in the 1984 movie *The Killing Fields*. As the narrative unfolds, Spalding Gray gives us an excellent on-location account of all the craziness that went on in Thailand, where the movie was filmed. And the Thailand that Gray conjures up for us actually rivals Hollywood in terms of the excess of all sensual pleasures: alcohol, drugs, money, and all the sex that Gray—along with everyone else—should ever hope to encounter. Still, for all that hedonistic excess, Gray doesn't ignore the darker implications of his tale. He presents us with shocking evidence of the profound devastation caused by Nixon's five-year saturation bombing campaign and the genocidal campaign implemented by the Khmer Rouge on the country and its people.

Doubtlessly, in reaction to this historical horror, Gray begins his search for what he refers to as "the perfect moment." But when he does finally get to embrace this magical, mystical "perfect moment," it has absolutely nothing at all to do with Hollywood and everything to do with a memory of Marilyn Monroe. On the airplane bound for America, Gray bids a fond farewell to all the beauty, pleasure, and craziness of Thailand. His mood grows pensive, causing him to remark, "I had a flash. An inkling. I suddenly thought I knew what it was that had killed Marilyn Monroe."[1] This is followed by an extended sequence from *The Killing Fields*. The smoldering wreckage of Cambodia becomes the apocalyptic-like backdrop against which all the Americans are escaping in helicopters into the clear, sun-drenched free skies above.

Gray's use of Marilyn Monroe is both subtle and most moving. In paying homage to her within this context, Marilyn is meant to evoke all the beauty and sadness of Gray's experiences in Thailand. And beyond that, Gray also juxtaposes her against all the confusion, nostalgia, and the profound sense of loss that he perceives as characterizing much of his generation. Although he does initially begin this reference to Marilyn in a recessing negative place, he (and director Demme's use of the mise-en-scène) soon alters that initial conceptual configuration, moving her into a more expansive, positive space. It is of Marilyn that Gray speaks as he describes his experiencing of "the perfect moment" as he heads back home to the woman he loves. Fittingly, the clear turquoise blue skies that Gray and the other American characters in *The Killing Fields* go flying off into become a signifier for Marilyn's own mythical ascent into a space of aesthetic peace and harmony.

The 1988 mock documentary *Mondo New York* purposefully connects itself to the scandalous 1965 Italian documentary *Mondo Cane*. The makers of *Mondo Cane* went out of their way to document all of man's cruelty to other men and women, to animals, to nature, and mostly to himself. After witnessing two hours of cinematic pain, degradation, and humiliation, we are left with an overpowering sense of dread. This same feeling is also experienced while viewing much of *Mondo New York*. Thus, we are presented with a sequence of a violent cockfight, a degrading auction in which young Chinese girls are sold off to the highest bidder, and a gruesome church scene featuring a demented priest who bites off the heads of two rats and eats them. Most amazingly, all this takes place in New York City.

The tone of this mock documentary is established at once in the opening monologue. Singer-actress Lydia Lunch recites a poem to the greedy New Yorkers. Following Lunch's recitation, we are then "escorted" through the underbelly of New York by a beautiful teenage girl named Shannah Loumeister. She is our personal tour guide, taking us from one outrageous episode to the next. Fortunately, *Mondo New York* features several Manhattan performance artists, many of whom turn out to be most entertaining. One of these acts features a riveting reference to Marilyn Monroe in the form of Phoebe Legere's performance. Perhaps it would be more accurate to describe Legere's performance as the collapsing of a whole cluster of pop references into the meaning of Marilyn. For besides suggesting just Marilyn Monroe—complete with platinum hair, glowing red lips, plunging décolletage, and stylish dark glasses—Legere also conjures up visions of Marlene Dietrich at her most world-weary and wryly insolent. As Legere's performance continues, she evokes glam rockers of the 1980s like David Bowie and Alice Cooper with all her highly suggestive body movements as she sings her song "Marilyn Monroe." But as she continues, Legere next sings of the foreboding appearance of dark, mysterious clouds that come to serve as a portent of all Marilyn's pain and suffering. And eventually, the song becomes a funeral dirge for Marilyn. After finishing, Legere intones Marilyn's name over and over until it becomes a haunting mantra, a lamentation for all that the world has lost in her passing. Legere next does something most unexpected: she throws her body to the floor; lifts up her miniskirt, revealing her sheer panties; and masturbates herself in full view of the camera.

In making this bold, unexpected move in *Mondo New York*, Legere collapses yet another pop reference into her depiction of Marilyn Monroe. She transforms the goddess of the silver screen into the porn queen of sexploitation movies. In this way, Legere has collapsed all the unruly content of porn standards (the high heels, the erotic posturing, the seamed stockings, the open-mouth expression, the explicit display) into the figure of Marilyn. Certainly, the appeal of Legere's curvaceous and long-legged dimensions on full display gets much attention, but there's more going on than just that alone. Because the artist has chosen to make her own body the site of her art, she offers a deeply internalized invocation of Marilyn Monroe. And with this artistic choice, Legere alienates herself from her own body as she reveals it so explicitly to us. It's as if she's forcing us to contemplate all the cruel, rough, jagged edges behind the seemingly smooth surface of Marilyn's Hollywood existence. For better or worse, Legere gives us the goddess descended, brought down, defiled, and ultimately destroyed.

But since the 1980s are about the goddess ascended, Legere doesn't conclude her performance with the image of a destroyed Marilyn. Just as quickly as she threw herself down to the floor, she is back on her feet again. Her clothes are no longer dishabilled, and her body is no longer on explicit display. She looks much as she did at the beginning of her performance. She no longer suggests the porn queen of sexploitation movies as she does the goddess of the silver screen triumphant.

In the 1990s, Marilyn Monroe's immortal, goddesslike aura becomes a resplendent cloak to be slipped on by mere mortals when they are in need of a touch of magic in their lives. For example, *Used People* begins in 1969 with Pearl Berman, a middle-aged Jewish woman, mourning the loss of her husband, Jack. She has two divorced daughters, the overweight Bobby and the profoundly unstable Norma, the latter of whom is grief stricken over the recent death of her child and the abandonment of her husband. In an attempt to get through her life, Norma incarnates the identities of various famous movie-star icons. While sitting Shiva for her husband, handsome Italian Joe Meledandri pays his respects to Pearl and asks her out on a date. After much reluctance, Pearl accepts Joe's offer. On the day of her date, Norma (dressed as Marilyn Monroe in the famous white dress from *The Seven Year Itch*) helps Pearl get dressed for Joe. Although the date turns out badly, Joe prevails on Pearl and her family to come to his brother's restaurant for a lavish Italian meal. This leads to further mishaps for both families that get resolved by the end of the movie when Pearl and Joe get married with both a priest and a rabbi presiding.

Essentially, *Used People* is an enjoyable if somewhat old-fashioned soap opera with various modernistic twists added in here and there to help spice up the plot a bit. One such plot twist consists of Marcia Gay Harden's character—the emotionally unstable and often hysterical Norma—who attempts to transform herself into various movie stars as a means of expressing her psychic limitations to the other characters in the movie and create for herself some sort of an identity for herself. In *The Interpretation of Dreams*, Freud explains that such behavior is often a hysterical symptom, particularly in the female (caused as the result of some form of unresolved pain or suffering that is turned inward against the self), that can even act as a point of articulation for a loss of identification. And so in *Used People*, the hysterical character of Norma is depicted as turning to various legendary cinematic role models to create for herself even a temporary sense of the identity for the one she no longer believes she possesses.

During the course of the movie, Norma acts out the identities of Judy Garland, Barbra Streisand, Audrey Hepburn, and Faye Dunaway; and then there is the transcendent moment she becomes Marilyn in *The Seven Year Itch*. Of course, we have by now seen this most iconic costume used in countless depictions, and its use here is loaded with significant meaning. For when Norma, in a most unhysterical state for a change, finally decides to begin the process of lifting herself from out of the dark identity crisis she has fallen into for so long, it is to Marilyn she turns for her inspiration. And almost as if by magic, with simply her donning of a platinum blonde wig, putting on a white dress, and assuming the role of Marilyn Monroe, Norma acquires the strength she needs to do what must be done. She not only reconnects with her estranged son, Sweet Pea, but also begins the healing process, which puts her on the road to the regaining of her own lost identity.

There is a distinctive cosmic absurdity to the 1992 live-action/animated movie *Cool World* directed by the talented Ralph Bakshi, who had previously scored successes with the 1972 animated movie *Fritz the Cat* and the 1973 *Heavy Traffic*. Both of those works were irreverent looks at the radical-hip lifestyles of the 1960s and 1970s. Each was also set in a grotesquely stylized, decaying metropolitan setting. Although *Cool World* does share a similar setting, sadly it is not of the same artistic level of those other works. Still, the rendering of the physical details of Cool World is not without interest. Consisting of richly stylized sculptural architecture, enlivened by all sorts of swelling curves and twists, these incredible structures are further decorated with gigantic human faces. And in keeping with the overall tone of the absurdly stylized, many of the faces on these buildings have huge, gaping mouths with jagged teeth and long tongues that swallow up the movie's characters as they enter and exit. Bakshi then juxtapositions these architectural wonders against garish-colored skies in a wild burst of nonnaturalistic colors—yellows, blues, greens, reds, and oranges—that all clash against the distorted spectacle that is Cool World.

This same stylized dynamic gets carried over into the movie's Marilyn Monroe–inspired character of Holli Would. For the entire first half of the movie, she exists only as this voluptuous and scantily clad "doodle" (*Cool World*'s term for its cool cartoon characters). But cartoon or not, Holli turns to her idol Marilyn Monroe for inspiration. Her idolization of Marilyn continues when she is brought to life, taking the stunning form of Kim Basinger (indeed, a whole other type of richly stylized Hollywood artifice entirely). Through a series of wild twists and turns of the plot, the now humanized Holli first succeeds at seducing her cartoon creator, Jack Deebs (Gabriel Byrne), then tricks him into bringing her back home to earth with him. The essentialist antirealism of *Cool World* gets carried over into the "real" world in the last part of the movie, with Holli in Las Vegas (as artificial and theatrical in its own right as Cool World). The skimpy, showgirl-like costumes Basinger wears in these Las Vegas scenes add to the excessive theatricality of the proceedings, as does the scene in which she pays a special musical homage to Marilyn Monroe by performing an eroticized version of the song "Let's Make Love" with Frank Sinatra Jr. (who acts as stand-in for Yves Montand) in a Las Vegas nightclub.

All the Las Vegas scenes are soon unfurled into a dramatically mythical context when Bakshi interjects traces of the mythic formulation of the quest myth into the narrative. This development occurs when Holli announces her desire to capture "The Spike of Power," a magical talisman located on top of the tallest gambling casino. In the capturing of this mythical prize, Holli will get to remain on earth in human form, performing her Marilyn-inspired routine in Las Vegas forever. The full impact of the introduction of an explicit mythical reference into the narrative network of the depicted Marilyn creates a tension between the modern and the mythical that will become even more significant in many of the new-millennial depictions of Marilyn.

The 1992 documentary *Legends* benefits from the presence of Susan Griffiths impersonating Marilyn Monroe. *Legends* offers a glimpse into the world of professional impersonators who make their living reincarnating great stars in the Las Vegas extravaganza "Legends." Role playing and theatrical artifice are established at the start of the narrative with scenes of Griffiths perfecting her expert impersonation of Marilyn Monroe, Jonathan Von Brana his Elvis Presley, and Monica Maris her Judy Garland. It is most important to stress here that the initial impression these scenes make leads us to believe that the plot of *Legends* is going to be determined largely by this continuous sense of antireality. Also, all the images seem to be under the manipulative control of John Stuart (the show's creator). He compulsively puts his three stars through all their paces to make reality his seemingly impossible vision of a star-studded parade of Las Vegas razzle-dazzle and slick surface polish all of the time.

In any case, both our initial impression of the documentary and Stuart's initial intent experience a devastating blow when reality intrudes, forcing the plot to take some unpredictable twists and turns. When this happens, the theatrically excessive suddenly dissolves, and a surprising emotional intensity takes over as we learn the following in quick succession: 1) Griffiths and Von Brana are in love and plan to marry; 2) since they have both grown dissatisfied at being billed as "Marilyn Monroe" and "Elvis Presley" imitators, the newlyweds inform Stuart they are quitting the show to go out on their own; and 3) Monica Maris discovers she is dying of lung cancer, and the documentary in fact concludes with Stuart putting a rose on her crypt. Thus, even though the world that *Legends* initially attempts to depict is a space of complete illusion and artifice (where Marilyn, Elvis, and Judy all live!) and despite all of Stuart's best efforts to sustain just such an illusion, both he and we are inevitably made to realize that, in the end, it must all give way to the real and the true.

In her own way, the character of Havana in *Holy Matrimony* (1994) is as lost and confused as is Norma in *Used People* and Monica Maris in *Legends* when John Stuart must tell her that her terminal illness is affecting the quality of her performance as Judy Garland and she must therefore leave his show. Yet the major difference between them all is that as Norma's loss of identity is linked to a series of unfortunate personal losses and Maris's comes from her no longer being able to do what she most loves, Havana's comes from her having lived an intensely unhappy existence, always on the margins of life. For the most part illegal and clandestine, Havana has learned to survive mostly by wits alone. When we first meet her, she's employed at a carnival, impersonating Marilyn Monroe. At the same time, she harbors vague dreams of one day acquiring Marilyn Monroe–like stardom (much as Carla did in *Kennedy's Children*). After Havana helps her outlaw boyfriend, Peter, rob the owner of the carnival, they make their escape into Canada to hide out in the strict Hutterite religious colony where Peter grew up. But the whole time Havana plays the role of loving wife, she's really trying to find out where Peter has hidden the stolen money so she can make her quick escape. Even after Peter is killed in an automobile accident, Havana remains hell-bent on finding that money. Mindful of the colony's strict adherence to the Bible, she even borrows a page from Deuteronomy, insisting on her right to remain in the colony by marrying Peter's twelve-year-old brother, Zeke. But rather than Havana, it is her new bridegroom who discovers the money. Realizing the money has been stolen, Zeke convinces the Hutterite elders that he and Havana should return it to its rightful owner. Also, crooked FBI agent Markowski follows after the couple to steal the money for himself. After Havana and Zeke lose Markowski, Zeke returns the stolen money and convinces the robbed carnival owner not to press charges against "his wife."

When Havana makes her first attempt at escaping from the limitations and sordidness of her sorry life, she does as Norma did in *Used People*; she turns to Marilyn Monroe for inspiration. In the movie's opening scene, Havana is working at the carnival pretending to be Marilyn in *The Seven Year Itch*. Standing high above the unruly carnival crowds, she's like some sacred goddess enthroned on her pedestal, atop a giant fan that is triggered off every time some vulgarian hits the target. Whenever this happens, Havana's dress gets blown high above her head, ruining the theatrical purity of her beautiful, tableaulike illusion. Although Havana acts as if she's enjoying herself, we later learn her real feelings about the way she is treated. While sitting in the dressing room, taking off her Marilyn Monroe wig and makeup, she complains bitterly how much she hates her life. After comparing herself to Marilyn, she resolves to do whatever it takes to become a star in her own right. Yet if it is Marilyn whom Havana wishes to be, in many ways, like Carla, she misuses the meaning of Marilyn in her obsessive drive to become her. True, Havana can assume the surface effects of Marilyn's meaning, but in her personal spin on Marilyn, she supercharges the role with even more of a narcissistic edge than Carla did in *Kennedy's Children*. Havana's version of Marilyn would then seem to owe much to Madonna's more ambitious 1980s revision of Marilyn.

This helps explain the reckless extravagance of the self-absorbed behavior Havana exhibits when she uses her alluring Marilyn-like body to seduce the owner of the carnival in order for Peter to beat and rob the man. And then there's her total self-absorption when she insists on finding the hidden money even after Peter is killed and when she selfishly insists on marrying the twelve-year-old Zeke, without any concern for the boy's welfare. But then, when Zeke later intervenes and insists on her returning the money, she most unexpectedly begins to develop deeper feelings for her pint-sized bridegroom.

In light of this development, Havana's narcissistic edge is smoothed over, and she goes from being the whore to a loving Madonna figure. However, even in her transformed Madonna-like state, Havana still retains her same compensatory lush eroticism. Only now, she also reveals what was hiding under that glittery seductive facade the whole time: secret maternal instincts, a natural goodness, and a generous heart.

The unfortunate circumstances of the homeless and gravely ill Simon in *With Honors* (1994) confine him to the same lowly margins of society that Havana occupies in *Holy Matrimony*. And like Havana, Simon too possesses an uncanny aptitude for self-preservation, as is evidenced when reactionary Harvard student Monty drops the only copy of his thesis down a grating at Harvard's majestic Widener Library. When he goes to retrieve it, he discovers Simon, who lives in the library's basement, burning it page by page in a furnace. Insulted by its politically reactionary content but sensing an excellent meal ticket to carry him through the long, hard New England winter, he offers a compromise: one page of the thesis returned for each good turn by Monty. In desperation, Monty even brings Simon home with him. Initially, his three roommates are not too thrilled with this development, although the sole female roommate, Courtney, does soon warm up to the idea.

With time, Monty forms a close bond with Simon. He is surprised to discover that the homeless man is well read and intelligent. At the same time, Monty and Courtney also begin to develop strong feelings toward one another. During the Christmas recess, all of Monty's roommates go back home, but he stays at school to work on his thesis. He also learns that Simon is dying from a terminal disease. To help cheer him up, he takes Simon to a pajama party where he is delighted to meet Marilyn Monroe. Not long after, Simon dies as his four young friends take turns reading to him from his favorite book—Walt Whitman's *Leaves of Grass*. Monty eventually turns in his new thesis too late, which prevents him from graduating with honors.

The family nexus (as it was in *Nobody Dies on Friday*) is presented as being emptied out in *With Honors*, and the figure of the father is nowhere to be found. If the four Harvard students appear to do a credible enough job at creating an alternative family nexus for themselves, their attempt at finding a surrogate for the absent father is problematical. Not only is the homeless Simon not much of a father figure, but he is also in need of some real parenting himself, which he seems to get from his four young friends. In the scene where Monty and his roommates take Simon to a lively pajama party, he is ecstatic to meet and most theatrically flirt with Marilyn Monroe, who is once again wearing her *Seven Year Itch* white dress. And in this depiction of her, Marilyn's warm presence has a lively, mercurial quality as she magically slips in and out of the edge of the movie frame just as smoothly as she did in *Calendar Girl*. Yet for all its brevity, Marilyn is used here to evoke a warm feeling of joyousness for both Simon and for us as viewers. Thus, we are made to appreciate the potential power that her presence can now have in terms of generating meaning and feeling in the most unexpected new ways.

In the movie *Blue Sky* (1994), we also see Marilyn Monroe evoked in a similar way, only this time that evocation is a matter of infinitely more visual and psychological complexity. The movie begins in Hawaii in 1962. Major Hank Marshall is embarrassed by the sexually provocative behavior of his beautiful but profoundly unstable wife, Carly. Something of a dreamer, Carly desperately longs for a more glamorous life than the one her husband provides for her. To compensate, she projects herself into a world of movie-star fantasy in which she transforms herself into famous sex goddesses. As a result of Carly's flamboyant behavior, she, Hank, and their two young daughters are transferred to another Army base in Alabama. Hoping to make a brand-new start, Carly transforms herself into Marilyn Monroe. Unfortunately, Carly soon makes more trouble for Hank when she goes to the Officer's Club, emulating the torrid vamp Rose whom Marilyn played in *Niagara*, and makes a play for Hank's superior Colonel Johnson. After he sends Hank off to work at a Nevada nuclear test site, Colonel Johnson begins a torrid, indiscreet affair with Carly. While in Nevada, Hank discovers a serious radiation leakage and returns home to report it to Colonel Johnson. When their dispute grows more personal, Colonel Johnson tricks Carly into having Hank committed to a psychiatric hospital. When Carly later goes to visit him, she is horrified to see Hank drugged senseless. She then moves into the most important action of her entire life, successfully negotiating her husband's release and discharge. The movie ends with the family heading to California. In preparation for her new life, Carly transforms herself into a new Hollywood sex goddess—Elizabeth Taylor.

The first sex goddess that the flamboyant Carly transforms herself into in *Blue Sky* is Brigitte Bardot in *And God Created Woman*. Her mimetic transformation of Bardot is so complete that it even includes sunbathing topless on the beach. When Carly's antics practically cause the military helicopters flying overhead to crash into one another, the Army brass transfers Hank and his family to another Army base in Alabama. Solemnly vowing to behave more like a real wife and mother, Carly discards the guise of Brigitte Bardot.

Carly next becomes Marilyn Monroe. But Carly's mood grows dark and ominous when she is confronted with the drab circumstances of her new life in Alabama. She grows hostile and throws a violent temper tantrum, lashing out at everything in sight and most particularly at her husband. As her means of revenge, Carly attends the dance at the Officer's Club, further tormenting Hank when she next metamorphoses into Rose, the excessively torrid vamp Marilyn played in *Niagara*. Like Rose, Carly also wears a skintight scarlet dress as she lapses into her most melodramatic mode and focuses all her unleashed sexuality on Hank's commanding officer Colonel Johnson. Her beauty and sexual allure take on a destructive force that sets in motion a series of disastrous occurrences that finally end with her being tricked into committing Hank to a psychiatric hospital. On realizing what she has done, Carly becomes the very incarnation of Marilyn in her post-Niagarean career in which Rose is humanized and cannot ever be resuscitated again, and the former Monroean femme fatale is completely dissolved away into the lusciously big-hearted Cherie of *Bus Stop* forever singing "That Old Black Magic" off key to the delight of a bunch of drunken, lonely cowboys. Then later, when Carly successfully gets Hank released from the hospital, she recalls Marilyn's accomplished acting as Roslyn at the end of *The Misfits* after she succeeds in her valiant quest to make the men free all the wild mustangs they have captured, thus saving the great, noble animals from being slaughtered. Finally, the performance of Jessica Lange as Carly is a spectacular creation of seemingly inexhaustible power and variety that is never less than first-rate and fully deserving of all the accolades and awards (including the Best Actress Oscar) she received in 1994.

First-rate, too, is the performance of Jane Horrocks in the movie *Little Voice* (1998). She plays LV (Little Voice), a reclusive girl who lives with her widowed mother, Mari, in an industrial town in England. To escape her mother's vulgarity and selfishness, LV never leaves her bedroom. She spends all her days listening over and over again to her late father's record collection, which is made up of albums by Judy Garland, Shirley Bassey, and Marilyn Monroe, among others. When Mari's newest boyfriend, Ray Say, a down-on-his-heels talent agent, enters the scene and overhears LV impersonating Judy Garland with great feeling, he convinces Mari that LV could be their ticket to the big time. But immobilized by stage fright, LV cannot perform. Then, inspired by the ghost of her late father, she is a smash hit imitating Marilyn Monroe and many other stars. On the second night of her performance, LV refuses to perform. Angered by LV's refusal, Ray explodes and viciously attacks Mari. Alternating between the voices of Monroe and Garland, LV tells him off. Later that same evening, LV's home burns down, but she is rescued by Billy, the young telephone repairman and keeper of pigeons whom she has recently fallen in love with. LV goes back to her burnt-out home to confront her uncaring mother, then she and Billy prepare to embark on a new life together.

As this description would attest, *Little Voice* has the shape and feel of a folktale or fable, and this is also carried over into the performance of Jane Horrocks as LV. The actress is as vulnerable and fragile as a Victorian waif. With cheeks that hollow into a gaunt, famished-looking, white face and immense wonder-struck eyes, Horrocks fills the screen with a pathos that verges on offbeat poise. Her LV is so painfully shy that she can communicate only with the ghost of her dead father. The way he communicates back is in the form of the old record collection he's left her. But LV doesn't simply listen to these legendary divas; she meticulously transforms herself into them. In this, she's like Norma in *Used People* and Carly in *Blue Sky*. The only difference is whereas those characters transformed themselves into legendary women to make public spectacles of themselves, LV's transformations are a totally private affair.

Of course, all that changes when her mother's new boyfriend, Ray Say, arrives on the scene and quickly realizes LV is that one great act he has spent his whole life searching for to finally make him rich and famous. He cleverly draws her out by simply mentioning Marilyn Monroe to her. And with just the mere mention of the name of Marilyn, LV suddenly comes to life and breaks out into an impersonation of her. After having experienced her Judy and then her Marilyn, Ray looks LV straight in the eye and, with an avuncular theatricality, emphatically declares, A star is born! Immediately following his declaration, he moves Heaven and Earth to create for his new star the perfect showcase to best display her extraordinary talent to the world. This consists of a glitzy, full proscenium stage, with gold trim and blue curtains. Flanked by a full orchestra and with her name spelled out in giant, flashing neon letters, LV appears encased in a huge golden cage (not unlike one of the cages her new boyfriend, Billy, keeps his pigeons in). When LV first leaves the cage, she nervously creeps to the front of the stage with her wonder-struck eyes blazing. Then, suddenly, she spots the ghost of her father out in the audience, and it's as if all the lights have been switched on from deep inside her being. From this point on, the orchestra can barely keep up with LV as she hurls about the stage, transforming herself into Marilyn Monroe, Marlene Dietrich, and a triumphant Judy Garland singing "Get Happy." At the end of LV's mimetic tour de force, the plans are made to make her a big star. The only problem is that LV wants no such thing for herself. Her refusal to go along with the plans of Ray and her mother sets in motion a series of events that dooms the pair of them. If they end up groveling in total defeat, LV ends up actually finding a new sense of identity for herself and a new freedom as she and Billy overcome the ossified imbecilities of her mother and Ray and establish both their love and a new life together along with Marilyn, Marlene, Judy, and the rest.

The majority of the 1990s depictions of Marilyn Monroe as referent (with the exception of *With Honors*) have featured a heroine going through a profound loss of identity. Although the trend continues with the 1998 *Finding Graceland*, once again, as in *With Honors*, it is a male protagonist who searches for his lost identity. Byron Gruman, a once successful doctor, now spends his days wandering aimlessly, driving about in his smashed-up 1959 Cadillac convertible. One day, he is surprised to meet Elvis Presley. Almost in spite of himself, he agrees to drive Elvis to Graceland, just in time for the annual commemoration of his August 16 "death." As they make their way toward Graceland, Elvis attempts to draw Byron out to no real avail. Because he holds himself responsible for the death of his young wife, Beatrice, in a car accident, nothing Elvis says or does has any discernible effect on him. But when Elvis introduces Byron to Marilyn Monroe impersonator Ashley, he finally manages to get a rise out of him. This even helps Byron accept the revelation that Elvis is in actuality a grief-stricken man named John Burrows who lost his wife and child in a plane crash. Still, Elvis does get Byron's Cadillac repaired, and so the two of them head for Graceland. The movie ends with the pair returning to Graceland, where a candlelight vigil is taking place. Byron and Ashley reunite as Elvis mysteriously disappears into the crowd.

As they were in the movie *My Fellow American*, the mythical figures of Elvis Presley and Marilyn Monroe are inextricably bound together once again in this cinematic fantasy *Finding Graceland*. And in this depiction, their iconographic images are spiritualized and imbued with special healing abilities. But unlike the scene from the movie *Tommy*, when Nora takes the young hero to be cured of his affliction at the church of St. Marilyn Monroe, the spirits of Marilyn and Elvis really do have the power to heal this time. Still, if Elvis is a legend in this depiction, he is a legend with the mission of helping all those in need. As it turns out, the one most in need of Elvis's help is Byron himself. Following the death of his beautiful, young wife, Beatrice, Byron, like a beleaguered figure from out of the melodramatic imagination, drops out of life and love completely. He comes to resemble a lifeless zombie, drained of all emotion, as he drives aimlessly about the highways and byways of America on his destination to nowhere. But unlike Byron, Elvis most certainly does have a destination: he's headed back home to Graceland. To reward him, Elvis introduces Byron to none other than Marilyn Monroe. She appears like a vision of loveliness in shimmering gold lamé: she's a fantasy girl in a fantasy film. Marilyn swoons, faints, and falls to the floor, and when Byron goes to help her, she kisses him on the mouth and exclaims that she loves doctors as much as she loves playwrights and baseball players. In kissing Byron as she does, the figure of Marilyn cleverly reverses the roles of such classic fairy tales as *Sleeping Beauty* and *Snow White*. Now it is the heroine rather than the handsome prince who has the magical power to awaken the sleeper. The full force of Marilyn's magicalness can be seen when she performs onstage at the Hollywood Casino. A vision of loveliness all in white, her performance is much appreciated by one member of the Hollywood Casino's audience in particular—Byron. Each individual move and mannerism of Marilyn stirs something deep within him. And as he responds to Marilyn's erotic energy, as it is being channeled through the delicious conduit of Ashley, it becomes clear that all is not lost for him. After all, where the blood stirs to such an extent, there is hope.

If the spirit of Elvis lives in *Finding Graceland*, then so too does the spirit of Marilyn. In this cinematic space, they both also do more than live. As stated, they have the power to resurrect the dead as they do in Byron's case. For, as Elvis must remind Byron, what man mistakes for mere coincidence is often instead the power of fate. Actually, this mysterious power is even provided with a shining signifier at the end of *Finding Graceland* in the form of Elvis's beloved Valhalla—Graceland. With its huge wrought-iron gates, elegantly curved drive, colonnaded entrance, and lush, velvety grounds, Graceland is the American Dream come true, made real, and it is the place where Elvis and Marilyn are finally home. In this, the movie perfectly reflects the full power of the melodramatic impulse of many of the depictions of Marilyn Monroe in the 1990s. And we are left with one final image of a basically moral universe restored and running most efficiently again.

The rock-and-roll musical *Spice World* features the lively antics of the popular English girls group of the 1990s—The Spice Girls (Ginger, Sporty, Scary, Posh, Baby). The movie essentially centers on how each of the five Girls responds to the sudden fame and fortune that has been thrust on them. Although the Girls do all they can to stoically endure the seemingly endless rounds of rehearsals, photo shoots, press conferences, and warm-up shows, they would much rather be riding around London on the Spicebus having a good time for themselves. This is just what happens in the exuberant scene at a high-fashion photo shoot. Bored with the photographer's instructions, the Girls choose "to do their own thing," which consists of their dressing up as and impersonating their favorite pop culture icons of the twentieth century. In the lively sequence, they transform themselves into Jackie Kennedy Onassis, Wonder Woman, anorexic 1960s supermodel Twiggy, Elvis Presley, and, of course, Marilyn Monroe. Ginger Spice wears the white dress from *The Seven Year Itch* and a pair of white high-heeled platform shoes (giving this late 1990s depiction a trace of the disco era of the 1970s). Assuming a series of excessively theatrical and exaggerated poses, her white dress is blown higher and higher up into the air. Thus, she and the other Girls turn what was intended to be a sophisticated high-fashion shoot into a moment of Marx Brothers–like slapstick comedy.

In the 2001 comedy *Town & Country*, Warren Beatty plays Porter Stoddard, a successful New York architect. Yet, despite his success and wealth and the love of his loyal wife of twenty-five years, Ellie, Porter is bored and restless. Not long after he and Ellie celebrate their anniversary, they learn that their best friends, Mona and the unfaithful Griffin, are divorcing. Even though Porter is having an affair himself with beautiful, young classical cellist Alec, he says nothing to Ellie and accompanies Mona to Mississippi in an attempt to comfort her. While there, he begins an affair with Mona. Meanwhile, back in New York, Ellie finds out about Alec and plans to leave Porter. When he later accompanies Griffin to Sun Valley, Porter has two more affairs with the wealthy Eugenie and the free-living Auburn. Eventually, Porter returns to New York to attempt to reconcile with Ellie. There, Griffin admits that he's gay, and Porter confesses of his additional affairs with Eugenie and Auburn. Although Ellie claims she still wants a divorce, the movie concludes with a strong suggestion of the couple reconciling.

In 1975, Warren Beatty scored one of his biggest hits with the stylish screen comedy *Shampoo*. In some ways, *Town & Country* looks like an attempt to take up where that movie left off, twenty-six years later. Rather than a womanizing hairdresser, Beatty is now a philandering architect. But rather than the sophisticated and laconic wryness of the earlier movie, there is instead a self-indulgent extravagance here. To compensate for some of this, director Peter Chelsom has created a visually splendid movie. Once again, we are then given another example of style winning out over substance as Porter hops from bed to bed. Not too coincidentally, most of these beds are well situated in a series of conspicuous haute society settings. These luxurious backdrops afford Chelsom the opportunity to produce movie imagery drenched in a profusion of rich color symbolism. Although white on white and earthy, pale tones predominate the order of the symbolic color scheme, the use of ever-brighter colors intensifies as Porter seduces his many conquests. All this coloration is further reinforced in the scene of Porter's final seduction of the free-living and free-loving Auburn. Something of the female counterpart to Porter, Auburn goes from chance encounter to chance encounter, and she is the one who picks him up and invites him to a Halloween party. Dressed as Marilyn Monroe from the "Diamonds Are a Girl's Best Friend" routine in *Gentlemen Prefer Blondes*, Auburn's hot pink gown contrasts expressively with the cool whiteness of the polar bear costume she makes Porter wear. And the absurdly comical scene of the two of them dancing passionately together transforms them (like Marilyn and Mr. Evil in *Evil Hill*) into a comic version of a Beauty and the Beast for the new millennium.

If Marilyn Monroe dances with an animal in *Town and County*, the makers of the 2001 movie *Monkeybone* find a way to top even that. The movie opens with cartoonist Stu Miley selling his animated series based on his own libidinal alter ego—the cartoon monkey named Monkeybone—to cable TV. Later, while driving home with his girlfriend Julie, whom he intends to propose to, Stu has an automobile accident and falls into a deep coma. He next finds himself in Downtown—a surrealistic realm of nightmarish visions—ruled over by Hypnos, the god of sleep. Stu stops in a nightclub where none other than his own creation Monkeybone is the star attraction. Monkeybone's act consists of transforming himself into Marilyn Monroe. While back in the real world, Stu's sister Kimmy wants him disconnected from life support. The ever-loyal Julie, who is a sleep researcher, remains convinced his brain is still active. She injects Stu with a chemical to induce nightmares and, it is hoped, shock him out of the coma. Instead, this causes all havoc to break out, allowing Monkeybone's escape to the real world in Stu's body. But in the end, Stu is eventually reunited with his own body and with Julie.

The director of *Monkeybone*, Henry Selick, made the 1993 animated movie *The Nightmare before Christmas*, and this movie feels like that earlier one, only projected from a two-dimensional onto a three-dimensional spacing. This is especially true in the case of Monkeybone. Quite literally the outrageous embodiment of Stu's penis, Monkeybone is a dirty Freudian joke sprung to life. Perhaps the biggest joke of all, however, is that although Monkeybone is a phallic symbol, he does not possess the phallus, all of which explains his lecherous and lewd behavior toward every woman he encounters after he escapes to Earth in Stu's anatomically correct human form. It is Monkeybone's extreme behavior (as well as the lavish use of artifice and color) that identifies this as a new-millennial depiction of Marilyn Monroe. The primary colors of red, yellow, and blue are foregrounded throughout the narrative. And it is the garish Day-Glo versions of these colors that carry much of the narrative along. This is most apparent in the Daliesque surrealist nightclub scene where Monkeybone pays tribute to Marilyn Monroe in what is, without question, along with *Dead Marilyn*, one of the more perverse depictions studied for this book. Against the torrid glow of red velvet drapery, Monkeybone performs his astonishing routine atop an electric blue piano while metamorphosing into an anthropomorphized version of Marilyn, complete with platinum blonde hair; pouty, glistening red lips; *Seven Year Itch* white dress; and white stiletto high heels. Monkeybone then pulls off his own two ears, which become two deflated balloons. After blowing up his ears, they are transformed into voluptuous breasts. He pops the breasts into his dress to complete his bizarre transformation. Jumping down to the keys of the piano, he sings "I Want to Be Loved by You." His routine so excites a particularly lecherous elephant out in the audience that he expresses his fervent approval with so much zeal that Monkeybone even ends up like Marilyn in *The Seven Year Itch*, with his dress blown up around his ears (although in this instance, his dress is blown up around where his ears used to be). If Monkeybone's act does carry the absurd millennial impulse to its maximum expression, we can nonetheless trace its steady progression from the pervasive absurdity in other 2000s depictions of Marilyn (*Company Man, Evil Hill,* and *Town & Country*). And with this same impulse, each text is released from the rigorous demands of reality and so is free to reflect its own purposiveness (no matter how artificial, antireal, or irrational that purposiveness appears).

Unlike *Monkeybone*, the 2004 "In Camelot" episode of *The Sopranos* adheres to the demands of reality. Veteran actress Polly Bergen is featured as Fran Felstein, the glamorous and mysterious ex-mistress of Mob boss Tony Soprano's late father. Something of a Judith Campbell–like party girl in her heyday, the most decidedly rational and still quite well preserved Fran retains an undeniable stature that makes her alluring and enticing even in her seventies. Yet as striking as she may very well be on a physical level to Tony, the most striking thing of all about Fran is just how much enthralling verbalization she does. Completely dominating the "In Camelot" episode, with her tasteful and harmonious beige-on-beige color scheme (both she and her dwelling place are rendered in warm earthy and womanly colors), Fran virtually holds Tony spellbound as she regales him with story after story of her colorful past when she was acquainted with JFK, Frank Sinatra, and Marilyn Monroe.

Therefore, it is through the power of language that Fran weaves her Scheherazade-like spell on others (much as Marilyn herself did with Rick and Lars in *The Final Hours of Norma Jeane*). What Fran adds is a perceivable verbal and referential mode that connects Tony and us, through her, directly back to the early 1960s and the legendary era of Kennedy's Camelot. The system of signs she constructs invokes her once having had erotic trysts with JFK and Frank Sinatra and her friendship with Marilyn. With the mention of Marilyn's name, Fran then transforms herself into Marilyn Monroe singing "Happy Birthday, Mr. President." And, all at once, she conjures up a magical dimension that momentarily carries Tony Soprano and us back to the mythical time of Camelot.

UPDATE

Since this book was written, there have been (or soon will be) several other depictions of Marilyn Monroe all worthy of future scrutiny. Naomi Watts pays tribute to Marilyn (while absurdly and hyperpatriotically dressed as Uncle Sam) in writer-director David O. Russell's existentialist comedy *I Heart Huckabees* (2004); the late Arthur Miller turns to Marilyn, yet again, for inspiration in his final play, *Finishing the Picture* (2004), based on the legendary difficulties involved with the filming of *The Misfits* (in this, Miller takes a similar dramatic approach to the one used by Robert Brustein in *Nobody Dies on Friday* since Marilyn never once appears on stage); a new documentary, *Marilyn's Man* (2005), about Marilyn's life with her first husband, the late Jim Dougherty, has been filmed; and cable network TNT has announced plans for a future six-hour miniseries based on the life of Mob boss Sam Giancana, featuring as characters JFK, Frank Sinatra, Judith Campbell, and, naturally, Marilyn Monroe.

NOTE

1. Excerpted from Spalding Gray, *Swimming to Cambodia* (New York: Theatre Communications Group, 1985), 59. Used by permission.

Appendix A

Marilyn Monroe Iconography

Note that representations of Marilyn Monroe are shown in **bold** type. Entries for theatrical performances refer to first commercial appearances and do not include revivals.

1953

Peter Pan (animated film; Marilyn Monroe as referent)
Walt Disney Productions (77m)
Directors: Clyde Geronimi, Wilfrid Jackson, Hamilton Luske
Writers: Milt Banta, Bill Cottrell, Winston Hibler, Bill Peet, Erdman Penner, Joe Rinaldi, Ted Sears, Ralph Wright
Cast (voices): **Bill Thompson (Tinkerbell)**, Bobby Driscoll (Peter Pan), Kathryn Beaumont (Wendy), Hans Conried (Captain Hook/Mr. Darling), Paul Collins (John), Tommy Luske (Michael), Heather Angel (Mrs. Darling)

1954

I Love Lucy (television series; Marilyn Monroe as referent)
Desilu Productions (30m)
"Ricky's Movie Offer" episode
Original Airdate: November 8, 1954
Director: William Asher
Writers: Bob Carroll Jr., Madelyn Pugh, Jess Oppenheimer

Cast: **Lucille Ball (Lucy Ricardo)**, Desi Arnaz (Ricky Ricardo), Vivian Vance (Ethel Mertz), William Frawley (Fred Mertz), Frank Nelson, James Dobson

1955

Will Success Spoil Rock Hunter? (Broadway play; Marilyn Monroe as roman à clef)
Original Run: October 13, 1955 (444 performances: Belasco Theatre, Shubert Theatre, New York, NY)
Director: George Axelrod
Writer: George Axelrod
Cast: **Jayne Mansfield (Rita Marlowe)**, Orson Bean (George MacCauley), Martin Gabel (Irving LaSalle), Walter Matthau (Michael Freeman), William Thourlby (Bronk Brannigan)

1957

Will Success Spoil Rock Hunter? (film; Marilyn Monroe as roman à clef)
20th Century-Fox (94m)
Director: Frank Tashlin
Writer: Frank Tashlin (play by George Axelrod)
Cast: **Jayne Mansfield (Rita Marlowe)**, Tony Randall (Rockwell Hunter), Betsy Drake (Jenny Wells), Joan Blondell (Violet), John Williams (Irving LaSalle), Mickey Hargitay (Bobo Branigansky)

And God Created Woman (film; Marilyn Monroe as roman à clef)
Kingsley International (97m)
Director: Roger Vadim
Writers: Roger Vadim, Raoul J. Levy
Cast: **Brigitte Bardot (Juliet Hardy)**, Curt Jergens (Eric Carradine), Jean-Louis Trintignant (Michel Tardieu), Christian Marquand (Antoine Tardieu), Georges Poujouly (Christian Tardieu), Jeanne Marken (Madame Morin)

1958

The Goddess (film; Marilyn Monroe as roman à clef)
Columbia (105m)

Director: John Cromwell
Writer: Paddy Chayefsky
Cast: **Kim Stanley (Emily Ann Faulkner/Rita Shawn)**, Lloyd Bridges
(Dutch Seymour), Steve Hill (John Tower), Betty Lou Holland (The
Mother), **Patty Duke (Young Emily)**

1961

The Misfits (film; Marilyn Monroe as roman à clef)
United Artists (124m)
Director: John Huston
Writer: Arthur Miller
Cast: **Marilyn Monroe (Roslyn Taber)**, Clark Gable (Gay Langland),
Montgomery Clift (Perce Howland), Thelma Ritter (Isabelle Steers), Eli
Wallach (Guido)

The Ladies Man (film; Marilyn Monroe as roman à clef)
Paramount (106m)
Director: Jerry Lewis
Writers: Jerry Lewis, Bill Richmond
Cast: **Dee Arlen (Marilyn Monroe look-alike)**, Jerry Lewis (Herbert H.
Herbert), Helen Traubel (Helen Wellenmellon), Pat Stanley (Fay), Kathleen
Freeman (Katie), Hope Holiday (Miss Anxious), George Raft (Himself),
Henry James (Himself), Marty Ingels (Marty)

1962

Venus at Large (Broadway play; Marilyn Monroe as roman à clef)
Original Run: April 12, 1962 (4 performances: Morosco Theatre, New York,
NY)
Director: Rod Amateau
Writer: Henry Denker
Cast: **Joyce Jameson (Olive Ogilvie)**, David Wayne (Sonny Stone), William
Prince (Alec Grimes), Sally Gracie (Betty Stone), Leon Janney (Jack Carr),
Jack Bittner (Mick Mandelbaum), Ernest Treux (J. B. Bannister)

Marilyn Monroe Why? (TV documentary; Marilyn Monroe as [documentary]
subject)

CBS-TV (30m)
Original Airdate: August 10, 1962
Director: Les Midgley
Writer: Les Midgley
Host: Charles Collingwood

Come on Strong (Broadway play; Marilyn Monroe as roman à clef)
Original Run: October 4, 1962 (36 performances: Morosco Theatre, New
    York, NY)
Director: Garson Kanin
Writer: Garson Kanin
Cast: **Carroll Baker (Virginia Karger)**, Van Johnson (Herb Lunquist), Ru-
    fus Smith (Arthur Murchison), Chad Black (Calvin Lundquist), True Elli-
    son (Sue Stewart)

1963

Marilyn Monroe (TV documentary; Marilyn Monroe as [documentary] subject)
ABC-TV (30m)
Original Airdate: March 24, 1963
Director: Art Lieberman
Writer: Malvin Wald
Narrator: Mike Wallace

Marilyn (documentary; Marilyn Monroe as [documentary] subject)
20th Century-Fox (83m)
Director: Harold Medford
Writer: Harold Medford
Host: Rock Hudson

1964

After the Fall (Broadway play; Marilyn Monroe as roman à clef)
Original Run: January 23, 1964 (208 performances: ANTA Washington
    Square Theatre, New York, NY)
Director: Elia Kazan
Writer: Arthur Miller
Cast: **Barbara Loden (Maggie)**, Jason Robards Jr. (Quentin), Salome Jens
    (Holga), Mariclare Costello (Louise), Michael Strong (Dan), David J. Stew-
    art (Lou), Hal Holbrook (Reverend Barnes), Faye Dunaway (Nurse)

1966

The Legend of Marilyn Monroe (TV documentary; Marilyn Monroe as [documentary] subject)
ABC–TV (60m)
Original Airdate: November 30, 1966
Director: Terry Sanders
Writer: Terry Sanders
Narrator: John Huston

The Apple Tree (Broadway play; Marilyn Monroe as roman à clef)
"Passionella" segment
Original Run: October 18, 1966 (463 performances: Shubert Theatre, New York, NY)
Director: Herbert Ross
Writers: Sheldon Harnick, Jerry Bock (book by Jules Feiffer)
Music: Jerry Bock
Lyrics: Sheldon Harnick
Cast: **Barbara Harris (Ella/Passionella)**, Alan Alda (Flip), Larry Blyden (Narrator), Robert Klein (Mr. Fallible)

1967

Valley of the Dolls (film; Marilyn Monroe as roman à clef)
20th Century-Fox (123m)
Director: Mark Robson
Writers: Helen Deutsch, Dorothy Kingsley (book by Jacqueline Susann)
Cast: **Sharon Tate (Jennifer North)**, Barbara Parkins (Anne Wells), Patty Duke (Neely O'Hara), Paul Burke (Lyon Burke), Susan Hayward (Helen Lawson), Toni Scotti (Tony Polar), Martin Milner (Mel Anderson), Lee Grant (Miriam Polar)

1969

Cop-Out (off-Broadway play; Marilyn Monroe as a character)
Original Run: April 7, 1969 (8 performances: Cort Theatre, New York, NY)
Director: Melvin Bernhardt
Writer: John Guare
Cast: **Linda Lavin (Marilyn Monroe and all female characters)**, Ron Leibman (Arrow and all male characters)

1971

The Life and Death of Marilyn Monroe (play; Marilyn Monroe as a character)
Original Run: June 1, 1971 (140 performances: Close Theatre, Glasgow, Scotland)
Director: Keith Hack
Writer: Gerlind Reinshagen (Translator: Anthony Vivis)
Cast: **Shirley Anne Field (Marilyn Monroe)**, James Aubrey (Johnny Hyde), David Hyman (James Dougherty), Peter Kelly (Arthur Miller), Ian McKenzie (Joe DiMaggio)

1972

Slaughterhouse-Five (film; Marilyn Monroe as roman à clef)
Universal (104m)
Director: George Roy Hill
Writer: Stephen Geller (book by Kurt Vonnegut)
Cast: **Valerie Perrine (Montana Wildhack)**, Michael Sacks (Billy Pilgrim), Ron Leibman (Paul Lazzaro), Eugene Roche (Edgar Derby), Sharon Gans (Valencia)

1973

The White Whore and the Bit Player (off-off-Broadway play; Marilyn Monroe as roman à clef)
Original Run: February 5, 1973 (26 performances: The Duo Theater, New York, NY)
Director: Manuel Martin
Writer: Tom Eyen
Cast: **Candy Darling (The White Whore), Hortensia Colorado (The Nun or Bit Player)**

1974

Marilyn Remembered (TV documentary; Marilyn Monroe as [documentary] subject)

ABC–TV (60m)
Original Airdate: February 27, 1974
Director: Terry Sanders
Writer: Terry Sanders
Narrator: John Huston

The Sex Symbol (TV film; Marilyn Monroe as roman à clef)
The Douglas S. Cramer Company, Columbia Pictures Television (90m)
Original Airdate: September 17, 1974
Director: David Lowell Rich
Writer: Alvah Bessie (book *The Symbol* by Alvah Bessie)
Cast: **Connie Stevens (Emmaline Kelly/Kelly Williams)**, Shelley Winters (Agatha Murphy), Don Murray (Senator Grant O'Neal), James Olson (Calvin Bernard), William Smith (Buck Wischnewski), Jack Carter (Manny Fox)

Fame (Broadway play; Marilyn Monroe as roman à clef)
Original Run: November 18, 1974 (1 performance: John Golden Theatre, New York, NY)
Director: Anthony J. Ingrassia
Writer: Anthony J. Ingrassia
Cast: **Ellen Barber (Diane Cook)**, Rudy Hornish (Louis B. Mayer), Robert Miano (Clark Gable), Nancy Reardon (Louella Parsons), Bibi Besch, Christine Lavren

After the Fall (TV film; Marilyn Monroe as roman à clef)
Gilbert Cates Productions (150m)
Director: Gilbert Cates
Writer: Arthur Miller
Cast: **Faye Dunaway (Maggie)**, Christopher Plummer (Quentin), Bibi Andersson (Holga), Mariclare Costello (Louise), Lee Richardson (Lou), Murray Hamilton (Mickey), Nancy Marchand (Rose)

1975

Hey, Marilyn! (radio play; Marilyn Monroe as a character)
Director: Cliff Jones
Writer: Cliff Jones
Cast: **Beverly D'Angelo (Marilyn Monroe)**

Tommy (film; Marilyn Monroe as a character)
Columbia (111m)
Director: Ken Russell
Writer: Ken Russell (rock opera by Pete Townshend)
Cast: **St. Marilyn Monroe Icon**, Oliver Reed (Frank Hobbs), Ann-Margaret
(Nora Walker), Roger Daltrey (Tommy Walker), Robert Powell (Captain
Walker), Elton John (Pinball Wizard), Jack Nicholson (The Doctor), Tina
Turner (Acid Queen)

Kennedy's Children (Broadway play; Marilyn Monroe as referent)
Original Run: November 3, 1975 (72 performances: John Golden Theatre,
New York, NY)
Director: Clive Donner
Writer: Robert Patrick
Cast: **Shirley Knight (Carla)**, Barbara Montgomery (Wanda), Don Parker
(Sparger), Michael Sacks (Mark), Kaiulani Lee (Rona), Douglas Travis (Bar-
tender)

The Marilyn Project (off-Broadway play; Marilyn Monroe as a character)
Original Run: December 25, 1975 (26 performances; The Performance
Garage, New York, NY)
Director: Richard Schnechner
Writer: David Gerard
Cast: **Joan MacIntosh, Elizabeth Le Compte (The Star)**, Debra Wanner
(The Bit Player), Jude Cassidy (The Cameraman), Ron Vawter (The Direc-
tor), Tom Whitaker (The Gaffer), Malcolm Costello (The Makeup Man),
Alise Salzman (The Script Girl)

1976

Goodbye, Norma Jean (film; Marilyn Monroe as a character)
Filmways (95m)
Director: Larry Buchanan
Writers: Lynn Hubert, Larry Buchanan
Cast: **Misty Rowe (Norma Jean Baker/Marilyn Monroe)**, Terrence
Locke (Ralph Johnson), Patch Mckenzie (Ruth Latimer), Preston Han-
son (Hal James), Marty Zagon (Irving Olbach), Andre Philippe (Sam
Dunn)

1979

Winter Kills (film; Marilyn Monroe as roman à clef)
Embassy Pictures (97m)
Director: William Richert
Writer: William Richert (book by Richard Condon)
Cast: **Belinda Bauer (Yvette Malone)**, Jeff Bridges (Nick Kegan), John Huston (Pa Kegan), Anthony Perkins (John Cerruti), Elia Wallach (Joe Diamond), Dorothy Malone (Emma Kegan), Sterling Hayden (Z. K. Dawson), Toshirô Mifune (Keith), Elizabeth Taylor (Lola Comante)

Hey, Marilyn! (play; Marilyn Monroe as a character)
Original Run: 1979 (Citadel Theatre, Edmonton, Alberta, Canada)
Director: Peter Coe
Writer: Cliff Jones
Cast: **Lenore Zann (Marilyn Monroe)**

1980

Moviola: This Year's Blonde (TV miniseries; Marilyn Monroe as a character)
David Wolper Productions (120m)
Original Airdate: May 18, 1980
Director: John Erman
Writer: James Lee (book by Garson Kanin)
Cast: **Constance Forslund (Marilyn Monroe)**, Lloyd Bridges (Johnny Hyde), William Frankfather (John Huston), Norman Fell (Pat Toledo), Vic Tayback (Harry Cohn), Michael Lerner (Jack Warner), John Marley (Joe Schenck), Lee Wallace (Samuel Goldwyn)

Can't Stop the Music (film; Marilyn Monroe as a character)
Associated Film (118m)
Director: Nancy Walker
Writers: Bronte Woodard, Allan Carr
Cast: **Maggie Brendler (Marilyn Monroe)**, The Village People, Valerie Perrine (Samantha Simpson), Bruce Jenner (Ron White), Steve Guttenberg (Jack Morell), Tammy Grimes (Sydney Channing), June Havoc (Helen Morell)

Marilyn, The Untold Story (TV film; Marilyn Monroe as a character)
Lawrence Schiller Productions (180m)

Original Airdate: September 28, 1980
Directors: John Flynn, Jack Arnold
Writer: Dalene Young (book by Norman Mailer)
Cast: **Catherine Hicks (Norma Jean/Marilyn Monroe)**, **Tracey Gold (Young Norma Jean)**, Richard Baseheart (Johnny Hyde), Frank Converse (Joe DiMaggio), Jason Miller (Arthur Miller), Sheree North (Gladys Baker)

Fade to Black (film; Marilyn Monroe as referent)
American Cinema (100m)
Director: Vernon Zimmerman
Writer: Vernon Zimmerman
Cast: **Linda Kerridge (Marilyn)**, Dennis Christopher (Eric), Tim Thomerson (Dr. Moriarity), Eve Brent Ashe (Aunt Stella), Mickey Rourke (Richie), Marcie Barkin (Stacy)

1981

Dances of Love and Death (dance; Marilyn Monroe as a character)
Original Run: November 18, 1981 (18 performances: The Sadler Wells Theatre, London)
Director: Richard Cohan
Composer: Richard Cohan
Cast: **Celia Hulton (Marilyn Monroe)**

1982

Insignificance (play; Marilyn Monroe as a character)
Original Run: July 8, 1982 (Royal Court Theatre, London)
Director: Les Waters
Writer: Terry Johnson
Cast: **Judy Davis (The Actress: Marilyn Monroe)**, Ian McDiarmid (The Scientist: Albert Einstein), Larry Lamb (The Ballplayer: Joe DiMaggio), William Hootkins (The Senator: Senator Joe McCarthy)

1983

Marilyn! (West End play; Marilyn Monroe as a character)
Original Run: March 17, 1983 (Adelphi Theatre, London)

Director: Larry Fuller
Writers: Jacques Wilson, Mort Garson
Cast: **Stephanie Lawrence (Marilyn Monroe)**

Marilyn, An American Fable (Broadway play; Marilyn Monroe as a character)
Original Run: November 20, 1983 (17 performances: Minskoff Theatre, New
   York, NY)
Director: Kenny Ortega
Music and Lyrics: Jeanne Napoli, Doug Frank, Gary Portnoy, Beth Lawrence,
   Norman Thalheimer
Cast: **Alyson Reed (Norma Jean/Marilyn Monroe)**, **Kristi Coombs
   (Young Norma Jean)**, Scott Bakula (Joe DiMaggio), Will Gerard (Arthur
   Miller), Steve Shocket (Lee Strasberg)

Strawhead (play; Marilyn Monroe as a character)
Original Run: September 3, 1983 (20 performances: Provincetown Summer
   Theater, Provincetown, Massachusetts)
Director: Marshall Ogilvy
Writer: Norman Mailer (book *Of Women and Their Elegance* by Norman
   Mailer)
Cast: **Karen MacDonald (Marilyn Monroe)**, Cam Wilder (Joe DiMaggio),
   Allen T. Davis (Arthur Miller), John Oliver (Milton Greene), Georgia Pa-
   pastrat (Amy Greene), John Jiler (Norman Norell, Edward R. Murrow,
   Laurence Olivier, Lee Strasberg), M. J. Pauly (Joan Crawford, Queen Eliz-
   abeth), Judy Brubaker (Paula Strasberg)

1984

Saturday Night Live (TV series; Marilyn Monroe as a character)
NBC (90m)
Opening Credits: 1984–1985 Season
Director: Herb Sargent
Cast: **Julia Louis-Dreyfus (Marilyn Monroe)**, Jim Belushi, Billy Crystal,
   Mary Gross, Christopher Guest, Harry Shearer, Martin Short

1985

The Last Days of Marilyn Monroe, a.k.a. *Say Goodbye to the President* (TV documentary; Marilyn Monroe as [documentary] subject)

BBC (60m)
Original Airdate: October 27, 1985
Director: Christopher Olgiati
Writer: Christopher Olgiati (book *Goddess* by Anthony Summers)

Material Girl (music video; Marilyn Monroe as a character)
Warner Brothers (5m)
Director: Mary Lambert
Writers: Peter Brown, Robert Rans
Cast: **Madonna (as Herself and Marilyn Monroe)**, Keith Carradine (The
    Director)

Jimmy James as Marilyn Monroe (one-man show; Marilyn Monroe as a character)
Circa 1985–1995
Cast: **Jimmy James (Marilyn Monroe)**

Insignificance (film; Marilyn Monroe as a character)
Island Alive (105m)
Director: Nicolas Roeg
Writer: Terry Johnson (play by Terry Johnson)
Cast: **Theresa Russell (The Actress: Norma Jean/Marilyn Monroe)**,
    Michael Emil (The Scientist: Albert Einstein), Tony Curtis (The Senator:
    Senator Joe McCarthy), Gary Busey (The Ballplayer: Joe DiMaggio),
    Cassie Stuart (Young Norma Jean)

1987

Marilyn Monroe: Beyond the Legend (documentary; Marilyn Monroe as [docu-
    mentary] subject)
A Wombat Production (60m)
Directors: Gene Feldman, Suzette Winter
Writers: Gene Feldman, Suzette Winter
Narrator: Richard Widmark

Hoover vs. The Kennedys: The Second Civil War (TV miniseries; Marilyn Monroe
    as a character)
Operation Prime Time (240m)
Original Airdates: November 18 and 25, 1987
Director: Michael O'Herlihy
Writer: Lionel E. Siegel

Cast: **Heather Thomas (Marilyn Monroe)**, Jack Warden (J. Edgar Hoover), Robert Pine (John F. Kennedy), Nicholas Campbell (Robert F. Kennedy), Richard Anderson (Lyndon Johnson), Le Land Gant (Martin Luther King)

Swimming to Cambodia (film; Marilyn Monroe as referent)
Columbia (87m)
Director: Jonathan Demme
Writer: Spalding Gray (play by Spalding Gray)
Cast: Spalding Gray

Rendezvous in Montreal (computer-animated film; Marilyn Monroe as a character)
(5m)
Directors: Nadia Magnenot Thalmann, Daniel Thalmann
Writers: Nadia Magnenot Thalmann, Daniel Thalmann
Cast: **computer-generated Marilyn Monroe**, computer-generated Humphrey Bogart

1988

Remembering Marilyn (TV documentary; Marilyn Monroe as a [documentary] subject)
ABC (60m)
Original Airdate: May 8, 1988
Director: Andrew Solt
Writer: Theodore Strauss
Narrator: Lee Remick

Dead Marilyn (off-Broadway play; Marilyn Monroe as a character)
Original Run: October 31, 1988 (20 performances: La Mama Theatre, New York, NY)
Director: Peter Stack
Writer: Peter Stack
Cast: **Peter Stack (Marilyn Monroe)**

Mondo New York (mock documentary; Marilyn Monroe as referent)
Island Pictures (83m)
Director: Harvey Keith
Writers: Harvey Keith, David Silver
Cast: **Phoebe Legere**, Joey Arias, Rick Aviles, Charlie Barnett, Karen Finley, Lydia Lunch, Ann Magnuson, John Sex, Shannah Laumeister

And God Created Woman (film; Marilyn Monroe as roman à clef)
Vestron Pictures (94m)
Director: Roger Vadim
Writer: R. J. Stewart
Cast: **Rebecca De Mornay (Robin Shay)**, Vincent Spano (Billy Moran), Frank Langella (James Tiernan), Donovan Leitch (Peter Moran), Judith Chapman (Alecandra Tiernan), Jamie McEnnan (Timmy Moran)

1989

Goodnight, Sweet Marilyn (film; Marilyn Monroe as a character)
Film Karl Spiels/Lisa Film Productions (94m)
Director: Larry Buchanan
Writer: Larry Buchanan
Cast: **Paula Lane (Marilyn Monroe), Misty Rowe (Norma Jean Baker)**, Jeremy Slate (Mesquite), Joyce Lower (The Psychiatrist), Phyllis Coates (The Ghost of Gladys Baker), Gerry Niles Berry (The Masseur)

Another Chance (film; Marilyn Monroe as a character)
Shining Armour Communications (99m)
Director: Jerry Vint
Writers: Jerry Vint, Roger Camras
Cast: **Arlen Lorre (Marilyn Monroe)**, Bruce Greenwood (John Ripley), Vanessa Angel (Jackie), Bernard Behrens (St. Peter), Barbara Edwards (The Temptress), Robert Sacchi (Humphrey Bogart)

1990

Twin Peaks (TV series; Marilyn Monroe as referent)
Lynch/Frost Productions, Inc. (60m per episode)
Airdates: April 18, 1990–June 10, 1991
Directors: David Lynch, Mark Frost, Tim Hunter, Caleb Deschanel, Uli Edel, Diane Keaton, etc.
Writers: David Lynch, Mark Frost, Harley Peyton, Robert English, Barry Pullman, Jerry Stahl
Cast: **Sheryl Lee (Laura Palmer)**, Kyle MacLachlan (Agent Dale Cooper), Michael Ontkean (Sheriff Harry S. Truman), Piper Laurie (Catherine Martell), Joan Chen (Josie Packard), Richard Beymer (Ben Horne), Lara

Flynn-Boyle (Donna Hayward), Sherilyn Fenn (Audrey Horne), Mädchen Amick (Shelly Johnson), Dana Ashbrook (Bobby Briggs), Peggy Lipton (Norma Jennings), Jack Nance (Peter Martell), Russ Tamblyn (Lawrence Jacoby)

Marilyn: Something's Got to Give (TV documentary; Marilyn Monroe as a [documentary] subject)
20th Century-Fox (60m)
Original Airdate: December 13, 1990
Director: Henry Schipper
Writer: Henry Schipper
Narrator: Henry Schipper

Bye Bye Baby (film; Marilyn Monroe as a character)
International Dean Film (80m)
Director: Enrico Oldoini
Writers: Liliana Betti, Paola Costella, Enrico Oldoini
Cast: **Liza Ross (The Voice of Marilyn Monroe)**, Carol Alt (Sandra), Luca Barbareschi (Paolo), Brigitte Nielsen (Lisa), Jason Connery (Marcello)

Everybody Wins (film; Marilyn Monroe as roman à clef)
Orion Pictures (98m)
Director: Karl Reisz
Writer: Arthur Miller
Cast: **Debra Winger (Angela Crispini)**, Nick Nolte (Tom O'Toole), Will Patton (Jerry), Judith Ivey (Connie), Kathleen Wilholte (Amy), Jack Warden (Judge Harry Murdoch), Frank Converse (Charley Haggerty), Steven Skybell (Father Mancini)

1991

The Discovery of Marilyn Monroe, a.k.a. *Marilyn Monroe, the Early Years* (documentary; Marilyn Monroe as [documentary] subject)
United American Video (50m)
Director: Clay Cole
Writer: Clay Cole
Narrator: Clay Cole

Red Dwarf (TV series, UK; Marilyn Monroe as a character)
BBC (30m)

"Meltdown" episode
Original Airdate: March 21, 1991
Director: Ed Bye
Writers: Rob Grant, Doug Naylor
Cast: **Pauline Bailey (Marilyn Monroe)**, Chris Barrie (Rimmer), Craig
    Charles (Lester), Danny John-Jules (Cat), Hattie Hayridge (Holly), Robert
    Llwellyn (Kryten), Clayton Mark (Elvis), Kenneth Hadley (Hitler)

Marilyn and Me (TV film; Marilyn Monroe as a character)
ABC (120m)
Original Airdate: September 22, 1991
Director: John Patterson
Writers: Robert Boris, Stu Samuels
Cast: **Susan Griffiths (Norma Jean/Marilyn Monroe)**, Jess Dabson
    (Robert Slatzer), Joel Grey (Darryl F. Zanuck), Sal Lindi (Joe DiMaggio)

A Woman Named Jackie (TV miniseries; Marilyn Monroe as a character)
Lester Persky Productions (360m)
Original Airdates: October 14, 15, and 16, 1991
Director: Larry Peerce
Writer: Roger O'Hirson (book by C. David Heymann)
Cast: **Eve Gordon (Marilyn Monroe)**, Roma Downey (Jacqueline Bouvier
    Kennedy Onassis), Stephen Collins (John F. Kennedy), William Devane
    (Black Jack Bouvier), Josef Sommer (Joseph P. Kennedy), Rosemary Mur-
    phy (Rose Kennedy)

1992

Marilyn: The Last Interview (TV documentary; Marilyn Monroe as [documen-
    tary] subject)
HBO Cable (30m)
Original Airdate: August 7, 1992
Director: Richard Meryman
Writer: Richard Meryman
Narrator: Richard Meryman

Death Becomes Her (film; Marilyn Monroe as a character)
Universal (103m)
Director: Robert Zemeckis
Writers: Martin Donovan, David Koepp

Cast: **Stephanie Anderson (Marilyn Monroe)**, Meryl Streep (Madeline Ashton), Bruce Willis (Ernest Menville), Goldie Hawn (Helen Sharp), Isabella Rossellini (Lisle Van Rhumans)

Madame Montand and Mrs. Miller (TV film, UK; Marilyn Monroe as a character)
BBC (50m)
Original Airdate: August 9, 1992
Director: Morag Fullarton
Writer: Sue Glover
Cast: **Debra Sandlund (Marilyn Monroe Miller)**, Pauline Larriere (Simone Signoret Montand), Libby Morris (Patti)

The Marilyn Files (TV documentary; Marilyn Monroe as a [documentary] subject)
Producers Video Inc. (120m)
Original Airdate: August 14, 1992
Director: Bill Foster
Writer: Robert Slatzer (book by Robert Slatzer)
Hosts: Bill Bixby, Jane Wallace

Used People (film; Marilyn Monroe as referent)
20th Century-Fox (115m)
Director: Beeban Kidron
Writer: Todd Graff (play *The Grandma Plays*)
Cast: **Marcia Gay Harden (Norma)**, Shirley MacLaine (Pearl Berman), Kathy Bates (Bibby), Jessica Tandy (Frieda), Marcello Mastroianni (Joe Melendandri), Sylvia Sidney (Becky), Joe Pantolino (Frank), Matthew Brenton (Sweet Pea)

Cool World (film; Marilyn Monroe as referent)
Paramount Pictures (102m)
Director: Ralph Bakshi
Writers: Michael Grais, Mark Victor
Cast: **Kim Basinger (Holli Would)**, Gabriel Byrne (Jack Deebs), Brad Pitt (Frank Harris), Michele Abrams (Jennifer Malley), Frank Sinatra Jr. (Himself)

Legends (documentary; Marilyn Monroe as referent)
Orion Home Video (54m)
Director: Ilana Bar-Din
Writer: Ilana Bar-Din

Cast: **Susan Griffiths (Marilyn Monroe Impersonator)**, Jonathan Von
  Brana (Elvis Presley Impersonator), Monica Maris (Judy Garland Impersonator), John Stuart (Himself)

1993

Netherworld (film; Marilyn Monroe as a character)
Full Moon Entertainment (91m)
Director: David Schmoeller
Writers: Billy Chicago, Charles Band
Cast: **Holly Butler (Marilyn Monroe)**, Michael Bendetti (Corey Thorn-
  ton), Holly Floria (Dianne), Denise Gentile (Delores), Anjanette Comer
  (Mrs. Palmer)

Calendar Girl (film; Marilyn Monroe as a character)
Columbia (90m)
Director: John Whitesell
Writer: Paul W. Shapiro
Cast: **Stephanie Anderson (Marilyn Monroe)**, **Cortney Page (the Voice
  of Marilyn Monroe)**, Jason Priestly (Roy Darpinian), Gabriel Olds (Ned
  Bleuer), Jerry O'Connell (Scott Foreman), Joe Pantoliano (Harvey Darpin-
  ian), Steve Railsback (Roy's Father)

Body (play; Marilyn Monroe as a character)
Original Run: January 24, 1993 (36 performances: The Players Ring,
  Portsmouth, New Hampshire)
Director: Gary Newton
Writer: David J. Mauriello
Cast: **Maliraya Smith (Marilyn Monroe)**, Chris Doubek (Tim), Thomas
  Noe (Gus), Jon Marvitt (Gonzo)

Marilyn: The Last Word (documentary; Marilyn Monroe as a [documentary]
  subject)
Paramount (60m)
Directors: Joe Tobin, Paul Nichols
Writer: Peter Brennan
Hosts: Barry Nolan, Terry Murphy

Quantum Leap (TV series; Marilyn Monroe as a character)
NBC (60m)

"Goodbye, Norma Jean" episode
Original Airdate: March 2, 1993
Director: Christopher Hibler
Writer: Richard C. Okie
Cast: **Susan Griffiths (Marilyn Monroe)**, Scott Bakula (Dr. Sam Beckett), Dean Stockwell (Al Calavicci), Liz Vassey (Barbara Whitmore), Larry Pennell (Clark Gable), Tony Young (John Huston)

Marilyn (opera; Marilyn Monroe as a character)
Original Run: October 6, 1993 (7 performances: The New York State Theatre, New York, NY)
Directors: Jerome Sirlin, Paul L. King
Libretto: Norman Rosten
Composer: Ezra Laderman
Cast: **Kathryn Gamberoni (Marilyn Monroe)**, Susanne Marsee (Rose), Michele McBride (Vinnie), Michael Rees Davis (The Senator), Ron Baker (The Psychiatrist), Philip Cokorinos (Rick), John Lankston, Jonathan Green (The Hollywood Moguls)

1994

Marilyn Monroe, Life after Death (TV documentary; Marilyn Monroe as [documentary] subject)
Showtime Cable (90m)
Original Airdate: June 4, 1994
Director: Gordon Freedman
Writer: Gordon Freedman
Narrator: Roscoe Lee Brown

Marilyn and Bobby: Her Final Affair (TV film; Marilyn Monroe as a character)
USA Cable (120m)
Original Airdate: August 4, 1994
Director: Bradford May
Writer: Gerald Macdonald
Cast: **Melody Anderson (Marilyn Monroe)**, James F. Kelly (Robert F. Kennedy), Thomas Wagner (Jimmy Hoffa), Richard Dysart (J. Edgar Hoover), Raymond Serra (Sam Giancana)

Pulp Fiction (film; Marilyn Monroe as a character)
Miramax (150m)

Director: Quentin Tarantino
Writers: Quentin Tarantino, Roger Avary
Cast: **Susan Griffiths (Marilyn Monroe)**, John Travolta (Vincent Vega), Samuel L. Jackson (Jules Winnfield), Uma Thurman (Mia Wallace), Bruce Willis (Butch Coolidge), Ving Rhames (Marsellus)

Holy Matrimony (film; Marilyn Monroe as referent)
Buena Vista (93m)
Director: Leonard Nimoy
Writers: David Weisberg, Douglas S. Cook
Cast: **Patricia Arquette (Havana)**, Joseph Gordon-Levitt (Zeke), Armin Mueller-Stahl (Wilhelm), Tate Donovan (Peter), John Schuck (Markowski)

With Honors (film; Marilyn Monroe as referent)
Warner Brothers (103m)
Director: Alek Keshishian
Writer: William Mastrosimone
Cast: **Sunshine H. Hernandez (Marilyn Monroe)**, Joe Pesci (Simon Wilder), Brendan Fraser (Monty Kessler), Moira Kelly (Courtney Blumenthal), Patrick Dempsey (Everett Calloway), Josh Hamilton (Jeff Hawkes), Gore Vidal (Professor Pitkannan)

Blue Sky (film; Marilyn Monroe as referent)
Orion (101m)
Director: Tony Richardson
Writers: Rama Laurie Stagner, Arlen Sarner, Jerry Leichtling
Cast: **Jessica Lange (Carly Marshall)**, Tommy Lee Jones (Hank Marshall), Powers Booth (Vince Johnson), Carrie Snodgrass (Vera Johnson), Amy Locane (Alex Marshall), Chris O'Donnell (Glen Johnson)

1996

My Fellow Americans (film; Marilyn Monroe as a character)
Warner Brothers (101m)
Director: Peter Segal
Writers: E. Jack Kaplan, Richard Chapman, Peter Tolan
Cast: **Jennifer Austin (Marilyn Monroe)**, Jack Lemmon (President Russell P. Kramer), James Garner (President Matt Douglas), Dan Aykroyd (President William Haney), John Heard (Vice President Ted Matthews), Lauren

Bacall (Margaret Kramer), Sela Ward (Kaye Griffin), Todd McDurmont (Elvis Presley)

Norma Jean and Marilyn (TV film; Marilyn Monroe as a character)
HBO Cable (125m)
Original Airdate: May 18, 1996
Director: Tim Fywell
Writer: Jill Isaacs
Cast: **Ashley Judd (Norma Jean)**, **Mira Sorvino (Marilyn Monroe)**, Ron Rifkin (Johnny Hyde), Josh Charles (Eddie Jordan), David Dukes (Arthur Miller), Peter Dobson (Joe DiMaggio), John Rubenstein (Darryl F. Zanuck), Lindsay Crouse (Natasha Lytess), Steven Culp (Robert F. Kennedy)

Marilyn, The Mortal Goddess (TV documentary; Marilyn Monroe as a [documentary] subject)
A&E Cable (120m)
Original Airdate: June 1, 1996
Director: Bill Harris
Writers: Kevin Burns, Jeff Scheftel, Andy Thomas
Host: Peter Graves

1997

Jackie: An American Life (Broadway play; Marilyn as a character)
Original Run: November 10, 1997 (Belasco Theatre, New York, NY)
Director: Gip Hoppe
Writer: Gip Hoppe
Cast: **Kristine Nielsen (Marilyn Monroe)**, Margaret Colin (Jacqueline Bouvier Kennedy Onassis), Bill Camp (Bobby Kennedy, Hugh Auchincloss, and others), Thomas Derrah (Teddy Kennedy, Truman Capote, and others) Gretchen Egolf (Lee Bouvier and others), Lisa Emery (Eunice Kennedy and others), Victor Sleazak (John F. Kennedy and others), Derek Smith (Frank Sinatra and others)

1998

Nobody Dies on Friday (play; Marilyn Monroe as a character)
Original Run: April 26, 1998 (35 performances: Hasty Pudding Theater, Cambridge, Massachusetts)

Director: David Wheeler
Writer: Robert Brustein
Cast: **Rachel Warren (The Voice of Marilyn Monroe)**, Alvin Epstein (Lee Strasberg), Annette Miller (Paula Strasberg), Emma Roberts (Susan Strasberg), Robert Kropf (John Strasberg)

Finding Graceland (film; Marilyn Monroe as referent)
Largo Entertainment (96m)
Director: David Winkler
Writer: Jason Horwitch
Cast: **Bridget Fonda (Ashley/Marilyn Monroe)**, Harvey Keitel (John Barrows/Elvis Presley), Johnathon Schaech (Byron Gruman), Gretchen Moll (Beatrice)

The Rat Pack (TV film; Marilyn Monroe as a character)
HBO Cable (120m)
Original Airdate: September 20, 1998
Director: Rob Cohen
Writer: Kario Salem
Cast: **Barbara Niven (Marilyn Monroe)**, Ray Liotta (Frank Sinatra), Joe Mantegna (Dean Martin), Don Cheadle (Sammy Davis Jr.), Angus MacFadyen (Peter Lawford), William Petersen (John F. Kennedy), Zeljko Ivanek (Robert F. Kennedy), Deborah Kara Unger (Ava Gardner), John Diehl (Joe DiMaggio)

Spice World (film; Marilyn Monroe as referent)
Polgram (92m)
Director: Bob Spiers
Writer: Kim Fuller
Cast: The Spice Girls: **Geri Halliwell (Ginger Spice)**, Melanie Brown (Scary Spice), Victoria Adams (Posh Spice), Melanie Chisholm (Sporty Spice), Emma Bunton (Baby Spice), Richard E. Grant (Clifford), Alan Cumming (Piers Cutherton-Smyth), Roger Moore (The Chief)

Little Voice (film; Marilyn Monroe as a referent)
Miramax (96m)
Director: Mark Herman
Writer: Mark Herman (play *The Rise and Fall of Little Voice* by Jim Cartwright)
Cast: **Jane Horrocks (Little Voice)**, Brenda Blethyn (Mari), Ewan McGregor (Billy), Michael Caine (Ray Say), Jim Broadbent (Mr. Boo)

1999

The Final Hours of Norma Jeane (play; Marilyn Monroe as a character)
Original Run: January 12, 1999 (25 performances: Edge Theatre, South Beach, Florida)
Director: Jim Tommaney
Writer: Jim Tommaney
Cast: **Naia Kelly (Norma Jeane/Marilyn Monroe)**, Elia Patrick (Lars), Harvey Guinon (Rick)

Introducing Dorothy Dandridge (TV film; Marilyn Monroe as a character)
HBO Cable (115m)
Original Airdate: August 14, 1999
Director: Martha Coolidge
Writer: Shonda Rhimes, Scott Abbott (book by Earl Mills)
Cast: **Kerri Randles (Marilyn Monroe)**, Halle Berry (Dorothy Dandridge), Brent Spiner (Earl Mills), Klaus Maria Brandauer (Otto Preminger), Obba Babatundé (Harold Nicholas), Loretta Devine (Ruby Dandridge), Cynda Williams (Vivian Dandridge), William Atherton (Darryl F. Zanuck)

The Underground Comedy Movie (film; Marilyn Monroe as a character)
Phaedra Cinema (87m)
Director: Vince Offer
Writer: Vince Offer
Cast: **Gena Lee Nolin (Marilyn Monroe)**, Vince Offer (Vince), Slash (Himself), Michael Clarke Duncan (The Gay Virgin), Joey Buttafuoco (Sonny), Lightfield Lewis (The Virgin Hunter/Juror), Karen Black (The Mother)

2000

The Death of Marilyn Monroe (documentary; Marilyn Monroe as [documentary] subject)
A&E Home Video (60m)
Director: Damian Weyand
Writers: Sean Geary, Seth Grahame-Smith
Narrator: David Ackroyd

E! True Hollywood Story: The Many Loves of Marilyn Monroe (TV documentary; Marilyn Monroe as [documentary] subject)
Director: Tracy Allan
Writer: William Neal
Narrator: Keri Tombazian

Company Man (film; Marilyn Monroe as a character)
Paramount Classics (81m)
Directors: Peter Askin, Douglas McGrath
Writers: Peter Askin, Douglas McGrath
Cast: **Meredith Patterson (Marilyn Monroe)**, Douglas McGrath (Allen Quimp), Sigourney Weaver (Daisy Quimp), John Turturro (Crocker Johnson), Ryan Philippe (Petrov), Denis Leary (Officer Fry), Alan Cumming (General Batista), Anthony LaPaglia (Fidel Castro)

Evil Hill (film; Marilyn Monroe as a character)
Quality Filmed Entertainment (10m)
Director: Ryan Schifrin
Writer: Timothy Dowling
Cast: **Kim Little (Marilyn Monroe)**, Timothy Dowling (Mr. Evil), Jed Gillin (President John F. Kennedy), Rick Burns, Adam Dalesandro (Secret Service Men)

2001

Jackie, Ethel, Joan: Women of Camelot (TV miniseries; Marilyn Monroe as a character)
NBC (240m)
Original Airdates: March 4 and 5, 2001
Director: Larry Shaw
Writer: David Stevens (book by J. Randy Toraborrelli)
Cast: **Sarah La Fleur (Marilyn Monroe)**, Jill Hennessy (Jackie Kennedy), Lauren Holly (Ethel Kennedy), Leslie Stefanson (Joan Kennedy), Matt Letscher (Ted Kennedy), Robert Knepper (Robert F. Kennedy), Harve Presnell (Joe Kennedy), Daniel Hugh Kelly (John F. Kennedy)

Blonde (TV miniseries; Marilyn Monroe as a character)
CBS (240m)
Original Airdates: May 13 and 16, 2001

Director: Joyce Chopra
Writer: Joyce Eliason (book by Joyce Carol Oates)
Cast: **Poppy Montgomery (Norma Jean/Marilyn Monroe)**, Patricia Richardson (Gladys Baker), Wallace Shawn (I. E. Shinn), Griffin Dunne (Arthur Miller), Titus Welliver (Joe DiMaggio), Patrick Dempsey (Cass Chaplin), Eric Borgosian (Otto Ose), Richard Roxburgh (Mr. R.), Jess Ackler (Eddie G.)

Marilyn Monroe: The Final Days (TV documentary; Marilyn Monroe as [documentary] subject)
AMC Cable (120m)
Original Airdate: May 30, 2001
Director: Patty Irvins Sheckt
Writers: Monica Bider
Narrator: James Coburn

Town & Country (film; Marilyn Monroe as referent)
Entertainment Film (104m)
Director: Peter Chelsom
Writers: Michael Laughlin, Buck Henry
Cast: **Jenna Elfman (Auburn)**, Warren Beatty (Peter Stoddard), Diane Keaton (Ellie Stoddard), Goldie Hawn (Mona Miller), Garry Shandling (Griffin Miller), Andie MacDowell (Eugenie), Natasha Kinski (Alex)

Monkeybone (film; Marilyn Monroe as referent)
20th Century-Fox (93m)
Director: Henry Selick
Writer: Sam Hamm (graphic novel *Dark Tower* by Kaja Blackley)
Cast: **John Turturro (the Voice of Monkeybone)**, Brendan Fraser (Stu Milley), Bridget Fonda (Julie McElroy), Giancarlo Esposito (Hypnos), Rose McGowan (Kitty), Megan Mullally (Kimmy), Lisa Zane (Medusa), Whoopi Goldberg (Death)

American Iliad (play; Marilyn Monroe as a character)
Original Run: June 6, 2001 (45 performances: Victory Theatre, Burbank, California)
Director: Maria Gobetti
Writer: Donald Freed
Cast: **Diane Costa (Marilyn Monroe)**, Al Rossi (Richard Nixon), David Clennon (John F. Kennedy)

2002

Killing Castro (Internet film; Marilyn Monroe as a character)
I Film (3m)
Director: Clark Westerman
Writer: Clark Westerman
Cast: **Michele Merseran (Marilyn Monroe)**, Nick Spano (Agent
    O'Connell), Tristan Roger (Agent X), Robert Berson (Mister X)

Just a Dream (TV film; Marilyn Monroe as a character)
Showtime Productions (97m)
Director: Danny Glover
Writers: Ken Topolsky, Melanie Wilson
Cast: **Marilyn B. Monroe (Marilyn Monroe)**, Carl Lumbly (J.M.), Robby
    Benson (Dr. Hank Starbuck), Ally Sheedy (Maureen Starbuck), Rodney
    Grant (Cecil Running Bear), Jeremy Sumpter (Henry Starbuck), Amy
    Madigan (Cindy)

2003

Timequest (film; Marilyn Monroe as a character)
Ardustry Home Entertainment (95m)
Director: Robert Dyke
Writer: Robert Dyke
Cast: **Shelly Marks (Norma Jean)**, Joseph Murphy (Raymond Mead), Vic-
    tor Slevak (John F. Kennedy), Caprice Beneditti (Jackie Kennedy), Vince
    Grant (Robert Kennedy), Ralph Waite (The Time Traveler)

L.A. Confidential (TV film; Marilyn Monroe as a character)
Trio Cable (60m)
Original Airdate: November 18, 2003
Director: Eric Laneuville
Writer: Wolan Green (book by James Elroy)
Cast: **Nectar Rose (Marilyn Monroe)**, Kiefer Sutherland (Jack Vincennes),
    David Conrad (Ed Exley), Josh Hopkins (Bud White), Eric Roberts (Pierce
    Patchett), Melissa George (Lynn Bracken)

Marilyn Monroe: Medical Secrets (TV documentary; Marilyn Monroe as a [doc-
    umentary] subject)

Discovery Channel Cable (60m)
Original Airdate: December 24, 2003
Director: Daniel Levitt
Writer: Daniel Levitt
Narrator: Christopher Hasson

2004

The Mystery of Natalie Wood (TV film; Marilyn Monroe as a character)
NBC (180m)
Original Airdate: March 1, 2004
Director: Peter Bogdanovich
Writer: Elizabeth Egloff (books by Suzanne Finstad, Warren G. Harris)
Cast: **Sophie Monk (Marilyn Monroe)**, Justine Waddell (Natalie Wood),
Michael Weatherly (Robert Wagner), Alice Krige (Maria Grudin), Colin
Friels (Nick Grudin), Matthew Settle (Christopher Walken)

The Sopranos (TV series; Marilyn Monroe as referent)
HBO Cable (60m)
"In Camelot" episode
Original Airdate: April 18, 2003
Director: Steve Buscemi
Writer: Terence Winter
Cast: **Polly Bergen (Fran Felstein)**, James Gandolfini (Tony Soprano), Edie
Falco (Carmela Soprano), Jamie Lynn Sigler (Meadow Soprano), Robert
Iler (Anthony Soprano Jr.), Dominic Chianese (Uncle Junior), Lorraine
Bracco (Dr. Jennifer Melfi), Michael Imperioli (Christopher Moltisanti)

Appendix B

Marilyn Monroe Filmography

Marilyn's roles are shown in **bold** type. (In addition to the films here, it is quite possible that Marilyn Monroe may have also appeared as an extra, laboring away somewhere off in the background of the following 20th Century-Fox movies: *The Shocking Miss Pilgrim*, 1946; *Mother Wore Tights*, 1947; and *Green Grass of Wyoming*, 1948.)

1947

Dangerous Years
20th Century-Fox (77m)
Director: Arthur Pierson
Writer: Arnold Belgard
Cast: William Halop (Danny Jones), Ann E. Todd (Doris Martin), Jerome Cowan (Weston), Anabel Shaw (Connie Burns), Richard Gaines (Edgar Burns), **Marilyn Monroe (Evie)**
Marilyn is given a couple of lines of dialogue as she plays Evie, a beautiful waitress slinging out hash to the teenaged punks hanging out at the greasy spoon where she works.

1948

Scudda Hoo! Scudda Hay!
20th Century-Fox (98m)
Director: F. Hugh Herbert

Writer: F. Hugh Herbert (story by George Agnew Chamberlain)
Cast: June Haver (Rad McGill), Lon McCallister (Snug Dominy), Walter Brennan (Tony Maule), Anne Revere (Judith Dominy), Natalie Wood (Bean McGill), **Marilyn Monroe (The Girlfriend)**
While a farmer's son carries on an absurd obsession with a pair of mules, Marilyn can be briefly glimpsed rowing a boat on a lake.

Ladies of the Chorus
Columbia (61m)
Director: Phil Karlson
Writers: Joseph Carole, Harry Sauber
Cast: Adele Jergens (Mae Martin), **Marilyn Monroe (Peggy Martin)**, Rand Brooks (Randy Carroll), Nana Bryant (Mrs. Carroll)
Marilyn is given a sizable part in a movie playing a leggy burlesque showgirl who has an act with her equally leggy mother (Adele Jergens).

1949

Love Happy
United Artists (85m)
Director: David Miller
Writers: Frank Tashlin, Mac Benoff (story by Harpo Marx)
Cast: Harpo Marx (Harpo), Chico Marx (Faustino the Great), Groucho Marx (Sam Grunion), Vera-Ellen (Maggie Phillips), Ilona Massey (Madame Egelichi), **Marilyn Monroe (Grunion's Client)**
The plot of this movie, such as it is, concerns Groucho Marx as an unlikely private eye, hot on the trail of the thief of a priceless necklace. Marilyn slinks her way across the screen as Groucho's most memorable client.

1950

A Ticket to Tomahawk
20th Century-Fox (90m)
Director: Richard Sale
Writers: Richard Sale, Mary Loos
Cast: Dan Dailey (Johnny), Anne Baxter (Kit Dodge Jr.), Rory Calhoun (Dakota), Walter Brennan (Terence Sweeney), Connie Gilchrist (Madame Adelaide), **Marilyn Monroe (Clara)**

A relatively painless spoof of movie Westerns with some eye-popping Technicolor scenery going for it and an even more eye-popping Marilyn as a
blonde chorus girl wearing a bright yellow dress.

The Asphalt Jungle
MGM (112m)
Director: John Huston
Writers: Ben Maddow, John Huston (book by W. R. Burnett)
Cast: Sterling Hayden (Dix Handley), Louis Calhern (Alonzo D. Em-
merich), Jean Hagen (Doll Conovan), James Whitmore (Gus Minissi),
Sam Jaffe (Doc Erwin Rieden-Schneider), **Marilyn Monroe (Angela
Phinlay)**
Powerfully directed and acted, this classic crime story about the robbery of a
jewelry store provided Marilyn with one of her best earlier roles playing the
sexy young "niece" of crooked lawyer Louis Calhern.

All About Eve
20th Century-Fox (138m)
Director: Joseph L. Mankiewicz
Writer: Joseph L. Mankiewicz (story by Mary Orr)
Cast: Bette Davis (Margo Channing), Anne Baxter (Eve Harrington), George
Sanders (Addison DeWitt), Gary Merrill (Bill Sampson), Celeste Holm
(Karen Richards), Hugh Marlowe (Lloyd Richards), Thelma Ritter (Birdie),
Marilyn Monroe (Miss Caswell)
A great story about the often traitorous backstage world of Broadway. Sharp
dialogue, the great Bette Davis, and Marilyn in the showcase role of Miss
Caswell add up to one of the all-time classic American movies.

The Fireball
20th Century-Fox (84m)
Director: Tay Garnett
Writers: Tay Garnett, Horace McCoy
Cast: Mickey Rooney (Johnny Casar), Pat O'Brien (Father O'Hare), Beverly
Tyler (Mary Reeves), **Marilyn Monroe (Polly)**
Looking especially blonde and willowy, Marilyn is ridiculously cast as (of all
things) a roller-derby groupie hot for Mickey Rooney.

Right Cross
MGM (90m)
Director: John Sturges
Writer: Charles Schnee

Cast: June Allyson (Pat O'Malley), Dick Powell (Rick Garvey), Ricardo Montalban (Johnny Monterez), Lionel Barrymore (Sean O'Malley), **Marilyn Monroe (Dusky Ledoux)**

Blink and you'll miss Marilyn in a bit part as Dick Powell's stunning girlfriend with the most memorable name of Dusky Ledoux.

1951

Hometown Story
MGM (61m)
Director: Arthur Pierson
Writer: Arthur Pierson
Cast: Jeffrey Lynn (Mike Washburn), Donald Crisp (John MacFarland), Alan Hale Jr. (Slim Haskins), **Marilyn Monroe (Miss Martin)**

Marilyn more than holds her own as an attractive office receptionist constantly having to dodge her lecherous boss's endless advances.

As Young as You Feel
20th Century-Fox (77m)
Director: Lamar Trotti
Writer: Lamar Trotti (story by Paddy Chayefsky)
Cast: Monty Woolley (John Hodges), Thelma Ritter (Della Hodges), David Wayne (Joe), Jean Peters (Alice Hodges), Constance Bennett (Lucille McKinley), **Marilyn Monroe (Harriet)**

Marilyn breezes her way through this generally breezy comedy, once again playing a shapely secretary on the prowl for rich, old geezers.

Love Nest
20th Century-Fox (84m)
Director: Joseph Newman
Writer: I. A. L. Diamond (book by Scott Corbett)
Cast: June Haver (Connie Scott), William Lundigan (Jim Scott), Frank Fay (Charley Patterson), **Marilyn Monroe (Roberta Stevens)**

The mere sight of Marilyn, as a former out-of-uniform WAC, proves potent enough to blow the cobwebs off of her old army buddy's (William Lundigan) marriage.

Let's Make It Legal
20th Century-fox (77m)
Director: Richard Sale

Writers: I. A. L Diamond, F. Hugh Herbert (story by Mortimer Braus)

Cast: Claudette Colbert (Miriam), Macdonald Carey (Hugh), Zachary Scott (Victor), Barbara Bates (Barbara), Robert Wagner (Jerry), **Marilyn Monroe (Joyce)**

Claudette Colbert and Macdonald Carey might be the stars of this cozy comedy about a middle-aged couple who divorce and reconcile, but Marilyn gets the attention as a voluptuous blonde on the hunt for a rich, old husband.

1952

Clash by Night
RKO (105m)
Director: Fritz Lang
Writer: Alfred Hayes (play by Clifford Odets)
Cast: Barbara Stanwyck (Mae), Paul Douglas (Jerry), Robert Ryan (Earl), **Marilyn Monroe (Peggy)**, J. Carroll Naish (Uncle Vince), Keith Andes (Joe)

Bringing sexiness to the role of a blue jean–clad young woman working in a fish cannery, Marilyn receives star billing for what is essentially a standout supporting part.

We're Not Married
20th Century-Fox (85m)
Director: Edmund Goulding
Writers: Nunnally Johnson, Dwight Taylor (story by Jay Dratler, Gina Kaus)
Cast: Ginger Rogers (Ramona Gladwyn), Fred Allen (Steve Gladwyn), **Marilyn Monroe (Annabel Norris)**, Eve Arden (Katie Woodruff), David Wayne (Jeff Norris), Paul Douglas (Hector Woodruff), Eddie Bracken (Willie Fisher), Zsa Zsa Gabor (Eve Melrose)

Marilyn makes every single second she's on screen count playing a married "Miss Mississippi."

Don't Bother to Knock
20th Century-Fox (96)
Director: Roy Baker
Writer: Daniel Taradash (book by Charlotte Armstrong)
Cast: Richard Widmark (Jed Towers), **Marilyn Monroe (Nell Forbes)**, Anne Bancroft (Lyn Leslie), Elisa Cook Jr. (Eddie Forbes), Jim Backus (Peter Jones)

As a deeply disturbed babysitter, Marilyn infuses her role with a dramatic edginess from start to finish.

Monkey Business
20th Century-Fox (97m)
Director: Howard Hawks
Writers: I. A. L. Diamond, Ben Hecht, Charles Lederer (story by Harry Segall)
Cast: Gary Grant (Barnaby Fulton), Ginger Rogers (Edwina Fulton), Charles Coburn (Mr. Oxley), **Marilyn Monroe (Lois Laurel)**
After a mischievous monkey spikes a watercooler with a youth potion, everybody (but Marilyn's sexy, nontyping secretary) is reduced to an infantile state of being.

O. Henry's Full House
20th Century-Fox (117m)
"The Cop and the Anthem" segment
Director: Henry Koster
Writer: Lamar Trotti (story by O. Henry)
Cast: Charles Laughton (Soapy), **Marilyn Monroe (The Streetwalker)**, David Wayne (Horace)
Even the great O. Henry himself would have fully approved of Marilyn's witty star turn as a Rubenseque, nineteenth-century streetwalker.

1953

Niagara
20th Century-Fox (89m)
Director: Henry Hathaway
Writers: Charles Brackett, Richard Breen, Walter Reisch
Cast: **Marilyn Monroe (Rose Loomis)**, Joseph Cotton (George Loomis), Jean Peters (Polly Cutler), Casey Adams (Ray Cutler)

Gentlemen Prefer Blondes
20th Century-Fox (91m)
Director: Howard Hawks
Writer: Charles Lederer (musical play by Joseph Fields, Anita Loos)
Cast: Jane Russell (Dorothy), **Marilyn Monroe (Lorelei Lee)**, Charles Coburn (Sir Francis Beekman), Elliott Reid (Malone), Tommy Noonan (Gus Esmond), George Winslow (Henry Spofford III)

How to Marry a Millionaire
20th Century-Fox (96m)
Director: Jean Negulesco
Writer: Nunnally Johnson (plays by Zoe Akins, Katherine Albert, and Dale Eunson)
Cast: **Marilyn Monroe (Pola)**, Betty Grable (Loco), Lauren Bacall (Schatze), David Wayne (Freddie Denmark), Rory Calhoun (Eben), Cameron Mitchell (Tom), William Powell (J. D. Hanley)
1953 was Marilyn Monroe's annus mirabilis. After starring in *Niagara*, *Gentlemen Prefer Blondes*, and *How to Marry a Millionaire*, she was finally catapulted into full-fledged Hollywood stardom. Henry Hathaway directed her starring vehicle, *Niagara*, with a masterful command of fluid screen narrative. And she responded to his direction with a star-making performance as a small-town adulteress (unhappily married to Joseph Cotten) with murder on her mind and a skintight blood-red dress on her body. Equally worthy is Marilyn's comedic playing of Lorelei Lee in Howard Hawks's *Gentlemen Prefer Blondes*, the definitive, archetypal sexy, dumb blonde—still clever enough to know that diamonds are a girl's best friend—opposite partner-in-gold-digging Jane Russell. If *How to Marry a Millionaire* is not quite in the same league as Marilyn's two other 1953 films, it's still an enjoyable enough movie on its own terms, with, besides Marilyn, Lauren Bacall, Betty Grable, and Joe MacDonald's luxurious Cinemascope photography of New York all going for it.

River of No Return
20th Century-Fox (91m)
Director: Otto Preminger
Writer: Frank Fenton (story by Louis Lantz),
Cast: Robert Mitchum (Matt Calder), **Marilyn Monroe (Kay)**, Rory Calhoun (Harry Weston), Tommy Retting (Mark Calder)
Although Marilyn dismissed this as being "a grade Z cowboy movie," it does offer Joseph La Shelle's gorgeously filmed scenery (in Cinemascope and Technicolor), and Marilyn delivers a quietly moving performance as a tough saloon singer (with a heart of gold) rather than portraying simply another gold-digging tough cookie.

There's No Business Like Show Business
20th Century-Fox (117m)
Director: Walter Lang
Writers: Henry Ephron, Phoebe Ephron (story by Lamar Trotti)
Cast: Ethel Merman (Molly Donahue), Donald O'Connor (Tim Donahue), **Marilyn Monroe (Vicky)**, Johnnie Ray (Steve Donahue), Mitzi Gaynor (Katy Donahue)

With small plotting but big, splashy musical numbers (songs by Broadway great Irving Berlin), this movie gives Marilyn an opportunity to bump and grind her way through "Heat Wave."

1955

The Seven Year Itch
20th Century-Fox (105m)
Director: Billy Wilder
Writers: George Axelrod, Billy Wilder (play by George Axelrod)
Cast: **Marilyn Monroe (The Girl Upstairs)**, Tom Ewell (Richard Sherman), Evelyn Keyes (Helen Sherman), Sonny Tufts (Tom Mackenzie)
As the beautiful Girl Upstairs, who loves the breeze from the New York subway blowing up her dress, Marilyn creates one of the most iconic scenes in the history of the movies.

1956

Bus Stop
20th Century-Fox (96m)
Director: Joshua Logan
Writer: George Axelrod (play by William Inge)
Cast: **Marilyn Monroe (Cherie)**, Don Murray (Bo), Arthur O'Connell (Virgil), Betty Field (Grace), Eileen Heckart (Vera), Robert Bray (Carl), Hope Lange (Elma)
Playing lonely, worn-at-the-edges saloon singer Cherie, Marilyn delivers one of her three great screen performances (the other two are in *Some Like It Hot* and *The Misfits*).

1957

The Prince and the Showgirl
Warner Brothers (117m)
Director: Laurence Olivier
Writer: Terence Rattigan (play *The Sleeping Prince* by Terence Rattigan)
Cast: **Marilyn Monroe (Elsie)**, Laurence Olivier (Charles, Prince Regent of Carpathia), Sybil Thorndike (The Queen Dowager), Richard Wattis (Mr. Northbrook), Jeremy Spenser (King Nicholas)

Marilyn is at her most beautiful playing a chorus girl opposite Olivier's stuffy prince in this literate, elegantly crafted, and mostly undervalued romantic comedy.

1959

Some Like It Hot
United Artists (122m)
Director: Billy Wilder
Writers: I. A. L. Diamond, Billy Wilder
Cast: Tony Curtis (Joe), Jack Lemmon (Jerry), **Marilyn Monroe (Sugar Kane)**, George Raft (Spats Colombo), Pat O'Brien (Mulligan), Joe E. Brown (Osgood Fielding III), Joan Shawlee (Sweet Sue)
As luscious lounge singer Sugar Kane, Marilyn plays her final—and best—dumb blonde movie role in director Billy Wilder's comic masterpiece.

1960

Let's Make Love
20th Century-Fox (118m)
Director: George Cukor
Writer: Norman Krasna (additional material by Hal Kanter, Arthur Miller)
Cast: **Marilyn Monroe (Amanda)**, Yves Montand (Jean-Marc Clement), Tony Randall (Howard Coffman), Frankie Vaughn (Tony Danton), Milton Berle, Bing Crosby, Gene Kelly (as themselves)
Despite a troubled shooting, numerous script problems, and her own shaky emotional state at the time, Marilyn does breathe some life into her role of an off-Broadway actress who catches the roving eye of swinging billionaire Montand.

1961

The Misfits
United Artists (124m)
Director: John Huston
Writer: Arthur Miller
Cast: **Marilyn Monroe (Roslyn Taber)**, Clark Gable (Gay Langland), Montgomery Clift (Perce Howland), Thelma Ritter (Isabelle Steers), Eli Wallach (Guido)

1962

Something's Got to Give
20th Century-Fox (unfinished)
Director: George Cukor
Writers: Nunnally Johnson, Walter Bernstein (remake of *My Favorite Wife* by Bella and Sam Spewack)
Cast: **Marilyn Monroe (Ellen Arden)**, Dean Martin (Nick Arden), Cyd Charisse (Bianca), Tom Tyron (Steven Burkett), Wally Cox (Shoe Clerk), Phil Silvers (Insurance Salesman), Steve Allen (Dr. Herman Schlick)
In the existing footage of what would have been her thirtieth movie, Marilyn glows as a shipwrecked woman who returns from the dead to the surprise of her newly remarried husband.

Bibliography

Barnes, Clive. "Marilyn: An American Fable." *New York Post*, November 21, 1983.

Baty, S. Paige. *American Monroe: The Making of a Body Politic*. Berkeley: University of California Press, 1995.

Baxter, John. "The Sixties." In *Hollywood: 1920–1970*, edited by Peter Cowie. New York: A. S. Barnes, 1977.

Bego, Mark. *Madonna: Blonde Ambition*. New York: Cooper Square, 2000.

Bessie, Alvah. *The Symbol*. New York: Random House, 1966.

Brustein, Robert. "Nobody Dies on Friday" (unpublished play).

———. *Seasons of Discontent*. New York: Simon and Schuster, 1965.

Carson, Neil. *Arthur Miller*. New York: Grove, 1982.

Curry, Ramona. "Power and Allure: The Mediation of Sexual Difference in the Star Image of Mae West" (unpublished dissertation).

Custen, George F. *BIO/PICS: How Hollywood Constructed Public History*. New Brunswick, N.J.: Rutgers University Press, 1982.

David, Catherine. *Simone Signoret*. Woodstock, N.Y.: Overlook, 1990.

Estrin, Allen. *The Hollywood Professionals: Frank Capra, George Cukor, Clarence Brown*. New York: A. S. Barnes, 1980.

Frame, Shelley. *The Actor's Studio: A History*. Jefferson, N.C.: McFarland, 2001.

Freud, Sigmund. *The Uncanny (On Creativity and the Unconscious: Papers on the Psychology of Art, Literature, Love, Religion)*. Edited by Benjamin Nelson. New York: Harper, 1950.

Glover, Sue. "Madame Montand and Mrs. Miller" (unpublished television play).

Gore, Chris. *The 50 Greatest Movies Never Made*. New York: St. Martin's, 1999.

Gottfried, Martin. "Fame." *New York Post*, November 19, 1974.

Gray, Spaulding. *Swimming to Cambodia*. New York: Theatre Communications Group, 1985.

Guare, John. *Cop-Out*. New York: Samuel French, 1969.

Higham, Charles. *The Art of the American Film, 1900–1971*. New York: Doubleday, 1973.

Hoppe, Gip. *Jackie: An American Life*. New York: Samuel French, 1998.

Johnson, Terry. *Insignificance*. London: Methuen, 1982.

Kael, Pauline. *Reeling*. Boston: Little, Brown, 1976.

Klinger, Barbara. *Melodrama and Meaning: History, Culture, and the Films of Douglas Sirk*. Bloomington: Indiana University Press, 1994.

Koenenn, Joseph C. "Marilyn: Alive and Kicking." *New York Post*, October 26, 1988.

Mauriello, David J. "Body" (unpublished play).

Nightingale, Benedict. "As Theater, 'Doonesbury' Lacks True Satirical Bite." *New York Times*, November 27, 1983.

Robinson, Jeffery. *Bardot: An Intimate Portrait*. New York: Donald I. Fine, 1996.

Rothstein, Edward. "New Milieu for Monroe: City Opera's 'Marilyn.'" *New York Times*, October 8, 1993.

Sante, Luc. "Her Story." *New York Review of Books*, June 15, 2000.

Sexton, Martha. *Jayne Mansfield and the American Fifties*. Boston: Houghton Mifflin, 1975.

Signoret, Simone. *Nostalgia Isn't What It Used to Be*. New York: Harper & Row, 1978.

Silverman, Debra. *Selling Culture*. New York: Pantheon, 1986.

Summers, Anthony. *Goddess: The Secret Lives of Marilyn Monroe*. New York: Macmillan, 1985.

Swed, Mark. "With Its World Premiere Festival, New York City Opera Found That the Public and Press Have an Appetite for New Work." *Opera News*, December 25, 1993.

Taraborrelli, Randy. *Jackie, Ethel and Joan: Women of Camelot*. New York: Rose, 2000.

Tommaney, Jim. "The Final Hours of Norma Jean" (unpublished play).

Trowbridge, Clifton W. "Arthur Miller: Between Pathos and Tragedy." In *Arthur Miller*, edited by Harold Bloom. New York: Chelsea House, 1987.

Variety. "The Life and Death of Marilyn Monroe." June 15, 1971.

Title Index

Note: The parentheses following each title identifies the type of work and provides the date of issue as well as (if applicable) the representation of Marilyn, both actor and role.

After the Fall (1964 Broadway play, Barbara Loden as Maggie), 95–98

After the Fall (1974 TV film, Faye Dunaway as Maggie), 106

American Iliad (2001 play, Diane Costa as Marilyn), 70–73

And God Created Woman (1957 original film, Brigitte Bardot as Juliet Hardy), 86–87

And God Created Woman (1987 remake film, Rebecca De Mornay as Robin Shay), 108–9

Another Chance (1989 film, Arlen Lorre as Marilyn), 31–32

The Apple Tree, "Passionella" (1966 Broadway play, Barbara Harris as Ella/Passionella), 98–100

Blonde (2001 TV miniseries, Poppy Montgomery as Marilyn), 66–70

Blue Sky (1994 film, Jessica Lange as Carly Marshall impersonating Marilyn), 151–52

Body (1993 play, Maliraya Smith as Marilyn), 43–45

Bye Bye Baby (1990 film, Liza Ross as the voice of Marilyn), 32–33

Calendar Girl (1993 film, Stephanie Anderson as Marilyn and Cortney Page as the voice of Marilyn), 42–43

Can't Stop the Music (1980 film, Maggie Brendler as Marilyn), 9–10

Come on Strong (1962 Broadway play, Carroll Baker as Virginia Karger), 94–95

Company Man (2000 film, Meredith Patterson as Marilyn), 62–63

Cool World (1992 film, Kim Basinger as Holli Would impersonating Marilyn), 147–48

Cop-Out (1969 off-Broadway play, Linda Lavin as Marilyn), 1–2

Dances of Love and Death (1981 dance, Celia Hulton as Marilyn), 12–13

Dead Marilyn (1969 off-Broadway play, Linda Lavin as Marilyn), 28–29

Death Becomes Her (1992 film, Stephanie Anderson as Marilyn), 39–40

The Death of Marilyn Monroe (2000 documentary), 130–32

The Discovery of Marilyn Monroe, Marilyn Monroe, the Early Years (1991 documentary), 120–21

E! True Hollywood Story: The Many Loves of Marilyn Monroe (2000 documentary), 132–33

Everybody Wins (1990 film), 190–211

Evil Hill (2001 film, Kim Little as Marilyn), 63–64

Fade to Black (1980 film, Linda Kerridge impersonating Marilyn), 142–43

Fame (1974 Broadway play, Ellen Barber as Diane Cook), 105–6

The Final Hours of Norma Jean (1999 play, Naia Kelly as Marilyn), 58–60

Finding Graceland (1998 film, Bridget Fonda as Ashley impersonating Marilyn), 154–55

The Goddess (1958 film, Kim Stanley as Emily Ann Faulkner / Rita Shawn), 87–90

Goodbye, Norma Jean (1976 film, Misty Rowe as Marilyn), 6–7

Goodnight, Sweet Marilyn (1989 film, Paula Lane as Marilyn and Misty Rowe as Norma Jean Baker), 29–31

Hey, Marilyn! (1976 radio play, Beverly D'Angelo as Marilyn), 3

Hey, Marilyn! (1979 play, Lenore Zann as Marilyn), 3

Holy Matrimony (1994 film, Patricia Arquette as Havana impersonating Marilyn), 148–50

Hoover vs. the Kennedys: The Second Civil War (1987 TV miniseries, Heather Thomas as Marilyn), 26–28

I Love Lucy, "Ricky's Movie Offer" episode (TV series, 1954 season, Lucille Ball as Lucy Ricardo impersonating Marilyn), 140–41

Insignificance (1982 play, Judy Davis as Marilyn), 13–17

Insignificance (1985 film, Theresa Russell as Marilyn), 25

Introducing Dorothy Dandridge (1999 TV film, Kerri Randles as Marilyn), 60–61

Jackie: An American Life (1997 Broadway play, Kristine Nielsen as Marilyn), 52–53

Jackie, Ethel, Joan: Women of Camelot (2001 TV miniseries, Sarah La Fleur as Marilyn), 64–66

Just a Dream (2002 TV film, Marilyn B. Monroe as Marilyn), 73–75

Kennedy's Children (1975 Broadway play, Shirley Knight as Carla, who wants to be Marilyn), 140–42

Killing Castro (2002 Internet film, Michele Merseran as Marilyn), 73–74

L.A. Confidential (2003 TV film, Nectar Rose as Marilyn), 76–77

The Ladies Man (1962 film, Dee Arlen impersonating Marilyn), 92–93

The Last Days of Marilyn Monroe, a.k.a. Say Goodbye to the President (1985 documentary), 115–17

The Legend of Marilyn Monroe (1966 documentary), 114–15

Legends (1992 documentary, Susan Griffiths impersonating Marilyn), 148

The Life and Death of Marilyn Monroe (1971 play, Shirley Anne Field as Marilyn), 3

Little Voice (1998 film, Jane Horrocks as Little Voice impersonating Marilyn, 152–54

Madame Montand and Mrs. Miller (1992 TV film, Debra Sandlund as Marilyn), 39–41

Marilyn Monroe (1963 documentary), 114

Marilyn (1993 opera, Kathryn Gamberoni as Marilyn), 44–45

Marilyn! (1983 play, Stephanie Lawrence as Marilyn), 17

Marilyn, an American Fable (1983 Broadway play, Alyson Reed as Marilyn), 17

Marilyn and Bobby: Her Final Affair (1994 TV film, Melody Anderson as Marilyn), 47–49

Marilyn and Me (1991 TV film, Susan Griffiths as Marilyn), 34–36

The Marilyn Files (1992 documentary), 123–25

Marilyn Monroe: Beyond the Legend (1987 documentary), 117–18

Marilyn Monroe: The Final Days (2001 documentary), 134–36

Marilyn Monroe, Life after Death (1994 documentary), 126–27

Marilyn Monroe: Medical Secrets (2003 documentary), 136–38

Marilyn Monroe: Why? (1962 documentary), 113

Marilyn, The Mortal Goddess (late 1990s documentary), 128–30

The Marilyn Project (1975 off-Broadway play, Joan MacIntosh and Elizabeth Le Compte as the two side of "the star" (Marilyn), 3

Marilyn Remembered (1974 documentary), 115

Marilyn: Something's Got to Give (1990 documentary), 119–21

Marilyn, The Last Interview (1992 documentary, 122–23

Marilyn: The Last Word (1993), 125–26

Marilyn, the Untold Story (1980 TV film, Catherine Hicks as Marilyn), 10–12

Material Girl (1985 music video, Madonna as Marilyn), 23–24

Mondo New York (1987 mock documentary, Phoebe Legere impersonating Marilyn), 144–46

Monkeybone (2001 film, John Turturro as the voice of an animated character impersonating Marilyn, 157–58

Moviola: This Year's Blonde (1980 TV miniseries, Constance Forslund as Marilyn), 7–9

My Fellow Americans (1996 film, Jennifer Austin as Marilyn), 49–50

The Mystery of Natalie Wood (2004 TV film, Sophie Monk as Marilyn), 78–80

Netherworld (1993 film, Holly Butler as Marilyn), 41–42

Nobody Dies on Friday (1997 play, Rachel Warren as the voice of Marilyn), 53–56

Norma Jean and Marilyn (1996 TV film, Ashley Judd as Norma Jean and Mira Sorvino as Marilyn), 50–52

Peter Pan (1953 animated film, character of Tinker Bell based on Marilyn), 139–40

Pulp Fiction (1994 film, Susan Griffiths as Marilyn), 49

Quantum Leap, "Goodbye, Norma Jean" episode (TV series, 1992 season, Susan Griffiths as Marilyn), 45

The Rat Pack (1998 TV film, Barbara Niven as Marilyn), 56–58

Red Dwarf, "Meltdown" episode (TV series, 1991 season, Pauline Bailey as Marilyn), 33–34

Remembering Marilyn (1987 documentary), 118–19

Rendezvous in Montreal (1987 animated film, character of Marilyn), 28–29

Saturday Night Live (TV series, 1984 season, Julia Louis-Dreyfus as Marilyn), 22–23

The Sex Symbol (1974 TV film, Connie Stevens as Emmaline Kelly / Kelly Williams), 104–5

Slaughterhouse-Five (1972 film, Valerie Perrine as Montana Wildhack, 101–3

The Sopranos, "In Camelot" episode (TV series, 2004 season, Polly Bergen as Fran Felstein impersonating Marilyn), 158

Spice World (1998 film, Geri Helliwell as Ginger Spice impersonating Marilyn), 155–56

Strawhead (1983 play, Karen MacDonald as Marilyn), 17–21

Swimming to Cambodia (1985 film, Spaulding Gray paying homage to Marilyn), 143–44

Timequest (2002 film, Shelly Marks as Marilyn), 77–78

Tommy (1975 film, Tommy being taken to the church of St. Marilyn Monroe to be cured), 4–5

Town & Country (2001 film, Jenna Elfman as Auburn impersonating Marilyn), 156–57

Twin Peaks (1990–91 TV series, Sheryl Lee as Laura Palmer), 111–12

The Underground Comedy Movie (1999 film, Gena Lee Nolin as Marilyn), 59

Used People (1992 film, Marcia Gaye Harden as Norma impersonating Marilyn), 146–47

Valley of the Dolls (1967 film, Sharon Tate as Jennifer North), 100–101

Venus at Large (1962 Broadway play, Joyce Jameson as Olive Ogilvie), 93–94

The White Whore and the Bit Player (1973 off-Broadway play, Candy Darling as The Star / The White Whore), 103–4

Will Success Spoil Rock Hunter? (1955 Broadway play, Jayne Mansfield as Rita Marlowe), 83–84

Will Success Spoil Rock Hunter? (1957 film, Jayne Mansfield as Rita Marlowe), 84–85

Winter Kills (1976 film, Belinda Bauer as Yvette Malone), 106–8

With Honors (1994 film, Sunshine H. Hernandez as Marilyn), 150–51

A Woman Named Jackie (1991 TV miniseries, Eve Gordon as Marilyn), 36–38

About the Authors

John De Vito holds a BA in visual studies from Harvard University. *The Immortal Marilyn: The Depiction of an Icon* is his first book.

Frank Tropea holds a BA in English literature and psychology from the University of Massachusetts, Amherst, and an MA in literature and psychology from Harvard University. His poetry has been published in numerous literary journals.